Anthony C. Thiselton is Emeritus Professor of Christian Theology at the University of Nottingham. He is also Emeritus Canon Theologian of Leicester and of Southwell and Nottingham. He has published 25 books, including a commentary on the Greek text of 1 Corinthians (Eerdmans, 2000), *A Concise Encyclopedia of the Philosophy of Religion* (Oneworld, 2002), *The Holy Spirit* (SPCK, 2013), *The SPCK Dictionary of Theology and Hermeneutics* (2015), *Systematic Theology* (SPCK and Eerdmans, 2015), *Discovering Romans* (SPCK, 2016) and *Approaching Philosophy of Religion* (SPCK, 2017). Three of these books have received awards for excellence. He has taught on four continents, and is a Fellow of the British Academy.

T0327247

APPROACHING THE STUDY OF THEOLOGY

An introduction to key thinkers, concepts, methods and debates

ANTHONY C. THISELTON

First published in Great Britain in 2017

Society for Promoting Christian Knowledge
36 Causton Street
London SW1P 4ST
www.spck.org.uk

British Library Cataloguing-in-Publication Data
A catalogue record for this book is available from the British Library

ISBN 978–0–281–07759–5
eBook ISBN 978–0–281–07760–1

Typeset by Manila Typesetting Company
First printed in Great Britain by Ashford Colour Press
Subsequently digitally reprinted in Great Britain

eBook by Manila Typesetting Company

Produced on paper from sustainable forests

Contents

Part 2: Concepts and issues

Part 3: Key terms

Preface

Once again I am indebted to Mr Philip Law of SPCK for devising the excellent structure of this book. As a teacher of Christian theology for over fifty years, I am convinced that this particular approach to the subject will serve very well both those who are in the midst of a course in theology, and those who are contemplating the study of theology to degree level. It may also inform clergy, pastors and teachers who are in a position to advise students about what a degree course in theology will involve.

In virtually every other book I have thanked my wife Rosemary for typing the MS. This time, as before, she has checked through indices and pages to check for errors. But this time, I have managed to type this book, by a combination of oral software and one-finger typing. I suppose that the time had to come, albeit that I remain part of the handwriting generation!

I am very grateful to my friend the Revd Stuart Dyas, whose proof-reading has been invaluable and whose meticulous attention to detail has been remarkable. In particular he has shown where tenses needed correction for accuracy and clarification.

Anthony C. Thiselton, FBA
Emeritus Professor of Christian Theology, Universities of Nottingham and Chester, and Emeritus Canon Theologian of Leicester and of Southwell and Nottingham

Abbreviations

ANF	*Ante-Nicene Fathers*
Aquinas,	
Summa Theologiae	Thomas Aquinas, *Summa Theologiae*, 60 vols (Lat. and Eng., Blackfriars edn, London: Eyre and Spottiswoode, 1963)
AV	Authorized (King James) Version
Barth,	
Church Dogmatics	Karl Barth, *Church Dogmatics*, 14 vols, (Eng., Edinburgh: T&T Clark, 1957)
BCP	Book of Common Prayer
Calvin, *Institutes*	*Institutes of the Christian Religion*, transl. H. Beveridge, 2 vols (Grand Rapids, Mich.: Eerdmans, 1989)
Eng.	English
Fr.	French
Ger.	German
Gk	Greek
Heb.	Hebrew
Lat.	Latin
LXX	Septuagint
NIDPCM	*New International Dictionary of Pentecostal and Charismatic Movements*
NIV	New International Version
NPNF	*Nicene and Post-Nicene Fathers*
NRSV	New Revised Standard Version
NT	New Testament
OT	Old Testament

Chronology

d. *c.* 101	Clement of Rome
c. 35 – *c.* 108	Ignatius of Antioch
d. *c.* 160	Marcion
c. 100 – *c.* 165	Justin Martyr
c. 130 – *c.* 200	Irenaeus
c. 150 – *c.* 215	Clement of Alexandria
c. 150 – *c.* 225	Tertullian
c. 185 – *c.* 254	Origen
c. 250–336	Arius
c. 272–337	Constantine
c. 296–373	Athanasius
c. 330–79	Basil of Caesarea
c. 330–90	Gregory of Nazianzus
c. 330–95	Gregory of Nyssa
c. 339–97	Ambrose of Milan
c. 347–407	John Chrysostom
354–430	Augustine
c. 500	Dionysius (Pseudo-Dionysius)
c. 810 – *c.* 895	Photius of Constantinople
c. 1033–1109	Anselm of Canterbury
1079–1142	Peter Abelard
1090–1153	Bernard of Clairvaux
c. 1100–60	Peter Lombard
1225–74	Thomas Aquinas
c. 1330–84	John Wycliffe
c. 1466–1536	Desiderius Erasmus
1483–1546	Martin Luther (95 Theses, 1517)
1484–1531	Ulrich Zwingli
1489–1556	Thomas Cranmer
1491–1551	Martin Bucer
c. 1494–1536	William Tyndale
1497–1560	Philipp Melanchthon
1509–64	John Calvin

1554–1600	Richard Hooker
1596–1650	René Descartes
1632–77	Baruch Spinoza
1632–1704	John Locke
1703–91	John Wesley
1711–76	David Hume
1724–1804	Immanuel Kant
1743–1805	William Paley
1762–1814	Johann G. Fichte
1768–1834	Friedrich D. E. Schleiermacher
1770–1831	Georg Wilhelm Friedrich Hegel
1775–1854	Friedrich W. J. von Schelling
1801–90	John Henry Newman
1804–72	Ludwig A. Feuerbach
1808–74	David F. Strauss
1809–82	Charles R. Darwin
1813–55	Søren Kierkegaard
1822–89	Albrecht Ritschl
1825–1901	Brooke Foss Westcott
1844–1900	Friedrich Wilhelm Nietzsche
1846–1922	Wilhelm Herrmann
1848–1921	Peter T. Forsyth
1851–1930	Adolf von Harnack
1866–1957	F. R. Tennant
1869–1937	Rudolf Otto
1871–1944	Sergei Bulgakov
1875–1965	Albert Schweitzer
1879–1977	Gustaf Aulén
1884–1973	Charles H. Dodd
1884–1976	Rudolf Bultmann
1884–1978	Étienne Gilson
1886–1965	Paul Tillich
1886–1968	Karl Barth
1889–1966	Emil Brunner
1889–1976	Martin Heidegger
1890–1978	Walther Eichrodt
1890–1978	Anders T. S. Nygren
1892–1971	Reinhold Niebuhr

1900–79	Joachim Jeremias
1900–2002	Hans-Georg Gadamer
1902–99	Oscar Cullmann
1903–83	Ernst Fuchs
1903–58	Vladimir Lossky
1904–84	Karl Rahner
1904–95	Yves M. J. Congar
1905–88	Hans Urs von Balthasar
1906–45	Dietrich Bonhoeffer
1906–98	Ernst Käsemann
1908–86	Helmut Thielicke
1912–2001	Gerhard Ebeling
1913–2005	Paul Ricoeur
1913–2007	Thomas Forsyth Torrance
1915–72	Ian T. Ramsey
1919–83	John A. T. Robinson
1921–2008	Krister Stendahl
1922–2012	John Hick
1924–2006	James Barr
1928–2014	Wolfhart Pannenberg
b. 1926	Jürgen Moltmann
b. 1928	Hans Küng
b. 1930	John Polkinghorne
b. 1931	John D. Zizioulas
b. 1932	Alvin Plantinga
b. 1932	Nicholas Wolterstorff
b. 1934	Eberhard Jüngel
b. 1934	Richard Swinburne
b. 1936	Rosemary Radford Ruether
b. 1939	James Dunn
b. 1940	Stanley Hauerwas
1941–2003	Colin Gunton
b. 1945	Oliver O'Donovan
b. 1946	Richard Bauckham
1955–2016	John Webster

Introduction:
Landmarks in the study of theology

1 Biblical roots

(a) Doctrine of God

From the earliest books and chapters of the Bible, its writers portray God as Creator of the world, and as One who communicates with humankind. Regardless of the date of Genesis 1, Genesis 1.1 declares, 'In the beginning . . . God created the heavens and the earth'. Isaiah regularly refers to God as Creator, as in Isaiah 40.28: 'The LORD is . . . the Creator of the ends of the earth', and in Isaiah 43.15, where he refers to the creation of Israel: 'I am the LORD . . . the Creator of Israel.' God's creation of humankind occurs in Genesis 1.27; 5.1–2; and 6.7; also in Deuteronomy 4.32 and about 20 passages in Isaiah.

Also in the earliest chapters of Genesis, God addressed humankind, and before the fall normally communicated with them, perhaps every day (Gen. 3.8–9). The commands of God presuppose the notion of God's self-disclosure or revelation, in contrast to human discovery of God. The frequent use of 'I' in direct address also constitutes an event of revelation. Thus in the time of Noah, God says, 'I will blot out the earth' (Gen. 6.7), and famously in Exodus 3.13–14, declares to Moses, 'I AM WHO I AM' (or more probably to reflect the Hebrew imperfect, 'I will be who I will be'). The prophets maintain this theme, as, for example, in Jeremiah 31.31, 33, 'I will make a new covenant with the house of Israel . . . I will put my law within them'.

These three fundamental biblical roots develop into doctrine: God as Creator, God as Communicator or Revealer, and God as regularly engaging with humankind. The implication is that God created us *because he loves us*. God chose not to remain in isolation, but from the first sought the company of humankind. In twentieth-century theology, Jürgen Moltmann has developed these themes.

Setting aside the Mosaic period, some of the oldest passages and traditions of the Old Testament (OT) come from the book of Judges, from the era when Israelite theology encountered the polytheism and the nature worship of the Canaanites. In contrast to the Canaanite deities, Israel's God was seen as *the living God*. This characterization of God never disappeared from Israelite faith. The Hebrew word *hayah*, living, underlined God's dynamic character, in contrast to the *ba'alim*, who were lifeless and static. Often people link the prohibition on making carved images of God, or 'idols' (Exod. 20.4–5), with the context of pagan idolatry. But a more likely context is God's decision to make humanity in his own image (Gen. 1.27), because to bear the image of God is the vocation of his people, and they were not to shift this responsibility on to artificial man-made constructs of an image. The contrast between the tabernacle and the Temple symbolized this, as Stephen explained in Acts 7. The tabernacle represented a place of meeting with God which could move from place to place, as the living God himself might move. The Temple signified a fixed dwelling-place. Some biblical passages suggest caution or partial reluctance to build a temple as a site for the worship of the living, moving, God.

God is also regarded as *holy*. In Exodus 3.5 God appeared on 'holy ground'. In Isaiah's call and vision, the angels cried, 'Holy, holy, holy, is the LORD of hosts' (Isa. 6.3). In the equally well-known tradition of Leviticus, God spoke to Moses, 'You shall be holy, for I the LORD your God am holy' (19.2). The tradition of the Day of Atonement (Lev. 16), and the system of varied sacrifices, underlined the holiness of God. This is linked with the characteristic of righteousness. In the Song of Moses, Moses declared, 'All his ways are just. A faithful God, without deceit, just and upright is he' (Deut. 32.4).

As OT thought developed, the character and characteristic actions of God became increasingly evident. By the period of the Psalms, God is omnipotent (or almighty), omniscient and omnipresent. Psalm 139 begins, 'O LORD, you have searched me and known me . . . You discern my thoughts from far away . . . and are acquainted with all my ways' (vv. 1–3). God is also all-knowing. His omniscience sometimes extends to a category of future acts: 'Before a word is on my tongue, O LORD, you know it completely' (v. 4). We shall show later that this does not entail radical determinism. God's omnipresence is seen in verses 7–10:

> Where can I go from your spirit?
>   Or where can I flee from your presence?
> If I ascend to heaven, you are there;
>   if I make my bed in Sheol, you are there.
> If I take the wings of the morning
>   and settle at the farthest limits of the sea,
> even there your hand shall lead me . . .

Traces of this tradition occur in Genesis when God said to Abraham regarding the birth of Isaac in his old age, 'Is anything too wonderful for the LORD?' (Gen. 18.14). In the New Testament (NT) this is linked to the notion of God as king: 'The Lord our God, the Almighty (Gk, *pantokratōr*) reigns' (Rev. 19.6). Luke recounts Jesus as saying, 'What is impossible for mortals is possible for God' (Luke 18.27).

In the OT God is also portrayed as sovereign in Isaiah 46.9–10 where he is depicted as declaring, 'I am God, and there is no other. I am God, and there is no one like me . . . My purpose shall stand, and I will fulfil my intention'. This echoes 2 Samuel 7.22, 'You are great, O LORD God, for there is no one like you.'

The most striking example of God's faithfulness is God's willingness to make a promise to, and a covenant with, Noah, Abraham, Moses, Israel, and the Church or humankind. To Noah, God promises, 'I will never again curse the ground because of humankind' (Gen. 8.21). A promise genuinely ties the speaker's hands, or limits his options, so that a more desirable course of action may be excluded if it countermands the promise. The OT specialist Walther Eichrodt rightly comments that by means of the covenant, 'With this God men know exactly where they stand; an *atmosphere of trust and security is created*, in which they find both the strength for a willing surrender to the will of God and joyful courage to grapple with the problems of life'.[1] Eichrodt contrasts this with lack of faithfulness and promise in polytheism, where fear constantly haunts the pagan world, by leaving people with the dread of arbitrariness and caprice in the godhead. The promises of Israel's God excluded this.

These basic characteristics of God (until recently often called 'attributes') feature in numerous discussions today. Richard Swinburne and Wolfhart Pannenberg, for example, have taken pains to show that these do *not* involve logical contradiction, do *not* lead to radical determinism and do *not* imply mere anthropomorphism.[2]

Biblical roots also assert God's *graciousness, goodness and love*, and God's being as *Spirit and light*, as eternal and *infinite*, and as *uniquely wise*. God is 'merciful and gracious, slow to anger, and abounding in steadfast love' (Exod. 34.6); 'God is spirit' (or better, 'Spirit', John 4.24); 'The LORD is the

---

1 Walther Eichrodt, *Theology of the Old Testament*, vol. 1 (London: SCM Press, 1961), p. 38 (his italics).
2 Richard Swinburne, *The Coherence of Theism* (Oxford: Clarendon Press, 1977), pp. 97–232; Wolfhart Pannenberg, *Systematic Theology* (Edinburgh: T&T Clark, 1991–8), vol. 1, esp. pp. 337–448.

true God; he is the living God and the everlasting King' (Jer. 10.10); 'From everlasting to everlasting you are God' (Ps. 90.2). Solomon declared, 'Even heaven and the highest heaven cannot contain you' (1 Kings 8.27). God is also 'the only (Gk, *mono*, solely or uniquely) wise God' (Rom. 16.27). All these characteristics are discussed at length in contemporary theology.

(b) Humankind

Genesis 2.7 reads, 'God . . . breathed into his nostrils the breath of life; and the man became a living being' (Heb., *nephesh chayyā*). The word *nephesh* occurs 755 times in the OT, and the Septuagint (LXX) translates it into Greek by the word *psychē* 600 times. Hans Wolff comments, 'Only in a very few passages [does] the translation *soul* correspond to the meaning of *nephesh*.' Indeed, he adds, 'Man does not *have* nephesh, he *lives* as nephesh' (his italics).[3] The Greek term *psychē* also usually denotes *life*; only occasionally it denotes *soul*.

This develops into the concept of the *unity* of human beings, in contrast to any *dualism* of mind (or soul) and body, as we find in Plato, Aristotle and Descartes. By the time this question becomes debated in late twentieth-century theology, Pannenberg affirms 'the biblical idea of psychosomatic unity', and rejects Plato's notion of 'liberation [of the soul] from the body at death'.[4] By the time of the NT, the Greek word *body* (Gk, *sōma*) usually comes to denote *the whole self* or *a person*. On the other hand, in Hebrew *nephesh* can even denote a corpse. James Dunn, a contemporary specialist on Paul, asserts, 'While Greek thought tended to regard the human being as made up of distinct parts, Hebrew thought [and Paul] saw the human being more as a whole person existing on different dimensions.'[5] He endorses D. E. H. Whiteley's contrast between Greek *partitive* views and Pauline *aspective* views of the human self. All this may seem strange to modern perceptions of the self. Yet in modern philosophy Gilbert Ryle has made a devastating and convincing attack on the dualistic views of the self in Descartes and Locke.[6]

Although we have focused on the unity of the body with the mind or spirit, both dimensions are hugely important in the biblical writings. In Hebrew culture, food and drink, health and sickness, physical pleasures

---

3 Hans Walter Wolff, *Anthropology of the Old Testament* (London: SCM Press, 1974), p. 11.
4 Pannenberg, *Systematic Theology*, vol. 2, p.184, cf. pp. 181–202; Plato, *Republic*, 611 e.
5 James D. G. Dunn, *The Theology of Paul the Apostle* (Edinburgh: T&T Clark, 1998), p. 54.
6 Gilbert Ryle, *The Concept of Mind* (London: Hutchinson, 1949 and Penguin, 1963), throughout.

and bodily and social relations, constitute a focus of regular attention.[7] *Body* denotes a human being in the *public* world of identity and recognition, as Ernst Käsemann elaborated in the mid twentieth century. In 1 Corinthians 6.20 Paul writes, 'Glorify God in your body.' It is noteworthy that the AV rendered this with the addition 'and in your spirit', against earlier Greek manuscript readings, supposing that Paul would not simply have focused on the body! The biblical writings also urge the God-given importance of *mind and reason.* In 1 Thessalonians 5.12, 14 and 2 Thessalonians 3.15, Paul urges that the Thessalonian Christians should have the right mind. He accuses the Galatians of becoming 'bewitched' or seduced by failing to use reason to see that they are defending a logical contradiction (Gal. 3.1–2). Christians need to renew their minds (Rom. 12.2). The Philippians must use their minds and think (Phil. 4.7). Many contemporary scholars make this clear.[8] On the social relation between individual human beings, Pannenberg rightly speaks of 'being with others as others', i.e. respecting the integrity of the other.[9]

Biblical writers also regard *the heart* as the core of a human being, and as having capacities not only for understanding and willing, but also for the keeping of secrets. In the context of Paul and the NT, Rudolf Bultmann and Gerd Theissen interpret this as authentically representing the notion of the unconscious or subconscious, even before Sigmund Freud.[10] Thus the Holy Spirit works within the heart, where his transforming influence is most needed. Paul says, 'God's love has been poured into our hearts through the Holy Spirit that (better, 'who') has been given to us' (Rom. 5.5). A moral dimension in humankind is found in biblical uses of *conscience (syneidēsis)*. Conscience, however, is not used in a Stoic way to denote ultimate moral guidance, but as a reactive response of pain (or sometimes pleasure) to an act *believed* to be right or wrong.[11]

---

7 John Macquarrie, *In Search of Humanity* (London: SCM Press, 1982), esp. pp. 47–55.

8 Stanley K. Stowers, 'Paul on the Use and Abuse of Reason', in D. L Balch and others (eds), *Greeks, Romans, Christians* (Minneapolis, Minn.: Fortress Press, 1990), pp. 253–86; Robert Jewett, *Paul's Anthropological Terms* (Leiden: Brill, 1971), pp. 358–90; Günther Bornkamm, 'Faith and Reason in Paul', in Bornkamm, *Early Christian Experience* (London: SCM Press, 1969), pp. 29–46; cf. also W. Pannenberg, *Basic Questions in Theology*, vol. 2 (London: SCM Press, 1971), pp. 34–5, 28–64.

9 Pannenberg, *Systematic Theology*, vol. 2, p. 193.

10 Rudolf Bultmann, *Theology of the New Testament*, vol. 1 (London: SCM Press, 1952), p. 223; Gerd Theissen, *Psychological Aspects of Pauline Theology* (Edinburgh: T&T Clark, 1987), pp. 57–114, 271–342.

11 C. A. Pierce, *Conscience in the New Testament* (London: SCM Press, 1955); Margaret Thrall, 'The Pauline Use of Syneidēsis', *New Testament Studies* 14 (1967), pp. 118–25; P. D. Gooch, 'Conscience in 1 Corinthians 8 and 10', *New Testament Studies* 33 (1987), pp. 244–54.

In the end the nature of humankind is determined by our relationship to God. In modern thought Migliore asserts, 'We cannot know our humanity without a new assurance of who God is'.[12] John Calvin makes a similar point. In the NT it becomes clear that Jesus Christ himself represents the true paradigm case of what it means to be fully human. In the OT this finds expression in the vocation to reflect 'the image of God' (Gen. 1.26–27). Vladimir Lossky is among many recent thinkers to insist that after the alienation of humankind from God in the 'fall', the image of God became no longer a natural possession, but a work of God's *grace*, which now needs to be rediscovered. Lossky calls people in general 'individuals', but those in whom the image of God is being restored 'persons'.[13] To bear the image of God now becomes a vocation. This may sound harsh, but is fully understandable in the light of the concept of 'image' in the ancient world. Pagan temples often contained an image of the deity which was meant to convey something of its character. Originally the image of God was intended to be borne by God's people to convey something of his qualities. Since that time when humankind lost its intimacy with God, this needed to be recovered. As humankind inherited a condition of alienation from God, human beings could hardly be said to bear the image of God. The significance of 'image of God' has long remained the subject of debate, even if the concept has always achieved a prominent place in Christian theology. Earlier theology selected particular qualities in humankind to explain the term 'image of God'. Thus Aquinas in the thirteenth century selected rationality, dominion over the animal creation, and other qualities which distinguished humankind from the animal creation. But while these remain relevant, the wider capacity to reflect the nature of God takes priority over these varied elements.[14]

(c) Human alienation from God

The biblical account began (in Genesis) with a human act of disobedience, the expulsion of humankind from Eden, and the sense of shame before God which led to our first ancestors seeking to hide themselves from God. Genesis implies that they hitherto had had intimate communion and

---

12 Daniel L. Migliore, *Faith Seeking Understanding* (Grand Rapids, Mich.: Eerdmans, 1991), p. 120.

13 Vladimir Lossky, *The Image and Likeness of God* (London and Oxford: Mowbray, 1974).

14 Cf. Anthony C. Thiselton, 'The Image and the Likeness of God: A Theological Approach', in Malcolm Jeeves (ed.), *The Emergence of Personhood: A Quantum Leap?* (Grand Rapids, Mich.: Eerdmans, 2015), pp. 184–201.

conversations with God (Gen. 3.1–24). From the narrative of Cain to the time of Noah (Gen. 4—8) human sin and alienation became cumulatively worse. There were moments of respite in the narrative, when God chose to enter into a covenant with Noah, Abraham, the patriarchs, Moses and Israel. A covenant, as we noted, enables humankind *to know where they stand* with God. The theme of covenant runs throughout the whole of Scripture, reaching perhaps the climax in Paul's discussion of God's covenant with Israel and with the remnant of Israel, or the Church, in Romans 9—11.

Although the word 'sin' is often regarded as distasteful today, this word takes many different forms in the biblical writings. The three most important ones to note are, first, *error* or missing one's way; second, *rebellion* against God as one might rebel against a king or parent; and third, a result of a condition of *distortion* or misdirected habit. The Hebrew terms for these are respectively *chatta't, pesha'* and *'āwon*. These can also be translated variously. *Pesha'*, for example, may mean *apostasy* in certain contexts. What is important is that all resonate with everyday modern situations. We all know what it is to miss a standard. We all know what it is to throw off an allegiance and be estranged. We all know what it is to become damaged by such acts, and to need to be reconciled. It is unfortunate that the term 'sin' often seems tasteless, and is frequently tied to some routine omission. The NT also abounds in a varied vocabulary. If Paul or Jesus use the general word 'sin', it fundamentally concerns our relationship, or lack of it, *to God*, not specific acts of omission or commission. Often in Paul it turns on alienation from God, and the need for reconciliation, and for matters to be put right. The technical term for this is justification through faith.

(d) Jesus Christ: Redeemer, Saviour and Lord

We cannot expect the OT to contain *explicit* descriptions of a later event. But we find two or more relevant streams of expectation of the Messiah. The *prophetic* tradition of expectation looked forward to an anointed king (Heb., *māshiach*) or Messiah (Gk, *ho Christos*, Anointed One). He would reverse the fortunes of Israel. Initially this referred to a prophet like Moses (Deut. 18.15), then to King David and to his successor, culminating in a king who would outshine all of David's qualities. The second tradition has usually been called the *apocalyptic* tradition. According to this, all earthly agents, including kings and priests, failed to bring in the new era of righteousness, and so it was believed that *God alone* would intervene in person to restore the kingdom of God. D. S. Russell comments, 'The triumph of God's predetermined purpose will provide the key to all life's mysteries and problems.'[15] Towards the end of the twentieth century, Pannenberg is among a number of writers who place these two expectations together, to see within them a picture which would result in the person of Christ, who is both God and his human agent.

Associated with the coming of a new era in Christ, OT expectations were well aware of such concepts as redemption, salvation, sacrifice and mediation. For an understanding of *redemption* Israel had only to reflect on its exodus from Egypt. Redemption always meant deliverance *from* plight and oppression *to* safety and security, *by* a mighty act of God. Sometimes God's action was costly. Two Hebrew verbs were used for 'to redeem': *pādāh* and *gā'al*. These usually denoted redemption from jeopardy to safety, usually by a costly act. *Salvation* was easily explained by recalling the exploits of the judges. Israel would sell itself into oppression under the Philistines, through wilful sin. Israel then cried to God for deliverance, and God raised up a series of 'saviours' in the person of successive judges. The whole book of Judges recounts a number of such cycles of oppression, deliverance, and the raising up of saviours to achieve it.

Several passages from the NT apply prophecies concerning David to Jesus Christ. In his sermon on the day of Pentecost, Peter uses Psalm 110.1, to apply David's 'throne', to Christ, and Hebrews does likewise (Heb. 5.5–10 and 7.1—8.7). This is the origin of Christ's three offices of prophet, priest and king, in Calvin, A. Osiander and Pannenberg.[16] In twentieth-century theology J. A. T. Robinson stresses the full humanity of Jesus Christ, while Pannenberg appeals to OT and apocalyptic expectation, and to the cosmic event of the resurrection simultaneously, to establish his divinity. In spite of certain reservations about the 'substance' language of Chalcedon (see Part 3), in his *Jesus – God and Man*, Pannenberg insists that 'the true divinity and true humanity of Jesus' are 'indispensable'.[17] In the post-resurrection era of Paul's theology, it is universally agreed that Paul's characteristic and favourite title for Jesus Christ is that of 'Lord'. A slave might belong to his lord. This could lead to hardship or the opposite depending on the identity of the lord. At best, if he had particular needs, or left his wife widowed, his lord would provide for him and any dependants. Bultmann and Taylor call it the dominating idea in Paul and the

---

15 D. S. Russell, *The Method and Message of Jewish Apocalyptic 200 B.C. – A.D. 100* (London: SCM Press, 1964), p. 106.

16 Pannenberg, *Systematic Theology*, vol. 2, p. 448.

17 Wolfhart Pannenberg, *Jesus – God and Man* (London: SCM Press, 1968), pp. 284–5.

term of religious veneration.[18] There is also no doubt that in the NT writings, the work of Christ in his Passion on the cross, as well as in his earthly ministry and resurrection, provides the key turning point in God's gift of salvation and redemption.

Debates about Christology were especially prominent in the first five centuries of the Church, and have been rekindled from the nineteenth to twenty-first centuries.

(e) The Holy Spirit

The term *the Holy Spirit* occurs only three times in the OT. But there are some 387 occurrences of *the Spirit of God*. In the sequence of the biblical canon, Genesis 1.2 indicates the creative work of God's Spirit (Heb., *rûach*). The NRSV translates the word in Genesis 1.2 as *wind*, which is indeed sometimes the meaning of *rûach*, although most writers rightly choose *Spirit* as the more appropriate translation here. The Spirit of God denotes *God in action*, and stresses the *transcendence* or *otherness* of God.[19] The Spirit falls upon humankind from *without* or *beyond*, not as a latent human capacity from within. For example, 'The spirit of the LORD rushed on him' (Judg. 14.6); and, 'the spirit of the LORD came mightily upon David' (1 Sam. 16.13). The Spirit of God stands in contrast to all that is merely human, finite or of this world. As Gordon Fee has shown, the Spirit is the presence and power of God himself, not some impersonal force.[20] One classic passage underlines this: 'The Egyptians are human, and not God; their horses are flesh, and not spirit' (Isa. 31.3). An extension of this theme concerns the Spirit as life-giver. In Ezekiel 37.14, God declares, 'I will put my spirit within you, and you shall live'. The gift of life from the Spirit is part of creation and the Spirit's creative capacities: 'The spirit of God has made me, and the breath of the Almighty gives me life' (Job 33.4). The Psalms declare, 'By the word of the LORD the heavens were made, and all their host, by the breath (Heb. *rûach*) of his mouth' (Ps. 33.6). In the late twentieth century, Moltmann entitled his book on the Holy Spirit, *The Spirit of Life*.[21]

Another feature of the work of the Spirit of God in the OT is the *empowerment of the individual*, especially for leadership, but also for

---

18 Rudolf Bultmann, *The Theology of the New Testament*, vol. 1 (London: SCM Press, 1952), p. 80; Vincent Taylor, *The Person of Christ in New Testament Teaching* (London: Macmillan, 1963), p. 42.

19 F. Brown, S. R. Driver and C. A. Briggs, *The New Hebrew and English Lexicon* (Lafayette, Ind.: Associated Publishers, 1980), pp. 924–6.

20 Gordon Fee, *God's Empowering Presence* (Milton Keynes: Paternoster, 1995), throughout.

21 Jürgen Moltmann, *The Spirit of Life: A Universal Affirmation* (London: SCM Press, 1982).

the benefit of the *community* of God's people. In Judges, the Spirit is given to Othniel (Judg. 3.7–11), to Ehud (3.12–30), to Deborah (4.1–24) and to Gideon (Judg. 6.11—8.28). Sometimes the Spirit gives particular gifts to humans, for example craftsmanship (Exod. 31.2–5). Most significantly, the Spirit of God anoints the messianic figure. 'The spirit of the LORD shall rest on him, the spirit of wisdom and understanding, the spirit of counsel and might' (Isa. 11.42). The Spirit also gives the gift of prophecy or proclamation, for example, to Micaiah (1 Kings 22.17). If we take all these references together, the Spirit is at very least 'personal', although not in the same sense as human beings are personal. For this reason, some have rightly suggested the term 'supra-personal' to describe the Spirit of God. Finally, Jeremiah, Ezekiel and Joel prophesy that the gift of the Spirit will be given to the whole community of God's people in the last day (Jer. 31.31–34; Ezek. 36.24–28; Joel 2.28–29).

In the NT, Peter proclaimed at Pentecost that Joel's prophecy has been fulfilled: 'In the last days it will be, God declares, that I will pour out my Spirit upon all flesh, and your sons and your daughters shall prophesy, and your young men shall see visions, and your old men shall dream dreams' (Acts 2.17). The Holy Spirit descended upon the 120 Christian believers in an audible, visible, tangible way. Those in the crowd saw the flames, they heard the sound of the wind, and they heard speaking in tongues or other languages. Whether this refers to speaking in tongues or to known languages is disputed, but virtually all the crowd present would have spoken Greek. At the very least this is a miracle of hearing, not primarily a miracle of speaking. Most interpreters regard this event as an anticipation of the universality of the gift of the Spirit to the community. It was visible and tangible, because arguably this was a unique *barrier-breaking* event. Although Acts subsequently records Pentecostal phenomena in the case of the Samaritans (Acts 8.4–25), these are usually explained as a 'catching up' on Pentecost for new recipients of the Spirit. In the case of Cornelius (Acts 10.1–48) this broke the barrier between Jews and Gentiles. In the case of the Samaritans, these were not fully Jews, but a halfway house to Gentile outreach.

It is important that in Paul the Holy Spirit is the possession of *all* Christians, not only an elite. Paul writes,

> Anyone who does not have the Spirit of Christ does not belong to him. But if Christ is in you, though the body is dead because of sin, the Spirit is life because of righteousness. If the Spirit of him who raised Jesus from the dead dwells in you, he who raised Christ from the dead will give life to your mortal bodies also through his Spirit that dwells in you. (Rom. 8.9–11)

10

Similarly, 'No one can say "Jesus is Lord" except by the Holy Spirit' (1 Cor. 12.3). Other passages in Paul confirm this. Paul writes much more about the gifts of the Holy Spirit in the Church, especially in 1 Corinthians 12—14. He asserts that God gives the Spirit's gifts to individuals 'for the common good' (1 Cor. 12.7). What each of these gifts amounts to today is widely debated, not least among Pentecostals. Is 'prophecy' the same as applied preaching? Many Pentecostals would deny this; but recently Thomas Gillespie and others have vigorously affirmed it.[22] Speaking in tongues, i.e. *glōssolalia*, has been variously interpreted. I have traced elsewhere some seven explanations and meanings for this phenomenon.[23]

(f) The Church, the sacraments and other theological themes

From earliest times it is clear that God calls to himself not simply individuals, but primarily a *people*, the people of God. Admittedly the process began with the call of an individual, Abraham, to whom God promised that he would be the ancestor of a great nation. God renewed this promise to, and covenant with, Isaac, Jacob and Moses. But from the time of Moses the biblical focus shifted to the *people* of Israel. The notion that a believer in God would be a lone individual was excluded from the very first. In the OT era the community was emphasized, for which the normal Hebrew word was *qāhāl*. In Judaism this became a synagogue, although Jews from all parts of the Roman Empire always looked to the Temple in Jerusalem as their true spiritual home. Deuteronomy and the Jewish *Haggadah* or narrative of the Passover both have a significant alternation between first person *singular* and first person *plural*. The confession of faith runs, '*We* were Pharaoh's slaves in Egypt, but the LORD brought *us* out of Egypt' (Deut. 6.20–24, my italics). But in Deuteronomy 26.5–9, the confession of faith begins, 'A wandering Aramaean was *my* ancestor', but continues in the plural, 'The LORD brought *us* out of Egypt' (my italics).

After the resurrection of Jesus, the day of Pentecost constituted a turning point. It became the birthday of the Christian Church (Gk, *ekklēsia*). The purpose of placing stress on the visible and audible presence and gift of the Holy Spirit was to show that the Church is not merely a human society, like a social club, but is the direct creation of God through the Holy Spirit. God enacts many of his purposes through the Church. This principle

---

22 Thomas W. Gillespie, *The First Theologians: A Study in Early Christian Prophecy* (Grand Rapids, Mich.: Eerdmans, 1994).
23 Anthony C. Thiselton, *The First Epistle to the Corinthians: A Commentary on the Greek Text* (Grand Rapids, Mich.: Eerdmans, 2000), pp. 970–88, 1098–1133.

abounds through virtually all NT books and passages. Immediately after the event of Pentecost, Luke recounts that the earliest Christians 'devoted themselves to the apostles' teaching and fellowship, to the breaking of bread and the prayers' (Acts 2.42). Paul declares, 'Do you not know that you (plural) are God's temple, and that God's Spirit dwells in you? . . . God's temple is holy, and you (plural) are that temple' (1 Cor. 3.16–17). In one of the later epistles of the NT Paul devotes Ephesians to the theme of the Church, emphasizing its unity as 'one new humanity' (Eph. 2.15). Later still, in the Pastoral Epistles, instructions are given for the appointment of bishops (or elders) and deacons, and their practical life (1 Tim. 3.1–13).

In the history of the Church through the centuries, no one has ever doubted the importance of the Christian Church for individual Christians and for the continuity and identity of the Christian message. Controversy concerns specific questions about the ministry and *organization* of the Church. For example, clearly the ministry of bishops is accepted by the Roman Catholic, Orthodox, Anglican and some Methodist churches. It is generally rejected by Baptists, Presbyterians (in explicit terms) and many Reformed churches.

The institution of the sacraments is well established in the Gospels and epistles, and the principle of covenantal signs is well established in the OT. In the OT and Judaism, circumcision is a *covenant sign*, which precedes the Christian ordinances of baptism and the Lord's Supper. Baptism is well established through a number of passages, and its theology is expounded in Romans 6.3–11. Paul writes, 'Do you not know that all of us who have been baptized into Christ Jesus were baptized into his death?' (Rom. 6.3). Paul expounds the sacrament of the Lord's Supper or Eucharist in 1 Corinthians 10.16–17, and especially in 1 Corinthians 11.23–33. Paul recites the words of institution from the Gospels, and concludes: 'As often as you eat this bread and drink the cup, you proclaim the Lord's death until he comes' (11.26). The importance of the sacraments has been universally agreed down the centuries. Only among some sects is it disputed. The Catholic Church multiplied the number of sacraments to seven, as in Aquinas (see Part 3, Sacrament). Protestant churches speak of the two dominical sacraments.

2 The era of the church fathers (*c.* AD 100 – *c.* 500)

(a) From the apostolic fathers to the Council of Nicaea

In the writings of the apostolic fathers, or sub-apostolic era, we find considerable continuity with the biblical writings. *1 Clement* (*c.* 96) emphasizes divine grace, appeals to redemption by the blood of Christ, and is rooted in Scripture and the Church (*1 Clem.*, 2.1; 16.14). Clement regards Scripture as inspired by the Holy Spirit (13.1). He pleads for the unity of the Church. Ignatius of Antioch (*c.* 35 – *c.* 108) eagerly awaits martyrdom (Ignatius, *To the Romans*, 2.2; 4.1). He stresses the reality of the Incarnation and the resurrection (Ignatius, *To the Trallians*, 9.1–2). He also expounds the unique role of the bishop as a focus of unity (2.1–2; 7.2).

The early apologists (*c.* 135–200) were keen to demonstrate to the Roman world that Christian faith was entirely rational and also soundly based on Scripture and the witness of the Church. Aristides and Quadratus addressed the emperor Hadrian (Antoninus Pius). The best-known apologist was Justin Martyr (*c.* 100 – *c.* 165). In his *Dialogue with Trypho*, he regarded knowledge of God as coming from the prophets, and dialogued with philosophy (*Dialogue*, 7). He cited the human birth of Jesus, urged conversion and baptism (14), and regarded the crucifixion and resurrection of Christ as uniquely saving (89, 95). Tatian, Athenagoras and Theophilus also defend Christians against false accusations, and defend the faith.

Irenaeus (*c.* 130 – *c.* 200), Bishop of Lyons, had roots in the Eastern and Western Church. He especially urged adherence to 'the rule of faith', i.e. to biblical and apostolic tradition. He opposed the secret tradition of the Gnostics, which he set in contrast with the *public tradition* of the apostles and the Christian Church. He regarded God as 'Creator of the world' (*Against Heresies*, 1.9.1), and spoke of God the Son and the Holy Spirit as the two 'hands of God' (4.20.3), and of the Holy Spirit as anointing Jesus Christ for his incarnate ministry (3.17–18). He also expounded the work of Christ as reversing sin and the fall, and as 'recapitulating' the destiny of humankind (see Part 3, Recapitulation). This was partly on the basis of Ephesians 1.10. Irenaeus also underlined the *unity and continuity* of the *Old and New Testaments*.

Tertullian (*c.* 150 – *c.* 225) of Carthage wrote apologetic and theological treatises, and later became a Montanist, stressing the immediate and direct influence of the Holy Spirit. Many of his writings were polemical. He rejected any wisdom from outside the one true Church. In this respect he was unlike the Alexandrians, Clement and Origen. He attacked Gnostic dualism, Marcion and the Valentinians. He had reservations about infant baptism, introduced traducianism (the belief in inherited sin) and resisted pagan philosophy, although he simultaneously drew on Stoic notions of the soul.

Alexandrian Christianity is represented in its early years by Clement of Alexandria (*c.* 150 – *c.* 215) and Origen (*c.* 185 – *c.* 254). Clement showed a remarkable knowledge of pagan literature, including its philosophy. He stressed that the Christian faith represents a fulfilment both of OT and of Greek philosophy. He even regarded Plato as 'Moses with an Attic [i.e. Athenian] accent'. He tended to view human sin as due to weakness. Origen produced a remarkable quantity of literature. This included textual criticism, biblical exegesis or commentaries, Christian doctrine and theology, and practical work on prayer and ethics. His major treatise on doctrine was *On First Principles* (*de Principiis*). In this he expounded the doctrine of God, Christology and the Holy Spirit. He described Christ as having deity (1.2.1), and as being the eternal Word. He quoted Colossians 1.15, 'In Christ all things exist'. He argued that the Holy Spirit was not created nor made (1.3.3). Christ is also the medium of divine revelation. Many have called him the greatest scholar and teacher of his time.

Hippolytus (*c.* 170 – *c.* 236) and Novatian (third century) were from the Roman Church. Hippolytus contributed some commentaries and liturgical formulations. In the persecution of the Emperor Decius, Novatian was a rigorist about the status of the lapsed. Cyprian (d. 258) of Carthage, by contrast, came to believe in the restoration of the lapsed, after a time of penance and delay. He also urged the importance of the episcopate and the institutional Church.

A turning point came with the Emperor Constantine (*c.* 280–337). He was proclaimed emperor at York in 306. He defeated his rival at the battle of the Milvian Bridge, and, according to Lactantius, his court theologian, fought under the sign of the cross. In 313 in the Edict of Milan he established freedom of religion. At the time the Church had become disunited over the question of Christology, when a substantial group followed Arius (*c.* 250–336) against the 'orthodox' bishops. In crude terms, Arius had argued that if Jesus Christ was God's 'Son', there must have been a time when the Son did not exist, but only the Father. Constantine convened the Council of Nicaea in 325, to resolve the dispute (see Part 3, Nicaea, Council of). Eusebius of Caesarea (*c.* 263–339) was one of the main opponents of Arius. The orthodox party appealed to the creed of the Palestinian community that Christ was 'of the same being' (Gk, *homoousios*) as God the Father. In conclusion the Council promulgated a revision of the Creed of Jerusalem, which is similar to today's Nicene Creed. Today's creeds in the Roman, Anglican and Orthodox traditions in practice represent a longer formulation, which was revised by the Council of Constantinople. The phrase 'proceeds from the Father and the Son' was later added by the Western Church, and is rejected by the Orthodox tradition. Over the next few years, theological issues did not entirely become disentangled from court politics.

(b) From the Council of Nicaea to AD 500

Over the fourth and fifth centuries further issues arose about Christology, the Holy Spirit and the Holy Trinity. Hilary of Poitiers (*c.* 315–68) and Ambrose of Milan (*c.* 339–97), together with Augustine of Hippo (354–430), constituted the major theologians of the Western or Latin tradition. Athanasius (296–373), Basil of Caesarea (*c.* 330–79), Gregory of Nazianzus (*c.* 330–90), Gregory of Nyssa (*c.* 330–95), John Chrysostom (*c.* 347–407) and Jerome (*c.* 345 – 420) were the major thinkers of the Eastern or Greek tradition.

Athanasius, Bishop of Alexandria, defended the orthodox notion that Christ is 'very God' and is 'eternally begotten'. In his *Epistle to Serapion* he replied forcefully to the *pneumatomachi* or 'Tropici', who had claimed that the Holy Spirit was merely a created thing or person (Gk, *ktisma*). He argued, by contrast, that the Holy Spirit comes forth or *proceeds* from God (*Epistle to Serapion*, 1.22). The Spirit, he urged, also raised Christ from the dead (Rom. 8.11; *Epistle to Serapion*, 1.23). He stated that Christ or the Word 'was made human that we might be made Divine' (*On the Incarnation*, 54). In the same work he also demonstrated how closely the person and work of Christ are intertwined. It is generally regarded as a classic. In the Western Church Hilary echoed many of his thoughts.

Basil defended an orthodox doctrine of Christology against Eunomius and Arius. Like Athanasius, he opposed the *pneumatomachi* on the Holy Spirit. One characteristic of Basil is his urging the use of the threefold Gloria: 'Glory be to the Father and to the Son and to the Holy Spirit'. He stressed the co-equality of the Persons (*On the Holy Spirit*, 17–22). Together with his brother and his friend, he and the two Gregories are known as the Cappadocian Fathers.

On the Trinity, Gregory of Nazianzus and Gregory of Nyssa made important points. Both insisted that *numerals* apply only to created and finite people or objects. Thus the numeral 'three' is irrelevant to debates about the Trinity. In the West, Ambrose firmly defended an orthodox view of the Holy Spirit and the Holy Trinity.

Augustine of Hippo remains arguably the most influential of the church fathers. He drew on the work of Gregory of Nazianzus in the Eastern Church, and the Latin fathers from Tertullian to Ambrose. He profoundly influenced the thought of the medieval Church, including Aquinas. In early years he studied rhetoric in Carthage, and became a Manichaean. He was then appointed to the imperial court in Milan, where the preaching of Ambrose, the prayers of his mother Monica, and his reading of Scripture with fresh eyes, led to his conversion to Christian faith. In his early anti-Manichaean writings (*c.* 388–400), he recognized that the rhetoric of the Manichaeans had initially seduced him. He appeals to the authority of Scripture for his acceptance of the Christian faith (*The Morals of the Manichaeans*, 12.55).

What are known as his anti-Donatist writings include *On Baptism* and the *Correction of the Donatists* (both *c.* 400). The Donatists had advocated a 'pure church', holding a rigorist view concerning those who had 'lapsed' under persecution. Augustine argued for the 'special gift of Catholic unity' (*On Baptism*, 16).

Nevertheless, probably his most distinctive writings were the anti-Pelagian writings, which include *On the Spirit and the Letter* (*c.* 412), *On Nature and Grace* (*c.* 415), *On Grace and Free Will* (*c.* 427) and *On the Predestination of the Saints* (*c.* 428). Here he coined the term 'prevenient grace', commenting, 'God anticipates us that we may be called . . . He anticipates us that we may lead godly lives' (*On Nature and Grace*, 35.31; Eng., *NPNF*, ser. 1, p. 425). He also defended infant baptism, describing this as the practice of the Catholic Church (chs 22–23). He wrote numerous commentaries, on passages from Romans, 1 Corinthians, Galatians, Ephesians and Colossians. He argued that through the law alone, though 'sin has abounded', 'grace did much more abound' (*On the Spirit*, 9.6; cf. Rom. 5.20–21). Augustine seeks to expound Paul's doctrine of faith and works, and grace and law.

Augustine's treatise *The City of God* expounds his philosophy of history. It was occasioned by the fall of Rome to the Goths in 410. He refutes pagan charges that Christians caused the fall of Rome because of their Christian faith. His autobiographical reflections occur in *The Confessions*, which contain a reasoned reflection on the psychology of the will and human sin. One of his most explicitly doctrinal treatises was his volume *On the Trinity*.

3 The medieval era

Sometimes the impression is given that Western medieval theology was a fairly dull, flat, continuation of the Augustinian tradition, with minor inputs from Aquinas and Anselm. The reverse was in fact true. It was a creative period for theology, influenced not only by Aquinas and Anselm, but also by Alcuin, Abelard, Bernard of Clairvaux, Peter Lombard, Bonaventure, Duns Scotus, William of Ockham, John Wycliffe and others. The earliest Christian thinker of the medieval era was Gregory of Rome (*c.* 540–604). He was an able administrator and pastor, although not a creative theologian.

Without question, Thomas Aquinas (1225–74) marks the most sig-nificant turning point between the earlier and later Middle Ages, and for Christian theology in the modern era, especially for Roman Catholic the-ology. Hitherto most thinkers had been educated in monastic foundations, but from the thirteenth century they began to benefit from the new uni-versities of Paris and Oxford, and elsewhere. Albert the Great, Aquinas' teacher, urged him to study the works of Aristotle, and this influence is evi-dent from Thomas' writings. His greatest work is the *Summa Theologiae*, which was arranged in three parts, each with a number of 'questions' or propositions, arranged for teaching students, with counter-propositions and replies in scholastic style. Under each question Aquinas wrote several 'articles', or subsections. Since his work constitutes a major systematic theology, we also consider him under 'Systematic theology' in Part 1.

Anselm (*c.* 1033–1109), Archbishop of Canterbury, remains the second most important theologian of the medieval period. He is well known for two particular insights. First, he expounded the ontological argument for the existence of God. This occurred in his *Proslogion*, or 'Address', avail-able in English in *A Scholastic Miscellany*.[24] Today Anselm's argument is still regarded as a classic formulation. Karl Barth has argued that it was not intended as a philosophical argument, but rather as a confession of faith in the context of prayer. His second, and perhaps more important, work is *Why God Became Man*. This is also available in English in *A Scholastic Miscellany*, and other editions. Anselm expounds the person and work of Jesus Christ as the God-man, and in relation to the divine governance of the world.

As for other medieval thinkers, Alcuin (*c.* 740–804) contributed works on biblical exegesis and a treatise on the Trinity. Peter Abelard (1079–1142) worked in several areas: philosophy, the doctrine of the Holy Trinity, the atonement and biblical exegesis. He mediated between philosophical nominalism and philosophical realism, and opposed Anselm's interpre-tation of the atonement. Bernard (1090–1153) founded the monastery of Clairvaux and the Cistercian order. He wrote such devotional works as *On the Love of God* and *On the Steps of Humility and Pride*, which sum-marized the rule of Benedict. Peter Lombard (*c.* 1100–60) is well known for his *Sentences*, a collection of patristic sources, and for his exegetical work. He was a sober and careful exegete. John Duns Scotus (*c.* 1266–1308) directly influenced William of Ockham (*c.* 1285–1349). He believed that

---

24 E. R. Fairweather (ed.), *A Scholastic Miscellany* (Philadelphia, Pa.: Westminster Press and London: SCM Press, 1956), pp. 69–96.

God could be known by natural reason, and also wrote a commentary on the *Sentences* of Peter Lombard. He wrote on freedom, finitude, causality and logically possible states of affairs. John Wycliffe (*c.* 1330–84) heralded the Reformation by stressing the inspiration and authority of the Bible, and by attacking the doctrine of transubstantiation in the Eucharist. His book *On the Eucharist* aroused hostility at Oxford.

4 The Reformation and afterwards

Martin Luther (1483–1546) was the founder of the Reformation. Initially he entered the University of Erfurt (1501) and its Augustinian monastery (1505), and was ordained priest in 1507. He lived as a devout monk before becoming a teacher in the University of Wittenberg in 1508, where he taught Aristotle and the Bible. He sought the reform of monasteries, and was sent to Rome to put this into operation. At Rome he was profoundly disillusioned by superficial religious observances, the search for freedom from purgatory, and the extravagant expenditure on pomp and ceremony by the Roman Curia. The years 1512–19 became a time of prayer and heart-searching. Luther was disillusioned by the 'ladders' of mysticism and the system of penance. In 1513 he began to lecture on the Psalms. The phrase, 'In your righteousness deliver me' (31.1), impressed him. He compared it with Romans 1.17: 'The righteousness of God [is] revealed through faith, as it is written, "The just shall live by faith"' (AV), or 'the one who is righteous will live by faith' (NRSV).

Luther came to see that the issue was not *his* righteousness, but *God's*. He studied commentaries on the Psalms by Augustine and Peter Lombard. He later recalled that in his reading of Romans, 'I hated Paul with all my heart', but then,

> by the mercy of God, meditating day and night, I gave heed to the context of the words . . . I began to understand the righteousness of God is that by which the righteous lives by *a gift* of God, namely faith . . . I felt that I was altogether born again and had entered paradise itself through open gates. Then a totally other face of the entire Scripture showed itself to me.[25]

He began to contrast ecclesial 'works', as in the sale of indulgences for money, together with prescribed works to escape purgatory, with the *generous, free,*

---

25 Martin Luther, *Luther's Works*, 55 vols (Eng., St Louis, Mo.: Concordia) vol. 34, pp. 336–7; quoted by Skevington Wood, *Captive to the Word* (Exeter: Paternoster, 1969), p. 52 (my italics).

grace of God. On 31 October 1517, Luther nailed up in public his 95 theses, which mainly focused on the seductions of indulgences, and on the pope's 'plenitude of power'. In Christ's new law, he urged, all things are free. A human being, he declared, is always a sinner, always penitent, always justified.

In 1518 Luther published his *Heidelberg Disputation*, which constituted his reply to the controversy raised by his attack on indulgences. While Johann Tetzel opposed him, he received warm support from Martin Bucer (1491–1551), and in due course William Tyndale (*c.* 1494–1536). Tyndale followed his theology, especially his emphasis on the biblical writings and on God's word as promise. In his *Heidelberg Disputation*, Luther appealed to Romans 3.21, 'The righteousness of God has been manifested without the law', and to Augustine, and emphasized the centrality of the cross. He wrote, 'The theologian of glory says bad is good and good is bad. The theologian of the cross calls them by their proper name.'[26] For the next few years Luther underwent three 'trials' or disputations. The first took place before Cardinal Cajetan in October 1518. A second disputation took place at Leipzig with John Eck in July 1519. Eck chose to attack the Wittenberg school of theology, and especially Andreas Karlstadt (1486–1541). On being asked about his credentials, Luther observed, 'I simply taught, preached, and wrote God's word . . . I did not do anything . . . I left it to the Word.'[27] His third 'trial' or disputation was the Diet of Worms in 1521. Luther had been condemned by a papal bull, and his excommunication was ratified at Worms. Luther was commanded to recant, and uttered his famous, but possibly legendary, reply: 'Unless I am convinced by the testimony of the Scriptures or by clear reason . . . I cannot and will not recant anything . . . May God help me.'[28]

In 1525 Karlstadt and Müntzer stirred up the peasants to revolt against the Saxon princes. Luther did not support the Peasants' Revolt. The peasants had been seduced by the so-called Radical Reformers, whom Luther regarded as opponents who undermined his doctrine of justification. Luther and Ulrich Zwingli (1484–1531) rejected their Montanist-like appeal to the immediate voice of the Holy Spirit. Luther remained controversialist, theologian, teacher, preacher, translator and reformer. In 1525, he published his classic reply to Erasmus, entitled *On the Bondage of the Will*, which became one of his most famous theological works. Desiderius

---

26 James Atkinson (ed.), *Luther: Early Theological Works,* Library of Christian Classics, vol. 16 (London: SCM Press, 1962), pp. 281, 291.

27 Cited in James Atkinson, *The Great Light* (Grand Rapids, Mich.: Eerdmans, 1968), p. 55.

28 Atkinson, *The Great Light,* p. 47.

Erasmus (*c.* 1466–1536) was a fine scholar, but a cautious one, who doubted the clarity of Scripture. Luther argued that Scripture was always clear enough for us to take the next step in practical action.

In 1529 it became clear that there were disagreements among the Reformers on the nature of the Lord's Supper. Deeply concerned for Reformation unity, Luther sought a friendly conference with Zwingli, Melanchthon and Bucer at Marburg. He did his best to achieve a united witness, but Zwingli and others held firm in their beliefs. At his death in 1546, he commended himself to God, murmuring 'God so loved the world . . .' (John 3.16).

John Calvin (1509–64) was a second-generation Reformer. But his theology constitutes a landmark because of its systematic and logical nature. Hence we shall set out in detail Calvin's systematic theology in Part 1, under 'Systematic theology'. Calvin published the *Institutes of the Christian Religion* (1st edn, 1536; subsequent edns, 1539, 1541 and 1559).[29] In the first part or 'Book' of the *Institutes*, Calvin expounds a doctrine of God, especially as sovereign and transcendent. In Book 2, he turns to Christology. He considers human sin and Christ's redemption, including Christ's work as mediator. Book 3 concerns the Holy Spirit, including his revelation of God. Book 4 concerns the Church and sacraments (see Part 1, Systematic theology).

The Reformers also included Thomas Cranmer (1489–1556), Philipp Melanchthon (1497–1560) and Heinrich Bullinger (1504–75). In the period following the Reformation, we may note Richard Hooker (1554–1600), John Owen (1616–83) and the Pietists Philipp Spener (1635–1705) and Albrecht Bengel (1687–1752), together with John Wesley (1703–91). After the Reformation, however, with Protestant scholasticism, theology tended to harden into a more uniform orthodoxy, in which relatively few creative landmarks appeared.

5 The modern period

(a) From Schleiermacher to Harnack

Friedrich D. E. Schleiermacher (1768–1834) is generally regarded as the father of modern theology. Karl Barth, one of his critics, declared, 'He did not found a school, but an era'.[30] In early years he embraced the Moravians, and never entirely lost his evangelical or Pietist roots. B. A. Gerrish has

---

29 Calvin, *Institutes.*
30 Karl Barth, *Protestant Theology in the Nineteenth Century* (London: SCM Press, 1972), p. 425.

described him as a liberal evangelical. But at the University of Halle, he began to see value in the Enlightenment and later in Romanticism. In addition to his work on the NT, Schleiermacher became especially noted for his creative and distinctive work on hermeneutics. He also described preaching as his proper office, which served to awaken faith.

Schleiermacher's earliest work was his *Speeches on Religion to Its Cultured Despisers* (1799). Germany's 'cultured despisers' of religion included the educated, artistic and philosophical minds of the Berlin salons. In his first speech he argued, 'Millions have been satisfied to juggle with its [religious] trappings; few have discerned religion itself'. Religion concerns 'the innermost springs of my being'.[31] The central core of religion, he argued, is *a feeling of dependence on God*. Germans, he argued, destroy their tenderest blossoms of the human heart, although they are not as bad as the French, who merely search for 'witty frivolity', and the English, who are obsessed with trade and gain![32] The heart of religion is an 'immediate sense of utter dependence on God (*Gefühl schlechthinniger Abhängigkeit*)'.[33] His emphasis lies not so much on 'feeling', as on *dependence*, in spite of many popular claims to the contrary. Piety cannot be 'the craving for . . . metaphysical and ethical crumbs'.[34] He declared, 'True religion is a sense and taste for the infinite.'[35] Religion, he asserted, is more than mere system of doctrine.

Schleiermacher produced notes on hermeneutics (1805) (see Part 1, Hermeneutical theology). He published a *Brief Outline on the Study of Theology* (1811; 2nd edn, 1830). But his magnum opus was *The Christian Faith* (Ger., *Glaubenslehre*, possibly *Doctrine of Faith*, 1821–2; 2nd edn, 1830–1). Some have compared this volume with Aquinas' *Summa Theologiae* and Calvin's *Institutes*, although it is far less detailed than these.

In *The Christian Faith*, Part 1, Schleiermacher endorses all that he has said earlier about Christian self-consciousness. He sees 'godlessness' as simply 'effective or arrested development'.[36] This has identified him as part of the liberal tradition. He also abandons 'the idea of the absolutely supernatural'.[37] In Part 2 he addressed consciousness of sin, grace and Christ. He

---

31 Friedrich D. E. Schleiermacher, *Speeches on Religion* (Eng., New York, N.Y.: Harper, 1958), pp. 1, 3.
32 Schleiermacher, *Speeches on Religion*, p. 23.
33 Friedrich D. E. Schleiermacher, *The Christian Faith* (Eng., Edinburgh: T&T Clark, 1989), pp. 132, 142.
34 Schleiermacher, *Speeches on Religion*, p. 31.
35 Schleiermacher, *Speeches on Religion*, p. 39.
36 Schleiermacher, *The Christian Faith*, p. 135.
37 Schleiermacher, *The Christian Faith*, p. 183.

asserts, 'We have fellowship with God only in fellowship with the Redeemer, such that in it his absolutely sinless perfection and blessedness represent a free, spontaneous activity . . . [and] a free assimilative receptivity.'[38] This reveals his evangelical or Pietist early years. However, his Christology has also been influenced by Kant, and remains controversial. He speaks of 'the exclusive dignity of the Redeemer', but also urges: 'The Redeemer is like all men in virtue of the identity of human nature, but is distinguished from them by the constant patency of his God-consciousness.'[39] John Macquarrie describes this as a humanist Christology. Some argue that the Trinity constitutes the climax of his work, but it occupies only a very few pages of the 750-page work.

Georg W. F. Hegel (1770–1831) was one of the most creative philosophers of the nineteenth century. He collaborated with Friedrich Schelling, and succeeded Fichte, first at Jenna, and then in Berlin. Hegel worked for a sophisticated recovery of rationality through his emphasis on *historical* reason. In this respect he became a rival of Schleiermacher (see Part 1, Philosophical theology). In the twentieth century he had relatively little influence in England, but more recently he has had considerable influence on Pannenberg and Küng.

Hegel's pupils split into two groups. The 'left-wing' Hegelians replaced Hegel's emphasis on Spirit (Ger., *Geist*) with an emphasis on the material, or on humankind. Among these left-wing Hegelians, Ludwig Feuerbach (1804–72) and David F. Strauss (1808–74) deserve note, among others. Feuerbach argued that God was no more than a human projection. The believer, he argued, projects and objectifies his or her human nature into a supposed celestial figure, thereby creating 'God' in his or her own image (*The Essence of Christianity*, 1841). He provided a seminal link with the materialism of Karl Marx and Friedrich Nietzsche. Strauss, who was a pupil of F. C. Baur (1782–1860), regarded Schleiermacher as too 'churchly'. When he was only 27, he published his first edition of *The Life of Jesus*. He denied any 'supernatural' dimension in the life of Jesus, regarding most of its events as 'myth', or as ideas recounted as narratives. In the fifth edition (1865) of his *Life of Jesus*, Strauss attacked Schleiermacher's work, and virtually rejected the Christian faith. Strauss also promoted a purely historical approach to the biblical writings, excluding a place for theology.

Søren Kierkegaard (1813–55) was entirely different. He is rightly regarded as the first Christian existentialist. He regarded faith as passionate

---

38 Schleiermacher, *The Christian Faith*, p. 371.
39 Schleiermacher, *The Christian Faith*, p. 385.

subjectivity, and emphasized will and decision, in contrast to reason and argument. He disliked the notion of founding a 'school' of theology, but in fact this has occurred. His approach to God influenced Barth and Bultmann.

Albrecht Ritschl (1822–89) has been widely regarded as belonging to the liberal school, together with Harnack. However, recently J. Richmond drew attention to his work *The Christian Doctrine of Justification and Reconciliation* (3 vols, 1870–4), which is not entirely a 'liberal' approach. That label might have been applied to his earlier work. But in 1864 he succeeded I. A. Dorner at Göttingen, and gave more attention to the work of Christ. On the other hand, 'the Ritschl School' included W. Herrmann and Adolf von Harnack.

Wilhelm Herrmann (1846–1922) argued that faith came not from doctrine, but from trust and truth. Like Schleiermacher, he relied on the immediacy of communion with God. Adolf von Harnack (1851–1930) was primarily a church historian. But his popular book *What Is Christianity?* became a flagship of liberalism. He argued that Paul was responsible for doctrine, in contrast to the 'simple' teaching of Jesus, who taught only 'the idea of God as Father, the brotherhood of humanity, and the infinite value of the human soul'.[40] His more serious contribution was his *History of Dogma* (7 vols). By contrast, the Scottish theologian Peter T. Forsyth (1848–1921) held a more evangelical viewpoint, and wrote on the person and work of Christ (1909–10). He is sometimes described as a Barthian before Barth.

(b) From Barth to Niebuhr

Karl Barth (1886–1968) remains one of the two or three most influential theologians of the modern era. He is a great champion of Protestant orthodox faith. His 14 volumes of *Church Dogmatics* remain an invaluable resource, though they are too complex and detailed for introductory reading. Barth began his career under the spell of liberal theologians, but when he became a pastor in Switzerland (1911–21), he found their theology grossly inadequate to meet people's needs. In 1914 he was shocked not only by the German invasion of Belgium, but notably by the 93 intellectuals who included 'almost all my German teachers', and had signed a manifesto in support of Germany and the Kaiser. Together with Eduard Thurneysen (1888–1974), he sought a new understanding of the

---

40 Adolf von Harnack, *What Is Christianity?* (Eng., London: Benn, 1958), pp. 54–5.

living God of the Bible. In 1917 he published his essay, 'The Strange New World within the Bible'.[41] This world, he said, provides 'not right human thoughts about God, but right divine thoughts about persons' (p. 43).

In 1919 Barth published his famous commentary on Romans (2nd rev. edn, 1922).[42] He drew on Kierkegaard to recognize the shallowness of nominal Christianity, and the sovereign grace and transcendence of God. God is 'Other', and not simply the focus of human 'religion'. All human aspirations to religiosity, and all human social groupings, become relativized by God's sovereign grace. God's word pronounces a 'no' on humanity under sin, and a 'yes 'to divine grace. It was commented that the impact of Barth's *Romans* was like a stone falling into a pool, whose ripples extended far and wide. In 1921 Barth published *The Resurrection of the Dead*, in which he argued that the Corinthians believed 'not in God, but in their own belief in God, and in particular leaders . . . Against this the clarion call of Paul rings out: "Let no man glory in men" (1 Cor. 3.21) . . . "Let him glory in the Lord (1 Cor. 1.31)"'.[43] This concludes with a detailed study of the resurrection. In 1930 he published *Anselm*, which he described as the 'key' to the church dogmatics. Belief, as Anselm held, is a process initiated by God, not a human construct.

Barth wrote his *Church Dogmatics* (Eng., 14 vols) from 1932 to 1967, and it was not quite finished at his death. In the first volume Barth declared,

> The Bible is the concrete means by which the Church recollects God's past revelation, is called to the expectation of his future revelation, and is thus summoned and guided to proclamation and empowered for it . . . The Bible . . . bears witness to past revelation.[44]

(For details, see Part 1, Systematic theology.)

To Barth's generation belongs the seminal thought of half a dozen major theologians: Gustaf Aulén (1879–1977); Rudolf Bultmann (1884–1976); Paul Tillich (1886–1965); Anders Nygren (1890–1978); Reinhold Niebuhr (1892–1971); and Dietrich Bonhoeffer (1906–45). Aulén has written distinctively on the atonement (see Part 2, Atonement). Bultmann was primarily an NT scholar, but inaugurated a school of thought in post-war

---

41 Karl Barth, *The Word of God and the Word of Man* (Eng., London: Hodder & Stoughton, (1928), pp. 28–50.
42 Karl Barth, *The Epistle to the Romans* (Eng., Oxford: Oxford University Press, 1933).
43 Karl Barth, *The Resurrection of the Dead* (London: Hodder & Stoughton, 1933), p. 17.
44 Karl Barth, *Church Dogmatics*, vol. 1, Pt. 1.1, sect. 4, p. 111.

Germany. He notoriously proposed a programme of 'demythologizing' of the NT, which has largely met with much criticism in the UK.[45] On a more positive note, he carried forward work on hermeneutics begun by Schleiermacher and Heidegger. His work on Paul in his *Theology of the New Testament*, volume 1, is also helpful. Dietrich Bonhoeffer is widely known for his latest work in his *Letters and Papers* from prison. But he also produced what Gerhard Ebeling and others would regard as more significant works in earlier years such as *Sanctorum Communio: A Theological Study of the Sociology of the Church*.[46] He also trained ordinands for the ministry of the Confessing Church in Germany, which had resisted the influence of Nazism.

Paul Tillich published an innovative *Systematic Theology* in three volumes.[47] He was a professor in Frankfurt, but had to flee from Germany to the United States when Hitler became Chancellor. He described his theology as 'answering theology', mediating theology and as 'a theology of correlation'. (For details see Part 1, Philosophical theology.)

Two seminal thinkers of roughly this era are Anders Nygren and Reinhold Niebuhr. Nygren's most famous book was *Agapē and Eros*. He argued that *agapē* was used in the NT to express the free, unmotivated, creative love of God, in contrast to human love. This often looked for something in return. Niebuhr wrote the classic, *The Nature and Destiny of Man* (2 vols, 1941), and his smaller *Moral Man and Immoral Society* was even more distinctive. He argued that we often disguise self-seeking as being 'for the sake of the family', 'for the nation' or 'for our class'. This thereby hides sin under the self-interest of communities.

(c) Four recent Roman Catholic theologians

Karl Rahner (1904–84), Yves Congar (1904–95), Hans Urs von Balthasar (1905–88) and Hans Küng (b. 1928) are four seminal Roman Catholic theologians, who greatly influenced Vatican II (1962–5) and subsequent Catholic thought (see Part 2, Catholicism).

---

45 Rudolf Bultmann, 'New Testament Mythology', in H.-W. Bartsch (ed.), *Kerygma and Myth*, vol. 1 (Eng., London: SPCK, 1964); cf. Bultmann, *Essays Philosophical and Theological* (London: SCM Press, 1955), and *Faith and Understanding* (London: SCM Press, 1969). For evaluations and criticisms see Anthony C. Thiselton, *The Two Horizons* (Exeter: Paternoster and Grand Rapids, Mich.: Eerdmans, 1980), pp. 252–82.

46 Dietrich Bonhoeffer, *Sanctorum Communio: A Theological Study of the Sociology of the Church* (Eng., Philadelphia, Pa.: Fortress Press, 1998).

47 Paul Tillich, *Systematic Theology*, 3 vols (Chicago, Ill.: University of Chicago Press and London: Nisbet, 1953, 1957, 1963).

(d) Recent Protestant thinkers

The earliest of these theologians was Thomas F. Torrance (1913–2007) of Edinburgh. He is known mainly for his defence and exposition of Barth, and also especially for his work on patristics and the Holy Spirit. His book *Theological Science* also majors on 'objectivity' in theology and knowledge of God. He is said to have produced some 600 writings.

Paul Ricoeur (1913–2005) contributed decisively to hermeneutics. Ricoeur studied philosophy at the Sorbonne in 1934, and came under the influence of G. Marcel and M. Merleau-Ponty. In 1939 he joined the French army, but in 1940 was taken prisoner by the Nazis. During the war years he studied German philosophy, including Jaspers, Husserl and Heidegger. In 1956 he produced his first books on the human will, guilt, finitude, freedom and symbol. He brings to a climax the hermeneutical tradition from Schleiermacher to Hans-Georg Gadamer (1900–2002). His thought on hermeneutics took a decisive turn with his reading of Freud and 'double meaning', and his two magisterial books were *Time and Narrative* (3 vols) and *Oneself as Another* (for details, see Part 1, Hermeneutical theology).

Just as we have mentioned Torrance all too briefly, we may also mention George Lindbeck (b. 1923). His book *The Nature of Doctrine* (1984) is widely quoted, especially in the USA. He attempts to present an ecumenical account of doctrine, but whether he is overrated, time will tell. Colin Gunton (1941–2003) should also be mentioned (see Part 2, Atonement). He has also published on the Trinity and the work of Christ.

The remaining two theologians to consider are Jürgen Moltmann (b. 1926) and Wolfhart Pannenberg (1928–2014). Personally, I rate them the most important and creative theologians of our day. Moltmann was profoundly influenced by his experiences of death in the Second World War, and by his time as a prisoner of war. He recalls 'the death of all my mainstays . . . and daily humiliation'. Eventually he came upon a Bible, which contained the words, 'If I make my bed in hell, you are there'. He recalls, 'God found me'. He came to believe in 'the power of hope, to which I owed my life'.[48]

For a time, Moltmann served as a pastor, and became influenced by van Ruler's eschatology, Weber's *Systematic Theology*, Luther's theology of the cross and Ernst Bloch's *Principle of Hope*. In 1964 he published his

---

48 Jürgen Moltmann, 'My Theological Career', in Moltmann, *History of the Triune God* (London: SCM Press, 1991), p. 166.

famous *Theology of Hope.*[49] He wrote, 'Faith, whenever it develops into hope, causes not rest, but unrest.'[50] He continues, 'Christianity stands or falls with the reality of the raising of Jesus from the dead by God.'[51] The cross, on the other hand, means 'the experience of god-forsakenness . . . that is, an absolute *nihil* embracing also God'.[52] Moltmann contrasts 'the deadliness of death' and 'promised life'.[53] Christ's resurrection conquers the deadliness of death.

In his next major work, Moltmann explored *The Crucified God.*[54] On the public world scene, signs of hope had collapsed. This included the Warsaw Pact invasion of Czechoslovakia, the Vietnam War and the assassination of Martin Luther King. On the death of Christ, Moltmann asks, 'What does Jesus' suffering and death mean for God himself?'[55] He has reservations about 'theism', whose God is too often seen as 'eternally with himself'.[56] The gospel is 'the Word of the Cross' (1 Cor. 1.18). Following Luther, he writes, 'the theology of the cross leads to criticism of self-glorification'.[57] He laments that the cross has become an item of ornamental jewellery: 'We have surrounded the scandal of the cross with roses.'[58] He even addresses the problem of suffering and the Trinity: 'Even Auschwitz is taken up into the grief of the Father, the surrender of the Son, and the power of the Spirit.'[59]

In *The Church in the Power of the Spirit* (1975) Moltmann shows how God goes out of himself, as it were, to create and engage with the world. It is a missionary Church. In his next major book, *The Trinity and the Kingdom of God*, he replaces the question, 'What does God mean to me?' by the more important one, 'What do I mean to God?'[60] Further, he expounds 'a social doctrine of the Trinity',[61] and he attacks the unfeeling God of theism. He writes, 'A God who cannot suffer cannot love either.'[62] He expounds the co-equality of the Holy Trinity: 'The Father sends the Son through the

---

49 Jürgen Moltmann, *Theology of Hope* (London: SCM Press, 1967).
50 Moltmann, *Theology of Hope*, p. 21.
51 Moltmann, *Theology of Hope*, p. 165.
52 Moltmann, *Theology of Hope*, p. 198.
53 Moltmann, *Theology of Hope*, p. 210.
54 Jürgen Moltmann, *The Crucified God* (Eng., London: SCM Press, 1974).
55 Jürgen Moltmann, *A Broad Place* (London: SCM Press, 2007), p. 182.
56 Moltmann, *The Crucified God*, p. 194.
57 Moltmann, *The Crucified God*, p. 70.
58 Moltmann, *The Crucified God*, p. 36.
59 Moltmann, *The Crucified God*, p. 278.
60 Jürgen Moltmann, *The Trinity and the Kingdom of God* (Eng., London: SCM Press, 1981), p. 3.
61 Moltmann, *The Trinity*, p. 19.
62 Moltmann, *The Trinity*, p. 38.

Spirit; the Son comes from the Father in the power of the Spirit; the Spirit brings people into the fellowship of the Son with the Father.'[63] He rejects a merely modal view of the Trinity. He continues his Trinitarian theme in *God in Creation* (1985). He declares, 'Creation is a Trinitarian process'.[64] He rejects the notion of human 'dominion' of the world; rather humans are stewards of creation (Gen. 1.26). In his next major work, *The Way of Jesus Christ* (1990), the 'way' indicates a process of travelling as disciples of Christ.

In *The Spirit of Life* (1991), Moltmann expounds a careful doctrine of the Holy Spirit, arguing that human beings are expected to be 'open to the Spirit'.[65] Moltmann stresses the personhood of the Holy Spirit, especially since personhood becomes most comprehensible in terms of relationship. Moltmann holds together divine immanence and divine transcendence. He also draws on Hegel's notion of 'God's self-distinction', and on the notion of *perichōrēsis*, drawn from the Cappadocian Fathers. He stresses the Spirit's anointing and empowerment. Moltmann also expresses reservations about any sharp distinction between 'supernatural' and 'natural' *charismata*, or free gifts of God.[66]

The last of Moltmann's major studies in dogmatic theology is his book *The Coming of God* (1996), which concerns Christian eschatology.[67] Moltmann argues that just as the raised Christ does not 'develop out of the crucified and dead Christ . . . the ultimate new thing does not issue from . . . the old'.[68] Yet the new has its own continuity: it gathers up the old, and creates it anew; God is faithful to his creation. Moltmann also includes a section on the foolishness of suppressed mourning for the dead, in stark contrast to the biblical understanding of mourning in the face of loss as crucial. Like Pannenberg, he insists that 'on the last day God will awaken the whole person, not just the soul-less body'.[69] Moltmann also urges that when Christ appears in glory, believers will be beside him, and will live eternally with him.[70] Death is not the end. Moltmann also

---

63 Moltmann, *The Trinity*, p. 75.

64 Jürgen Moltmann, *God in Creation: An Ecological Doctrine of Creation* (Eng., London: SCM Press, 1985), p. 9.

65 Jürgen Moltmann, *The Spirit of Life: A Universal Affirmation* (Eng., London: SCM Press, 1991), p. 27.

66 Moltmann, *The Spirit of Life*, p. 183.

67 Jürgen Moltmann, *The Coming of God: Christian Eschatology* (Eng., London: SCM Press, 1996).

68 Moltmann, *The Coming of God*, p. 28.

69 Moltmann, *The Coming of God*, p. 101.

70 Moltmann, *The Coming of God*, p. 105.

considers the background of apocalyptic and millenarianism, and the new heaven and new earth of cosmic eschatology.

Pannenberg remains no less significant and creative than Moltmann. The latter's exceptional gifts include his pastoral sensitivity. On the other hand Pannenberg's encyclopaedic knowledge and wisdom, his philosophical insights and biblical exegetical skill, are staggering, and cannot be bettered. The one pity is that his immense learning sometimes leads to dense and difficult passages for some readers.

Pannenberg's early work on the theology of history and his many essays in his *Basic Questions in Theology* (3 vols) already mark him out as the major new alternative to Bultmann and existentialism.[71] The volume edited by Robinson and Cobb (cited below) makes this clear. In the first volume of *Basic Questions* Pannenberg comments, 'This universality of theology is unavoidably bound up with the fact that it speaks of God . . . It belongs to the task of theology to understand all being in relation to God.'[72] From the first, Pannenberg asserts that hermeneutics remains a primary concern. He also explains that Gerhard von Rad on Israelite tradition has been a primary influence upon him. He also insists that many NT issues can only be understood in terms of that tradition and 'the one history of God which binds them [the two Testaments] together'.[73] He further comments,

> The basis for all . . . Christological statements about Jesus of Nazareth is formed by the dependence of the meaning of Jesus on the fact that [he] is understood in the framework of the history of God with Israel attested in the Old Testament.[74]

This constitutes a theme which re-echoes throughout Pannenberg's works.

Pannenberg recognizes the legitimacy of historical-critical methods, but also speaks of their 'anthropocentricity'. The public history of God's dealings with the world is also different from what he calls the ghetto of redemptive history. Indeed he devotes an essay to 'Hermeneutic and Universal History', alluding to the history of Schleiermacher, Dilthey and Gadamer. In his second volume he discusses the nature of truth,

---

71 Wolfhart Pannenberg, *Basic Questions in Theology*, 3 vols (Eng., London: SCM Press, 1970, 1971, 1973); and Pannenberg, 'The Revelation of God in Jesus of Nazareth', in James M. Robinson and John B. Cobb (eds), *New Frontiers in Theology*, vol. 3, *Theology as History* (New York, N.Y.: Harper & Row, 1967), pp. 101–33.

72 Pannenberg, *Basic Questions*, vol. 1, p. 1.

73 Pannenberg, *Basic Questions*, vol. 1, p. 25.

74 Pannenberg, *Basic Questions*, vol. 1, p. 26.

referring to the contingent nature of God's revelation of his acts in history, i.e. it was not timeless and abstract. Pannenberg has two characteristic essays on faith and reason. In our day faith must be *rational*, as the early apologists and Aquinas saw. He declares,

> An otherwise unconvincing message cannot attain the power to convince simply by appealing to the Holy Spirit . . . Argumentation and the operation of the Spirit are not in competition with each other. In trusting in the Spirit, Paul in no way spared himself thinking and arguing.[75]

In volume 3 Pannenberg discusses atheism, philosophical questions, and meaning and eschatology. On Hegel, he declares, 'Hardly any of the great thinkers of the modern age have done as much as Hegel to set the Christian religion back upon the throne from which the Enlightenment had removed it'.[76] In his essay on meaning, he rightly quotes Dilthey to the effect that: 'What formerly seemed insignificant perhaps appears later as of fundamental importance . . . The final significance of the events of our life can be measured only at the end of our lives, in the power of death'.[77] This fully accords with Pannenberg's conviction that genuine meaning presupposes a grasp of the *whole*, which, in Christian terms, means the revelation of God and the end.

Two other major books intervene before the publication of Pannenberg's magisterial three-volume *Systematic Theology*. The first is *Jesus – God and Man*. One central thesis is, 'If Jesus has been raised, then the end of the world has begun'.[78] The resurrection of Jesus Christ derived its meaning from the history of traditions to which it belonged. He rejects Bultmann's view that the Easter faith of the Church caused faith in the resurrection. On the contrary he affirms his belief in the empty tomb.[79] The resurrection of Jesus Christ establishes the divinity of Jesus from a retrospective viewpoint, and also confirms the divinity of God the Father in raising him from the dead. Yet the Incarnation and the cross fully confirm the genuine humanness of Jesus.

The second work is Pannenberg's *Theology and the Philosophy of Science*.[80] Theology remains a science, because we need to defend 'the truth

---

75 Pannenberg, *Basic Questions*, vol. 2, pp. 34–5.
76 Pannenberg, *Basic Questions*, vol. 3, p. 158.
77 Pannenberg, *Basic Questions*. vol. 3, p. 201.
78 Wolfhart Pannenberg, *Jesus – God and Man* (Eng., London: SCM Press, 1968), p. 67.
79 Pannenberg, *Jesus*, p. 109.
80 Wolfhart Pannenberg, *Theology and the Philosophy of Science* (Philadelphia, Pa.: Westminster Press, 1976).

of Christianity by generally accepted criteria'.[81] But he attacks logical positivism and inadequate forms of sociology. He defends general hermeneutics as a whole from Schleiermacher through Dilthey to Gadamer; but he has strong reservations about Fuchs, Heidegger and Bultmann.[82] Like Torrance, he discusses theology as the science of God. He declares, 'The reality of God is always present only in subjective anticipations of the totality of reality'.[83] We see this in the utterances of believers and theologians. He concludes by demonstrating the coherence of theology.

We finally arrive at Pannenberg's magisterial three-volume *Systematic Theology*, which we discuss in Part 1, under 'Systematic theology'.

---

81 Pannenberg, *Theology*, p. 13.
82 Pannenberg, *Theology*, pp. 157–224.
83 Pannenberg, *Theology*, p. 310.

Part 1

APPROACHES

1

Biblical theology

The term *biblical theology* can be understood in at least three ways. One way refers simply to theology of the Bible. This substantially overlaps with our material under the heading 'Biblical roots' in the Introduction. A second way of understanding biblical theology would be to describe and evaluate the origin and eventual decline of what was called the 'Biblical Theology Movement'. This amounted to being an identifiable school of theology, and included such names as Brevard Childs, John Bright, G. E. Wright. We focus on this meaning. A third way of understanding the term is to describe and evaluate the major works of OT and NT theology. On the OT, such works as those by Gerhard von Rad, Walther Eichrodt, Edmond Jacob and others would be included. On the NT, those by Rudolf Bultmann, Ethelbert Stauffer, Alan Richardson and Joachim Jeremias would feature.

In the history of the Christian Church, Martin Luther in his *Large* and *Small Catechisms*, John Calvin in his *Institutes*, and to a large measure Karl Barth in his *Church Dogmatics*, sought to provide summaries or expositions of biblical themes. Strictly, however, as a distinctive discipline, in 1787 Johann Philipp Gabler (1753–1826) distinguished between 'a true biblical theology', which was a *historical* account of the views of different biblical writers, and 'a pure biblical theology', which abstracted *lasting and universal* biblical concepts from history. The so-called timeless truths would be presented to dogmatic theologians for their work, while the historical approach remained strictly disciplined for biblical studies.

In the nineteenth century and during the first half of the twentieth, OT theology tended to become separated from NT theology. By the early or mid twentieth century, Walther Eichrodt (1890–1978) had produced a theology of the OT centred on God's covenantal relationship with Israel. Gerhard von Rad (1901–71) produced a theology of the OT largely based on a tradition of redemptive history. In one sense this provoked a biblical theology which embraced both Testaments. In an opposite sense, their emphasis on the unity of each Testament encouraged the rise of biblical theology.

The rise of the biblical theology school is usually dated from the end of the Second World War and on until the early 1960s. Brevard Childs (1923–2007) described it as a reaction against certain tendencies. He wrote,

> Critical scholars were faulted for having lost themselves in *the minutiae of literary, philological, and historical problems. As a result the Bible had been hopelessly fragmented* and the essential unity of the gospel was distorted and forgotten. *Biblical scholarship had deteriorated into an exercise in trivia,* in which . . . the profound theological dimensions were overlooked (my italics).[1]

The biblical theology movement only temporarily suspended this regrettable tendency. Admittedly there were notable exceptions: for example, B. F. Westcott, J. B. Lightfoot and F. J. Hort (between about 1890 and 1910) provided such an exception, combining critical studies with theological concerns, which served the Christian Church. Childs also cited reaction against the radical criticism of such scholars as Wrede, Weiss and Schweitzer.[2]

More positively, Childs cited the work of H. H. Rowley, Alan Richardson, Floyd Filson and Paul Minear.[3] Childs also mentioned the work of James Muilenburg and Bernhard Anderson. We may further mention the work of William F. Albright (1891–1971), who was primarily an orientalist. In 1940 he published *From Stone Age to Christianity*, in which he set out a coherent narrative from Abraham and Moses to the birth of Christianity.[4] Childs also cited the more positive theological background associated with Barth, Brunner and Richard Niebuhr (1894–1962) and their critique of liberalism. Niebuhr described liberalism as teaching that 'a God without wrath brings men without sin into a kingdom without judgment through a ministry of a Christ without a cross'.[5] Childs mentions Edwin Hoskyns, C. H. Dodd and A. M. Hunter, from the UK, and alludes to Anton Fridrichsen of Uppsala, Sweden. Otherwise he regarded the movement as largely American.[6]

---

1 Brevard S. Childs, *Biblical Theology in Crisis* (Philadelphia, Pa.: Westminster Press, 1970), p. 15.
2 Childs, *Biblical Theology in Crisis*, p. 19.
3 Childs, *Biblical Theology in Crisis*, p. 14; H. H. Rowley, *Rediscovery of the Old Testament* (2nd edn, London: James Clarke, 1948).
4 William F. Albright, *From Stone Age to Christianity: Monotheism and the Historical Process* (Baltimore, Md.: Johns Hopkins University Press, 1940).
5 H. Richard Niebuhr, *The Kingdom of God in America* (San Francisco, Calif.: Harper, 1937; rp. 1959), p. 193.
6 Childs, *Biblical Theology in Crisis*, p. 31.

In 1952, G. Ernest Wright (1909–74), one of the founders of the biblical theology movement, published *God Who Acts: Biblical Theology as Recital.*[7] He wrote, 'One of the most important tasks of the Church today is to hold upon a Biblically-centred theology . . . It is difficult to find a leading graduate school in the world where students can profitably specialise in biblical theology.'[8] He was concerned to demonstrate God's revelation and action in history. He wrote,

> There is, first, the peculiar attention to history and to historical traditions as the primary sphere in which God reveals himself. To be sure, God also reveals himself and his will in various ways . . . Yet the nature and content of this revelation is determined by the outward, objective happenings in history.[9]

He defines God's action in history especially as his election of special people through whom he could accomplish his purposes. His emphasis on public historical tradition is not dissimilar to that of Irenaeus. He continues, 'The election and its implications were confirmed and clarified in the event of the covenant ceremony at Sinai . . . The central problem of Israel was envisaged as the problem of true security in the midst of covenant violation.'[10] He argues, 'The confessional recital of the redemptive acts of God in a particular history is the chief medium of revelation.'[11]

Two other keynote books, published before *God Who Acts*, were published in 1944 and 1950.[12] Some describe the earlier book as a primer of the biblical theology movement. It stresses God's revelation through history, the unity of the two Testaments, and the importance of the OT for Christians. The second book challenges the notion that Israel simply assimilated the cultural and sociological environment of its neighbours, and convincingly demonstrates the distinctiveness of Israel's faith as God's revelation.

Wright subsequently wrote *The Old Testament and Theology* (1969), in which he chronicled his development as a scholar, and expounded his basic beliefs. By the time of his death in 1974, he was admired as an

---

7 G. Ernest Wright, *God Who Acts: Biblical Theology as Recital* (London: SCM Press, 1952).

8 Wright, *God Who Acts*, p. 112.

9 Wright, *God Who Acts*, p. 55.

10 Wright, *God Who Acts*, p. 56.

11 Wright, *God Who Acts*, p. 13.

12 G. Ernest Wright, *The Challenge of Israel's Faith* (Chicago, Ill.: University of Chicago Press, 1944); and G. Ernest Wright, *The Old Testament against Its Environment* (London: SCM Press, 1950).

exceptional American biblical scholar, who inaugurated the era of 'biblical theology'.

A second leading American biblical scholar who contributed to the biblical theology movement was John Bright (1908–95). He taught for many years at Union Theological Seminary, New York. In 1953 he published *The Kingdom of God*, which shows the relevance of biblical faith for the Christian Church. But probably the best known of his works is *A History of Israel* (1959), in three editions, which updates reconstruction in the light of archaeology. In *Early Israel in Recent History Writing* (1956), he wrote: 'I am not among those who are inclined to sneer at a reverence for Scripture.'[13] He defended the authenticity of many historical traditions. Israel's faith, he argued, centred on the covenantal relation with God, which embodied God's election and his commands.

Another leading scholar whom we must note is Brevard Childs (1923–2007), the chronicler of the movement. He mounted a counter-reply to criticisms of the movement as a whole. His defence of biblical theology, however, represents his most distinctive contribution on the biblical canon. Childs had worked under Walther Eichrodt, and owed much to Karl Barth at Basel. Nevertheless, from 1958 to his retirement in 1999, he taught at Yale Divinity School. Two features further link him with the biblical theology movement. First, he insists on the unity of the Old and New Testaments. Second, he regards the OT (as well as the New) as acutely relevant to the Christian Church. His *Myth and Reality in the Old Testament* (Ger., 1957; Eng., 1960) defended a relation between myth and history.[14] He explicitly described the biblical use of what was previously myth as now 'broken myth', thereby anticipating George Caird.[15] By this phrase he means to say that the biblical writers may indeed use imagery that was *once* myth, but now no longer functions as myth. Some years later, Childs' *Biblical Theology in Crisis* conceded that the earlier biblical theology movement had passed its peak, and even needed to be carefully qualified. He admits, 'The Biblical Theology Movement underwent a period of slow dissolution beginning in the late fifties.'[16] Nevertheless, its strength lay in its stressing the importance of both the OT and NT for the Church.[17] He adds, 'The

---

13 John Bright, *Early Israel in Recent History Writing* (London: SCM Press, 1956), p. 124.
14 Brevard Childs, *Myth and Reality in the Old Testament* (London: SCM Press, 1960), esp. pp. 75–8.
15 Childs, *Myth and Reality*, p. 96.
16 Childs, *Biblical Theology in Crisis*, p. 87.
17 Childs, *Biblical Theology in Crisis*, p. 99.

text of Scripture points faithfully to Christ.'[18] On the other hand, he admits, biblical theology requires greater discipline, and greater attention to the historical diversity of the Bible, albeit within the context of the canon.[19]

Childs published his classic commentary on Exodus in 1974.[20] In addition to textual criticism, this offered literary and form-critical analysis, exegesis within an OT context, a NT context, a history of exegesis and theological reflection. This works well, including the section on the call of Moses.[21] Childs goes further in *Introduction to the Old Testament as Scripture*.[22] Most chapters end with theological and hermeneutical reflections. The sections on Samuel, Isaiah, Jeremiah and Hosea especially repay study.[23] He followed this by *The New Testament as Canon* (1984), and finally *Biblical Theology of the Old and New Testaments* (1992). Here he frankly acknowledged the need for a new approach. Yet he did much both to confirm and modify the older 'biblical theology' approach, especially on the unity of the two Testaments, and on their status and address to the Christian Church.

Much of the earlier critique of this movement came from James Barr (1924–2006). Barr was born in Glasgow and taught at Edinburgh, Manchester and Oxford. His strongest criticism was to disabuse his colleagues concerning an exaggerated contrast between 'Greek' and 'Hebrew' thought. His targets included Wright, Albright and T. Boman. Barr undertook a meticulous conceptual and linguistic examination in *The Semantics of Biblical Language* (1961), and in *Old and New in Interpretation* (1966). He argued convincingly, 'Divergencies in vocabulary grids themselves are ultimately irrelevant . . . The idea that the grammatical structure of a language reflects the thought structure . . . has very great difficulties.'[24] Barr illustrates and demonstrates this point by appealing not only to Greek and Hebrew, but also to French, German, Turkish and Chinese. He rejects the notion that all Hebrew thought is 'dynamic', and that all Greek is 'static'. In particular he criticizes Boman's *Hebrew Thought Compared with Greek* (1960), and some of the earliest volumes of Kittel's *Theological Dictionary of the New Testament*.[25] He also discusses Hebrew 'stative' verbs. In his

18 Childs, *Biblical Theology in Crisis*, p. 103.
19 Childs, *Biblical Theology in Crisis*, pp. 107–14, 143–7.
20 Brevard Childs, *Exodus: A Commentary* (London: SCM Press, 1974).
21 Childs, *Exodus*, pp. 47–89.
22 Brevard Childs, *Introduction to the Old Testament as Scripture* (London: SCM Press, 1979).
23 Childs, *Introduction*, pp. 263–80, 311–38, 339–54, 374–94.
24 James Barr, *The Semantics of Biblical Language* (Oxford: Oxford University Press, 1961), pp. 38, 39.
25 Thorlief Boman, *Hebrew Thought Compared with Greek* (London: SCM Press, 1960).

comments on the difference between genuine gender and more superficial grammatical gender he comments:

> No one would suppose that the Turks, because they nowhere distinguish gender in their language, not even in the personal pronouns as we do in English, are deficient in the concept of sexual difference; nor would we seriously argue that the French have extended their legendary erotic interests into the linguistic realm by forcing every noun to be either masculine or feminine. The absence of correlation between linguistic types of masculine, feminine and neuter and the real or conceptual distinctions of male, female and inanimate is very obvious in German and other languages.[26]

This point, of course, has additional significance for discussions about the supposed gender of God and the Holy Spirit. Barr rightly distinguishes between words and sentences in the context of Kittel's *Dictionary*. He comments, for example, 'If Kittel had only said "sentences", it would not have been quite so bad; but a dictionary is a book of words not a dictionary of sentences.'[27] In his subsequent book *Old and New in Interpretation*, Barr sums up the general point about Hebrew and Greek thought. He observes:

> There is no reason to deny or to minimize any more than there is to absolutize the difference between Hebrew and Greek thought; but if we wish to give a historically valid statement, we should first of all have to say that no unitary contrast, no simple contrast, no contrast capable of being grasped within a single philosophical antithesis, could ever be given.[28]

Later Barr turned his criticisms towards fundamentalism within the Protestant tradition in *Fundamentalism* (1977), but returned to his earlier theme in *The Concept of Biblical Theology* (1999).[29] Barr's publications are too numerous to enumerate. His forceful criticisms of some of the problems in the biblical theology school are valid, but given these modifications, we cannot simply sweep aside the contribution of scholars such as Wright, Bright, Childs and others. Perhaps it is no longer viable in its original form produced in the 1950s. But few would wish to put the clock back, and to ignore the biblical theology movement without its needed modifications.

---

26 Barr, *Semantics of Biblical Language*, p. 39.

27 Barr, *Semantics of Biblical Language*, p. 213.

28 James Barr, *Old and New in Interpretation: A Study of the Two Testaments* (London: SCM Press, 1966), p. 49.

29 James Barr, *The Concept of Biblical Theology* (Minneapolis, Minn.: Fortress Press, 1999).

2

Hermeneutical theology

Although interpretation of texts took place from the Stoics onwards, and biblical interpretation from the NT, Origen and other church fathers, hermeneutical theology proper did not emerge until after the Reformation, and decisively in the modern era. Origen proposed that most passages carried a literal, allegorical and spiritual meaning, analogous with body, mind or soul, and spirit.[1] At the Reformation, Martin Luther (1483–1546) argued that Scripture was always sufficiently clear to enable us to take action, and his German translation presupposes hermeneutics. William Tyndale (c. 1494–1536) argued that Scripture not only instructed, but also performed *actions*, such as promising, appointing, healing, saving, and so on.[2] Matthias Flacius Illyricus published *Clavis Scripturae Sacrae* (1567), arguing that each biblical text should be interpreted in the whole. Johann Martin Chladenius published his work on interpretation in 1742, introducing the concept of 'point of view' or perspective, which a writer or reader might bring to the biblical text. This was developed in the twentieth century by Roman Ingarden (1893–1970) and Wolfgang Iser (1926–2007).

The effective founder of modern hermeneutics, however, was Friedrich D. Schleiermacher (1768–1834). He produced notes for teaching in 1805, then a draft of a longer manuscript (1809–10), and a developed study of hermeneutics (1819). Hermeneutical understanding, he urged, arises not from logical deduction, but from the *interrelation between the general and the particular*. He called these respectively 'grammatical' hermeneutics (on the basis of shared language), and 'psychological' hermeneutics (on the basis of how particular authors *use* language). He related these two interrelated poles of understanding respectively to the masculine and feminine principle. He declared, 'Divinatory knowledge is the feminine strength in knowing people; comparative knowledge, the masculine.

---

1 Origen, *On First Principles*, 4.2.4.
2 William Tyndale, *A Pathway into the Holy Scripture*, in *Doctrinal Treatises* (Cambridge: Cambridge University Press, 1846), pp. 7–29.

Each method refers back to the other.[3] He also argued, 'Hermeneutics is a part of the art of thinking, and is therefore philosophical.'[4] Further, every understanding builds on a preliminary or provisional understanding (Ger., *Vorverständnis*). He concluded, 'Our initial grasp of the whole is only provisional and imperfect.'[5] A process of revision in our understanding constantly continues. He concludes, 'Even after we have revised our initial concept, it remains provisional: this is universally known as the hermeneutical circle.'

'To divine' without comparative philological or critical study, Schleiermacher insisted, is to become a hermeneutical 'nebulist'; while to engage in comparative or philological questions without a living, intuitive, perception of the spirit of the subject matter is to remain a hermeneutical 'pedant'.[6] The divinatory aspect uses imagination and empathy to understand the author and text; the comparative aspect uses rules of grammar, syntax and vocabulary to ensure that this understanding is accurate. In his capacity as a NT scholar, Schleiermacher insists, 'Only historical interpretation can do justice to the rootedness of the New Testament authors in their time and place.'[7]

Wilhelm Dilthey (1833–1911) applied hermeneutics not only to texts, but also to life and social institutions. He was primarily a secular philosopher, but his influence on hermeneutical theology remains permanent.

Martin Heidegger's (1889–1976) hermeneutics profoundly influenced Rudolf Bultmann and existentialist theology. Heidegger, in turn, was heavily indebted to Kierkegaard, Husserl and Jaspers. From them Heidegger learned to emphasize the priority of 'existence' as a given which preceded and conditioned the nature of understanding. He argued that it determines the conditions on which the possibility of any ontological investigation depends.[8] He also insisted, first, that 'the horizon for the understanding of being' is time.[9] Second, he argued that all interpretation and understanding must take account of 'historicality', i.e. ways in which texts, interpreters and readers are historically conditioned. Third, following

---

3 Friedrich D. E. Schleiermacher, *Hermeneutics: The Handwritten Manuscripts*, ed. H. Kimmerle (Eng., Missoula, Mont.: Scholars Press, 1977), p. 97.

4 Schleiermacher, *Hermeneutics*, p. 150.

5 Schleiermacher, *Hermeneutics*, p. 200.

6 Schleiermacher, *Hermeneutics*, p. 205.

7 Schleiermacher, *Hermeneutics*, p. 104.

8 Martin Heidegger, *Being and Time* (Eng., New York, N.Y.: Harper & Row, 1971), pp. 62, 39.

9 Martin Heidegger, *On the Way to Language* (Eng., New York, N.Y.: Harper & Row, 1971), p. 85; Heidegger, *Being and Time*.

Dilthey, Heidegger stressed the difference between understanding objects in terms of objectification, and understanding human life (*Dasein*, being-there) in terms of *existentialia*. Objectification amounts to depersonalization.[10] Interpretation is never presuppositionless, but depends on pre-understanding (*Vorverständnis*). He insists that the hermeneutical circle must not be understood as a vicious one, but as a key to understanding.

In Christian theology, Rudolf Bultmann (1884–1976) insisted, with Heidegger, that the interpretation of biblical exegesis can never be presuppositionless or value-neutral, but always depends on what has so far been understood. The necessary 'presupposition' for understanding is '*the interpreter's relationship in his life to the subject which is . . . expressed in the text*'.[11] For example, 'I can only understand a text of music in so far as I have a relationship to music'.[12] In *The Two Horizons*, I have attempted to show in detail how Bultmann has been influenced by the hermeneutical tradition, existentialism and neo-Kantian dualism.[13] Bultmann believed that NT writers never intended to describe objects, but to indicate stances, attitudes and values. This shaped his programme of 'demythologizing'.[14] His conception of *myth* leads to a devaluation of historical events, and their interpretation in terms of existential attitudes. This has two sides. For example, on the lordship of Christ Bultmann is brilliant at expounding its existential side. Jesus' lordship is interpreted in terms of *belonging to Christ*, and his having *the care of us*. On the other hand, scant attention is given to *Christ's ontological status* as one whom *God made Lord* (Rom. 1.3–4; Phil. 2.6–11). John Macquarrie suggests that Bultmann's disparagement of miracle implies 'a pseudo-scientific view of a closed universe that was popular half a century ago'.[15] On the other hand, Bultmann rightly notes that Paul never regards body and soul or spirit as 'components', but as modes of being in the world. Thus Bultmann's debt to Heidegger and existentialism made a huge impact on hermeneutics.

---

10 Heidegger, *Being and Time*, pp. 95–107.

11 Rudolf Bultmann, *Essays Philosophical and Theological* (London: SCM Press, 1955), p. 241 (his italics).

12 Bultmann, *Essays Philosophical and Theological*, pp. 242–3.

13 Anthony C. Thiselton, *The Two Horizons: New Testament Hermeneutics and Philosophical Description* (Exeter: Paternoster and Grand Rapids, Mich.: Eerdmans, 1980), pp. 205–92.

14 Rudolf Bultmann, *New Testament and Mythology and Other Basic Writings*, ed. Schubert Ogden (Philadelphia, Pa.: Fortress Press, 1984), esp. pp. 1–44.

15 John Macquarrie, *An Existentialist Theology: A Comparison of Heidegger and Bultmann* (London: SCM Press, 1955), pp. 168.

Karl Barth (1886–1968) held strong reservations about Bultmann's hermeneutics, especially, in effect, his dissolving history and ontology into existential attitudes. But he agreed with Bultmann's maxim that 'objective' interpretation was inadequate.

Hans-Georg Gadamer (1900–2002) represents the next milestone in hermeneutics. His major work is his magisterial volume *Truth and Method*.[16] He was a friend and for a time colleague of Heidegger, and studied Schleiermacher and Dilthey, but his work signals a decisive advance in hermeneutics. In *Truth and Method*, he attacked the abstract rationalism and individualism of both Descartes and the Enlightenment. In contrast to Descartes, Gadamer cites the work of Giambattista Vico (1668–1744), who stressed both community and history. Rationalism, Gadamer argued, might be adequate for the natural sciences alone, but a historical and hermeneutical method is necessary to understand the humanities or *Geisteswissenschaften*.

Hermeneutics is characterized by keeping oneself 'open to what is other'.[17] He illustrates the importance of history and art with reference to games, festivals and concerts, each of which cannot be precisely *replicated* without undermining their very identity. He writes, 'Play fulfils its purpose only if the player loses himself in the play . . . It is the game that is played – it is irrelevant whether or not there is a subject who plays it.'[18] Even more strikingly he writes, '*The primacy of play over the consciousness of the player is fundamentally acknowledged*' (his italics).[19] Thus in hermeneutics, the emphasis lies on the interpreter as *participant*, not merely as observer. Just as a player or performer is absorbed in the game, festival or concert, so a participant always has a different viewpoint and horizon from the neutral spectator or observer.

In the second main part of *Truth and Method*, Gadamer examines questions of truth, understanding and historical reason more deeply. He commends Dilthey's notion of life-world, although he also criticizes Schleiermacher for undue subjectivism. He introduces Heidegger's notion of temporality (*Zeitlichkeit*), and his own well-known concept of prejudices or prejudgments (*Vorurteile*). He concludes, 'The pre-judgements of the individual, far more than his judgements, constitute the historical

---

16 Hans-Georg Gadamer, *Truth and Method* (Eng. 2nd edn, London: Sheed & Ward, 1989; Ger., 1960).
17 Gadamer, *Truth and Method*, p. 17.
18 Gadamer, *Truth and Method*, pp. 102, 103.
19 Gadamer, *Truth and Method*, p. 104.

reality of his being.'[20] In his section on the rehabilitation of authority and tradition, he writes that authority 'rests on an acknowledgement, and hence on an act of reason itself, which, aware of its own limitations, trusts in the better insight of others'.[21] This leads him to expound his special concept of effective history, or the history of effects (*Wirkungsgeschichte*).

Further, Gadamer rightly explains the distinctive value of the term *horizon*. He observes that a horizon is 'something into which we move and that moves with us. Horizons change for a person who is moving. Thus the horizon of the past . . . is always in motion'.[22] This is easily understandable if we actually imagine travel in a train or a car. It yields a quite different concept from 'presupposition'. The latter seems by comparison often to be fixed, or not negotiable, whereas horizons may *expand* or become modified as we ourselves progress in knowledge and understanding. Indeed in Pannenberg's hermeneutical theology, the notion of expanding horizons becomes pivotal. Gadamer also emphasizes the importance of asking questions, rather than simply stating problems. 'Problems', he says, usually concern fixed abstractions, like 'fixed points'. Questions 'acquire the pattern of their answer from the genesis of their meaning', i.e. they are not 'fixed', and imply a context of enquiry.[23] He draws on R. G. Collingwood (1889–1943) for his 'Logic of Question and Answer'.

In Part 3, Gadamer expounds what he calls 'ontological hermeneutics', which is the term often used for his distinctive approach. He speaks of what might 'emerge' from a conversation, especially when the partner in the conversation is 'other'. The aim of the conversation partners is to bring their respective horizons as closely and creatively together as possible. This may produce a third perspective. He aims here to build on a theory of language, although he draws mainly on German theorists such as Ernst Cassirer, Wilhelm von Humboldt and others.

Simultaneously in the 1960s and 1970s, two theologians, Ernst Fuchs (1903–83) and Gerhard Ebeling (1912–2001) were producing what became known as the 'new hermeneutic'. Like Gadamer, they are concerned with the relation between the text and the reader of today. They ask, 'How does the word strike home (*treffen*) to the modern hearer?' The word of God, they argue, must *create* faith, not *presuppose* it. Ebeling insists, 'The same word can be said to another time only by being said

---

20 Gadamer, *Truth and Method*, pp. 276–7.
21 Gadamer, *Truth and Method*, p. 279.
22 Gadamer, *Truth and Method*, p. 304.
23 Gadamer, *Truth and Method*, p. 377.

differently.'[24] How can the word speak to us *anew*? Fuchs argues that understanding must become a common understanding or empathy (*Einverständnis*) between the reader and the text, akin to the common understanding that exists within a close-knit family.[25] He comments, '*At home one does not speak so that people may understand, but because people understand*' (his italics).[26] He declares, 'The truth has ourselves as its object.'[27] It is not the text that is 'object', but us. The subject–object relation is reversed.

Fuchs illustrates this with Jesus' parable of the labourers in the vineyard (Matt. 20.1–16). Jesus tells the parable of the labourers in such a way that the people in the crowd immediately *feel in their bones* the natural injustice apparently perpetrated on those who have worked the longest hours of the day. The landowner begins by paying the last, who had worked for one hour (Matt. 20.8). As those who have worked only a few hours receive a day's wage, those who have worked all day long in the burning heat assume that they will receive something extra. However, they are dismayed to receive the same day's wage, and the crowd is utterly on their side. The employer remonstrates with them: 'Did you not agree with me for the usual daily wage?' (v. 13). It takes a revelation for the crowd to realize that generosity and grace to the least deserving eclipse supposed natural justice. Love, Fuchs says, does not simply blurt out. The way of Jesus is far more effective than a conceptual sermon on grace.

The new hermeneutic became fashionable for a decade until it was generally realized that while Fuchs readily applied this method to interpreting the teaching of Jesus and to poetic passages, he tended to expound these in a one-sided way, and to ignore the more didactic passages of Paul. Worst of all, he understood the resurrection as a 'linguistic' event, rather than a historical one.

It was otherwise with the hermeneutics of Paul Ricoeur (1913–2005). Ricoeur made a decisive and lasting contribution to theological hermeneutics, perhaps even more important than that of Hans-Georg Gadamer.

---

24 Gerhard Ebeling, 'Time and Word', in James Robinson (ed.), *The Future of Our Religious Past* (London: SCM Press, 1971), p. 265.

25 Ernst Fuchs, 'The New Testament and the Hermeneutical Problem', in James M. Robinson and John B. Cobb (eds), *New Frontiers in Theology*, vol. 2, *The New Hermeneutic* (New York, N.Y.: Harper & Row, 1964), pp. 124–5; cf. pp. 111–45.

26 Fuchs, 'The New Testament and the Problem', in Robinson and Cobb (eds), *The New Hermeneutic*, p. 124.

27 Fuchs, 'The New Testament and the Problem', in Robinson and Cobb (eds), *The New Hermeneutic*, p. 143.

He writes as a philosopher, but his personal faith is as a committed Protestant. We alluded in the Introduction to his early influences, notably to his study of Jaspers, Husserl and Heidegger during the years of the Second World War.

A turning point for Ricoeur came later with his reading of Freud. He published his earlier thought on hermeneutics in his book *Freud and Philosophy* (1965; Eng., 1970).[28] As a Christian, he rejected Freud's materialist and mechanistic world-view. However, he regarded Freud's work on interpretation of dreams as a classic in hermeneutics. When a patient described his or her dreams, Freud understood that this description could *not be taken at face value*. The dream as *actually dreamed* ('the dream thoughts') is not exactly the same as the patient's report of the dream ('the dream text'). Another text lies *beneath* the text that is described. Freud argued that displacement, condensation and scrambling resulted in what he called over-determination. Ricoeur endorsed this approach.[29] He sums up the key point:

> Hermeneutics seems to me to be animated by this double motivation: *willingness to suspect, willingness to listen*; vow of rigour, vow of obedience. In our time we have not finished doing away with idols, and we have barely begun to listen to symbols (his italics).[30]

The use of these two axes leads to both explanation (*Erklärung*) and understanding (*Verstehen*). Gadamer had stressed only understanding, without explanation. Idols, Ricoeur argued, constituted distorted understandings in our own image; symbols constituted the positive and creative axis of understanding: 'The idols must die so that symbols may live.'[31]

Ricoeur produced a stream of publications, which are all full of insights. But the two major are *Time and Narrative* and *Oneself as Another*.[32] In *Time and Narrative*, he begins by comparing Augustine on time as expectation, attention and memory (i.e. extended duration), and Aristotle on temporal logic and its organized approach. Augustine represented 'discordance', and Aristotle, 'concordance'. If we place these together, we arrive at *plot*: 'Emplotment gives shape and organization to what otherwise would

---

28 Paul Ricoeur, *Freud and Philosophy* (Eng., New Haven, Conn.: Yale University Press, 1970).
29 Ricoeur, *Freud and Philosophy*, p. 93.
30 Ricoeur, *Freud and Philosophy*, p. 27.
31 Ricoeur, *Freud and Philosophy*, p. 531.
32 Paul Ricoeur, *Time and Narrative*, 3 vols (Eng., Chicago, Ill.: University of Chicago Press, 1984, 1985, 1988); and *Oneself as Another* (Eng., Chicago, Ill.: University of Chicago Press, 1992).

be bare extension.'[33] Temporality (*Zeitlichkeit*) is vital to narrative, and allows for 'refiguration'. In volume 2, Ricoeur discusses narrative voice and fiction; in volume 3, the poetics of narrative. Together with other narrative theorists (especially G. Genette), he has transformed the understanding of biblical narrative and reading. Narratives, he constantly insists, are not always simply chronological reports of facts.

In *Oneself as Another*, Ricoeur grapples with the philosophical problem of selfhood and its continuity. With great care, he takes us through the classic philosophical discussions of self, including those of Descartes, Locke, Hume, Strawson, Anscombe and Recanati. He provides an excellent critique of inadequate attempts, noting also where the debate has been positive and helpful. Ricoeur majors on the difference between 'who' and 'what', including speech-act theory and issues of personal identity. In the end, he rightly bases *human identity* on the *ethical* question of responsibility and accountability. He explores narrative-identity. In the course of discussion he comments, 'Otherness is not added onto selfhood from outside, as though to prevent its solipsistic drift', but belongs to the 'ontological constitution of selfhood'.[34] The inter-subjective world partly defines the self. Among Ricoeur's shorter books on biblical interpretation, his *Interpretation Theory* (1976) also contributes to theological hermeneutics; chapter 3 examines symbol and metaphor. Chapter 1 of *Essays on Biblical Interpretation* refers to hymnic texts, narrative texts, wisdom texts and others, within the biblical writings.

---

33 Ricoeur, *Time and Narrative*, vol. 1, p. 33.
34 Ricoeur, *Oneself as Another*, p. 317.

3

Historical theology

In his *Brief Outline of the Study of Theology* (Ger., 1850), Schleiermacher (1768–1834) includes several categories.[1] He calls historical theology 'indispensable'. It includes the social and historical context of theological formulations. However, it also includes the NT apostolic fathers, the emergence of Protestant theology, hermeneutical understanding of divergent traditions, and modern theology. A more recent treatment of the subject is Gerhard Ebeling (1912–2001), *The Study of Theology*.[2] Ebeling conflates historical theology and church history. He begins by pointing out the difficulties of the subject, not least the immense quantity of material in the study of sources. He even quotes Goethe as arguing disparagingly, 'The whole of church history is a mishmash of error and power'.[3]

Ebeling highlights the *confessional* conception of church history, which embraces both the classic Catholic and Protestant conceptions of church history. He also cites a Pietistic conception of the Church. Church history, he argues, can also be part of general *historical and secular* study. As a theological discipline, Ebeling regards *hermeneutics* as a necessary framework for the study of church history.[4] This includes recognition of the historical conditioning of the contemporary theologian or historian. He also regards church history as 'The History of the Exposition of Scripture'.[5] He sees systematic theology as a threat to the historical nature of Christian theology, transforming it into 'timeless truth'. Nevertheless, he writes, 'Every aspect of theological study must subserve the interpretation of Scripture'.[6]

---

1 Friedrich Schleiermacher, *A Brief Outline of the Study of Theology* (Eng., Edinburgh: T&T Clark, 1850), pp. 120–86.
2 Gerhard Ebeling, *The Study of Theology* (Eng., London: Collins, 1979), pp. 67–79, on church history.
3 Ebeling, *The Study of Theology*, p. 68.
4 Ebeling, *The Study of Theology*, pp. 77–8.
5 Gerhard Ebeling, *The Word of God and Tradition* (Eng., London: Collins, 1968), pp 11–31.
6 Ebeling, *Word of God*, p. 15.

E. Gordon Rupp wrote on 'The Study of Church History', and T. H. L. Parker, on 'Creeds and Confessions of Faith' in 1971, in a collection edited by F. G. Healey.[7] Like Ebeling, Rupp rightly stresses the necessity for the study of history, but comments,

> At the heart of this discipline must be intellectual integrity . . . The historian must be dedicated to the pursuit of truth to follow it wherever it leads and at whatever cost . . . No university can be without its history departments.[8]

He cites the value of archaeology, such events as the success of the early Church against persecutions, and the emergence of Byzantine faith and early British Christianity. In Christian terms, we can see the providence of God in the history of God's people. Parker traces the emergence of declaratory creeds in their historical context. He specifically traces the Apostles' Creed and the Niceno-Constantinopolitan Creed (381). He then discusses the Church's use of the creeds up to the Protestant confessions of the Reformers.[9]

Schleiermacher rightly insisted that the early part of historical theology should stress the direct continuity between the NT and the apostolic fathers. Clement, the earliest of the apostolic fathers (d. *c.* 101), quotes many of the OT passages that Paul and others quote (*1 Clem.*, 13.1–2; 15.2; 16.3; 17.5; 18.2–5; 20.5; 27.5; among others). Ignatius (*c.* 108–12) brackets Christ and the Holy Spirit (Ignatius, *Eph.*, 9.1), exhorts prayer continuously (*Eph.*, 10.1), and commends newness of life (*Eph.* 19.3). Believers have the stamp (Gk, *charaktēr*) of God (Ignatius, *To the Magnesians*, 5.2). Ignatius rebukes those who are 'puffed up' (Gk, *phusioumenois*; Paul's word in 1 Cor. 8.1). Above all, he acknowledges Jesus Christ, 'who was of the family of David and of Mary, who was truly born, both ate and drank, was truly persecuted under Pontius Pilate, was truly crucified and died . . . was also truly raised from the dead, when his Father raised him up'.[10] He longs for martyrdom at the hands of the wild beasts (Ignatius, *To the Romans*, 4.1.5–23). He several times stresses the bodily resurrection of Christ (e.g. *To the Smyrnaeans*, 3.1–3). The *Didachē* (probably *c.* 100–120) teaches the two ways of life and death, and following Matthew 28.9,

---

7 E. Gordon Rupp, 'The Study of Church History', and T. H. L. Parker, 'Creeds and Confessions of Faith', in F. G. Healey (ed.), *Preface to Christian Studies* (London: Lutterworth Press, 1971), pp. 105–22 and 123–52.

8 Rupp, 'The Study of Church History', in Healey (ed.), *Preface to Christian Studies*, pp. 108–9.

9 Parker, 'Creeds and Confessions', in Healey (ed.), *Preface to Christian Studies*, pp. 137–49.

10 Ignatius, *To the Trallians*, 9.1–2, Gk and Eng., in Kirsopp Lake (ed.), *Apostolic Fathers*, 2 vols (London: William Heinemann, 1912–17), vol. 1, pp. 220–1.

urges baptism in the threefold name of the Holy Trinity (*Didachē*, 7.1–3). The *Epistle of Barnabas* (date uncertain) quotes the passage on the atonement from Isaiah: 'He was wounded for our transgressions and bruised for our iniquities; by his stripes we were healed. He was brought as a sheep to the slaughter, as a lamb dumb before its shearer'(*Ep. Barnabas*, 5.2). There is also much other quotation from the OT.

Irenaeus (*c.* 130 – *c.* 200) was bishop of Lyons in 180, and is often regarded as the first theologian of the Christian Church. He had roots in both the Eastern and Western Church. He urged observance of biblical and apostolic *public* tradition, or 'the rule of faith', especially as against the Gnostic system of private traditions. He argued that God was the Creator of the world (*Against Heresies*, 1.9.1), and opposed the notion of emanations of the deity (1.12.7). He urged that the Holy Spirit anointed Christ for his incarnate ministry (3.17–18). His most distinctive notion was that of 'recapitulation' (Gk, *anakephalaiōsis*) on the basis of Ephesians 1.10 (see Part 3, Recapitulation).

It is valuable to compare the Latin church father Tertullian (*c.* 150 – *c.* 225) and the Alexandrian or Greek church father Origen (*c.* 185 – *c.* 254). Tertullian produced probably more works than any other Christian writer of the third century. Although Stoic philosophy strongly influenced his treatise *On the Soul*, he also argued that biblical and apostolic tradition should not be compromised by secular philosophy. One of his most memorable sayings was: 'What has Jerusalem to do with Athens?'[11] By contrast, Origen sought to find common ground between much Greek and some secular philosophy, and Christian thought. Like Philo, he often used allegorical interpretations of the Bible. His interests extended to textual criticism, to exegetical works and homilies, and to doctrine, especially in his treatise *On First Principles*, and his works on prayer and exhortation to martyrdom (see Introduction, above).

In the period after Nicaea, the creeds and doctrinal formulations emerged, especially about Christology, the Holy Spirit and the Holy Trinity (see Introduction, above). The Christological controversies began with opposition to Arius (*c.* 250–336), and affirmations of the personhood of the Holy Spirit emerged under the Cappadocian Fathers, Basil of Caesarea (*c.* 330–79), Gregory of Nazianzus (*c.* 330–90) and Gregory of Nyssa (*c.* 330–95). With various bishops and Roman emperors supporting different sides of the controversy, it became a live issue in historiography

---

11 Tertullian, *Prescriptions against Heretics*, 7.

to assess whether the primary motivations were genuinely theological or partly political. The Eastern and Western churches held different views of what was called 'the double procession' of the Holy Spirit. Did the Spirit proceed from the Father (the Eastern view) or from the Father and the Son? The Eastern view protected the equality of the persons of the Trinity; the Western view protected the close connection between the Holy Spirit and Jesus Christ. This hardened into an East–West division of Christendom under the uncompromising leadership of Photius of Constantinople (*c.* 810 – *c.* 895).

The medieval era was creative in various ways. This is often under-rated. The thirteenth century saw the transition from monastic education to that of the great universities. To this era belongs Thomas Aquinas (1225–74), who composed the magisterial *Summa Theologiae*.[12] This has long been regarded as a standard work of theology for all Roman Catholics, alongside the Bible and Augustine. Aquinas intended the *Summa* to be a textbook for theological students, and arranged it into three parts. Part 1 contains 119 'questions' in the scholastic manner of question and answer. It concerns the nature of Christian theology, the existence of God (including the major arguments for this), knowledge of God, God's will and power, questions about the Trinity, creation, angels, cosmogony, humankind and providence. Each 'question' is divided into several articles. One of the most famous sections concerns the formulation of the 'five ways', which include the cosmological argument for the existence of God. Part 2 concerns the virtues, sin and law, faith, hope, love and justice, as well as the social virtues. Part 3 concerns the Incarnation, Christ as the one mediator, the Virgin Mary, the Passion of Christ, the resurrection and the sacraments.

The historian of theology may note, first, that the dominance of the scholastic method determined the shape of the work. Second, this was the era of the revival of the study of Aristotle, especially following the translation of Aristotle by Arabic philosophers. Aquinas heavily depends on both the philosophy of Aristotle and the theology of Augustine. His theology of the Eucharist depended on Aristotle's philosophical distinction between substance and accidents.

Also during this period, Anselm of Canterbury (*c.* 1033–1109) is noted for his formulation of the ontological argument for the existence of God, and for his exposition of the atonement (see Part 2, Atonement). Peter Abelard (1079–1142), Peter Lombard (*c.* 1100–60), John Duns Scotus

---

12 Aquinas, *Summa Theologiae*.

(*c.* 1266–1308) and William of Ockham (*c.* 1285–1349) all deserve note for their contribution to historical theology or philosophical thought. Further, John Wycliffe (*c.* 1330–84) was an advocate of reform, even before the Reformation.

The primary founder of the Reformation was Martin Luther (1483–1546). We introduced his work in the Introduction (see The Reformation and afterwards, p. 18) and need not repeat this material. John Calvin (1509–64) belonged to the second generation of Reformers. He systematized Reformation theology in his masterly *Institutes of the Christian Religion* (see Introduction, and Part 1, Systematic theology).

It is often said that the post-Reformation era hardened into Protestant scholasticism. Nevertheless, such theologians as Richard Hooker (1554–1600) and John Owen (1616–83) brought advances. But many believe that more creative advances came in the nineteenth century. New attempts to wrestle with Christian theology emerged with Friedrich Schleiermacher (1768–1834) and Georg W. F. Hegel (1770–1831) (see Introduction, above, and Part 3, Hermeneutical theology; Philosophical theology; Systematic theology). Towards the end of the century, liberal theology arguably emerged with Albrecht Ritschl (1823–89), Wilhelm Herrmann (1846–1922) and Adolf von Harnack (1851–1930). Many might contest this generalizing label, and perhaps we should add such American theologians as Horace Bushnell (1802–76).

During the twentieth century, the major orthodox or conservative theologian Karl Barth (1886–1968) published his magisterial *Church Dogmatics* (14 vols; see Introduction, and Part 1, Systematic theology). Two other notable theologians are Rudolf Bultmann (1884–1976; see Part 1, Hermeneutical theology) and Paul Tillich (1886–1965; see Part 1, Philosophical theology). With them we might mention Reinhold Niebuhr (1892–1971), Oscar Cullmann (1902–99), Karl Rahner (1904–84), Yves Congar (1904–95), Hans Urs von Balthasar (1905–88). These last three are Roman Catholic theologians of weight (see Part 2, Catholicism). Among more recent major theologians stand Wolfhart Pannenberg (1928–2014), Jürgen Moltmann (b. 1926) and Hans Küng (b. 1928). (On these three, see Introduction, and Part 1, Systematic theology.)

4

Moral theology

Many regard moral theology as a synonym for Christian ethics, although Shaftesbury and Santayana insist that ethics and morality are not synonymous. C. H. Dodd (1884–1973) insists that ethics in the Graeco-Roman world often coincides with Paul's injunctions to moral conduct in *content*, even if the *motivation* of each is radically different.[1] Paul urges abstinence from sexual immorality, promoting family affection, minding one's own business, and working hard (1 Thess. 4.1–12).[2] In 2 Thessalonians, again he enjoins work (3.10–12) and uses the whole catechetical ethical tradition. He lists vices to be avoided (Gal. 5.16–21).[3] Dodd traces common features of this tradition. This included attitudes to authorities and the state, patience, non-provocative behaviour, and so on. On the other hand, *motivation* concerns eschatology, new creation, the new life and belonging to the body of Christ (Eph. 5.14–17). Unlike pagan ethics, the system is not self-contained. Dodd also appealed to Hebrews, 1 Peter and portions of the Gospels.

This principle remains relevant to moral theology today. Several moralists urge that Christians should seek common ground with Muslims on ethical *content*, even if ethical *motivations* remain distinctive to each group. Plato and Aristotle defend an 'objective' ethic, even if it is also mixed with self-realization and virtue ethics. Thomas Aquinas advocated ethical behaviour in terms of 'virtues'.[4] John Calvin promoted a 'command ethics', based on the Decalogue and biblical commandments, but also stressed that Christian *motivation* stemmed from gratitude for grace and salvation.[5] Most moral decisions made by Christian theologians draw on *both* de-ontological ethics (duty and obligation) *and* consequential ethics (the

---

1 C. H. Dodd, *Gospel and Law* (Cambridge: Cambridge University Press, 1951), pp. 19–20.
2 Dodd, *Gospel and Law*, p. 13.
3 Dodd, *Gospel and Law*, p. 16.
4 Thomas Aquinas, *Summa Theologiae*, II.II, qu. 1–46.
5 John Calvin, *Institutes*, 3.7–8.

well-being of one's neighbour). This exposes common ground with Kant on duty, and Bentham and Mill on the well-being of society.

Christian ethics must not be reduced to 'general ethics'. Notable examples of moral theology include especially the work of Dietrich Bonhoeffer, Helmut Thielicke, Oliver O'Donovan and the 2003 findings of the Church of England Doctrine Commission. The writers on Christian morals are numerous, ranging from Reinhold Niebuhr and Paul Ricoeur to Joseph Fletcher's *Situation Ethics* (1966). But four are especially creative.

First, Dietrich Bonhoeffer (1906–45) reflected on moral theology, shaped on one side by Luther's Christology and his theology of the cross, and on the other by his well-known resistance to Nazism, culminating in his imprisonment and death on the orders of Adolf Hitler. Heinrich Ott comments that he equated 'Christ and reality . . . Ethical "principles" miscarry'.[6] The key to his antipathy to 'ethical principles' was 'responsible action'.[7] Ethics demands fixing 'one's eyes solely on the simple truth of God . . . [The Christian] belongs solely to God and to the will of God'.[8] Thus Christian moral theology cannot be reduced to general ethics. The reason why Bonhoeffer opposed 'ethical principles' is because they are too abstract. He sought to avoid the Scylla of ethical formalism and the Charybdis of casuistry; ethical activity involves recognition of concrete reality.[9] This entails becoming conformed to Christ. Bonhoeffer wrote, 'Formation comes only by being drawn into the form of Jesus Christ.'[10] He also considered guilt and shame, which he called the sign of humankind's disunion with God.[11]

Bonhoeffer never finished his *Ethics*, although he longed for time to do so. It is clear, however, that responsible action stands at the heart of his moral theology, coupled with his concept of Christ as our ultimate reality.[12] Christians must imitate the pure moral life of Jesus. It is, he claims, the Pharisees for whom categories of good and evil are important. Bonhoeffer supplements his moral theology with his work on the sociology of the Church, namely *Sanctorum Communio*.[13] In 1934 he signed the Barmen

---

6 Heinrich Ott, *Reality and Faith: The Theological Legacy of Dietrich Bonhoeffer* (Eng., Philadelphia, Pa.: Fortress Press, 1972), p. 246.

7 Dietrich Bonhoeffer, *Ethics* (Ger., 1949; Eng., London: SCM Press, 1959), p. xv.

8 Bonhoeffer, *Ethics*, p. 7.

9 Bonhoeffer, *Ethics*, p. 8.

10 Bonhoeffer, *Ethics*, p. 18.

11 Bonhoeffer, *Ethics*, p. 148.

12 Bonhoeffer, *Ethics*, pp. 198, 224.

13 Dietrich Bonhoeffer, *Sanctorum Communio: A Theological Study of the Sociology of the Church* (Eng., Minneapolis, Minn.: Fortress Press, 2009); and Bonhoeffer, *The Communion of the Saints* (London: Harper-Collins, 1963).

Declaration in support of the Confessing Church, initiated by Barth and led by Martin Niemöller; it was one of his most personal concrete, responsible, risky ethical decisions.

Second, Helmut Thielicke (1908–86) was professor and rector of the University of Hamburg from 1960 to 1978. The war years were difficult, owing to his support for the Confessing Church. When the Nazis removed him from his chair at Erlangen, he held a post at Heidelberg from 1937 to 1940. His classic work on moral theology was his three-volume *Theological Ethics*.[14] He also published numerous other works, including apologetics, theology and sermons.[15] He entitled the three volumes of his *Theological Ethics* respectively *Foundations*, *Politics* and *Sex*. His work was profoundly theological, since he constantly refers to the biblical writings, to Luther and to the Christian tradition.

In Thielicke's volume on foundations, he avoided clear-cut ethical directives, regarding ethics in terms of dialectic between freedom and bondage. In his volume on sex, he addressed issues of Christian marriage and divorce, birth control, abortion, homosexuality, artificial insemination and even the Greek words for love, *agapē* and *eros*. In his volume on politics, he declared, 'The state is simply the institutionalized form of God's call to order. It is a "remedy required by our corrupted nature".'[16] He again quotes Luther: 'There is nothing greater on the whole earth than a state.'[17] God, he argues, thereby puts a stop to self-destruction, although democracy puts the people in control of the state. Nevertheless, ideologies can distort the purpose of laws. In ideological law, law can become 'an instrument of the will to power, a political weapon'.[18] On the NT Thielicke recognized that Romans 13 and Revelation 13 stand in tension. Paul's urging of obedience to the authorities presents a norm in normal times. But the colourful language of Revelation and its beasts from the sea concern 'ideological tyranny in an authoritarian state'.[19] He is clearly thinking of the terrors of Nazism. By contrast, he commends the United Nations' Declaration of Human Rights in December 1948. In the remainder of this volume he discusses the nature of power and authority, the theology of the state, and war in the atomic age.

---

14 Helmut Thielicke, *Theological Ethics*, 3 vols (Eng., Philadelphia, Pa.: Fortress Press, 1966–9).

15 Helmut Thielicke, *Modern Faith and Thought* (Eng., Grand Rapids, Mich.: Eerdmans, 1990), and many others.

16 Thielicke, *Theological Ethics*, vol. 2, *Politics*, p. 17; his quotation is from Luther.

17 Thielicke, *Theological Ethics*, vol. 2, *Politics*, p. 16.

18 Thielicke, *Theological Ethics*, vol. 2, *Politics*, p. 42.

19 Thielicke, *Theological Ethics*, vol. 2, *Politics*, pp. 53–69.

Third, we include Oliver O'Donovan (b. 1945) among the most creative thinkers in moral theology. He was formerly Professor of Moral Theology at Oxford (1982–2006), and then became Professor of Christian Ethics at Edinburgh (2006–13). He is a Fellow of the British Academy, and an Anglican. He published the first of his major books on moral theology, *Resurrection and the Moral Order*, in 1986.[20] In this he defends the objectivity of the moral order in Christ, especially against the 'virtue ethics' of Alasdair MacIntyre. His second major work, *The Desire of Nations* (1996), carefully listens to Scripture, tracing the continuity between the Hebrew Scriptures and the Christian New Testament, applying the revelation of God's kingship to Christian redemption and to political and ethical questions.[21] He declares, 'The Gospel of the Kingdom offers liberation to an imprisoned political culture.'[22] Craig Bartholomew comments, 'O'Donovan describes [*Desire of Nations*] as a work in political theology . . . [but] Scripture is never left behind . . . O'Donovan insists that there are objective orders in creation.'[23]

O'Donovan next produced *The Ways of Judgment* (2005).[24] Arguably this book complements *The Desire of Nations*, because it presupposes biblical foundations, and begins with contemporary situations in the political realm. These concern the United Nations after the Cold War, and the expansion of the European Union. He pleads for 'detailed attention to the structures of authority' and warns us that democracy is vulnerable to mass communication.[25]

Finally, O'Donovan is producing a trilogy, which is set to crown his career. Volume 1 is *Self, World, and Time* (2013), continuing the theme of *Ethics as Theology*.[26] He considers how Christian ethics is related to the humanities, including philosophy, theology and the social sciences. He regards faith, hope and love as the foundational Christian virtues which relate to contemporary issues within the horizon of time. Ethics must be the crowning theme of all theology. Volume 2 is *Finding and Seeking: Ethics*

---

20 Oliver O'Donovan, *Resurrection and the Moral Order* (Leicester: IVP, 1986; 2nd edn, Grand Rapids, Mich.: Eerdmans, 1994).

21 Oliver O'Donovan, *The Desire of Nations: Rediscovering the Roots of Political Theology* (Cambridge: Cambridge University Press, 1996), pp. 32, 80 and throughout.

22 O' Donovan, *Desire of Nations*, p. 119.

23 Craig Bartholomew and others (eds), *A Royal Priesthood? The Use of the Bible Ethically and Politically* (Carlisle: Paternoster, 2002), pp. 21, 23.

24 Oliver O'Donovan, *The Ways of Judgment* (Grand Rapids, Mich.: Eerdmans, 2005).

25 O'Donovan, *Desire of Nations*, pp. 18–19.

26 Oliver O'Donovan, *Self, World, and Time*, vol. 1, *Ethics as Theology: An Introduction* (Grand Rapids, Mich.: Eerdmans, 2013).

as Theology (2014). Objectivity is reaffirmed. Volume 3, *Entering into Rest: Ethics as Theology,* does not yet appear to be published. O'Donovan has also published numerous minor studies. One, for example, discusses homosexuality with pastoral sensitivity.[27] He points out that every way of Christian discipleship entails self-denial, whether for married or single people.[28] He has also supported the traditional Christian tradition of the 'just war', in spite of Anabaptist or Mennonite arguments to the contrary.[29]

Fourth, it may seem unusual to include the 2003 report of the Church of England Doctrine Commission alongside such prestigious thinkers as Bonhoeffer, Thielicke and O'Donovan, especially when we have omitted Brunner, Niebuhr, Hauerwas and such Mennonites as John Yoder. But under the chairmanship of Stephen Sykes, this report considers power, money, sex and time as crucial issues in moral theology in our era.[30]

The Commission begins by pointing out that ethics arises from a Christian doctrine of humankind and God's revelation. It recommends an 'open-eyed realism about the misuse of power'.[31] *Power*, for the Christian, is *not worldly* power, and all who exercise power must protect themselves from pride by vigorous self-examination.[32] Paul speaks of power *in weakness*, although we must not renounce the exercise of power for the protection of the weak. On *money*, the Commission concluded, 'Money is not the problem . . . We are the problem. It is not money that defines us theologically or spiritually, but our personal attitudes.'[33] Peter Selby, a member of the Commission and author of *Grace and Mortgage* (1997), points out that such developments as 'fractional reserve banking' increase the amount of money that could be lent, erode reference to a reality outside the system, and lead to borrowing against projected future wealth.[34] The Commission, in effect, anticipated the economic problems of 2008–9.

On *sex*, the Commission bewailed the negative image of sex promoted by some parts of the Church, but also took account of the dangers of sexual repression. Its members pointed out that God 'desires and accepts

---

27 Oliver O'Donovan, *Church in Crisis: The Gay Controversy and the Anglican Communion* (Eugene, Ore.: Cascade Books, 2008).

28 O'Donovan, *Church in Crisis*, p. 109, cf. pp. 105–9.

29 Oliver O'Donovan, *The Just War Revisited* (Cambridge: Cambridge University Press, 2003).

30 Stephen Sykes (ed.), *Being Human: A Christian Understanding of Personhood Illustrated with Reference to Power, Money, Sex and Time: Report of the Doctrine Commission* (London: Church House Publishing, 2003).

31 Doctrine Commission, *Being Human*, p. 18.

32 Doctrine Commission, *Being Human*, p. 51.

33 Doctrine Commission, *Being Human*, p. 57.

34 Doctrine Commission, *Being Human*, p. 60.

love as well as giving it. God chooses not to be self-contained, but deeply involved with others [whom] God has made to be his partners in the world'.[35] At its best, they argued,

> Sexual engagement is mutually involving. It entails give-and-take, desire and delight, loss of control and surrender, the assumption of responsibility for each other . . . Sexual union can be not only joyful and fulfilling but also painful and disappointing. At worst it becomes a place of cruelty and perversion, mutual torment or ruthless exploitation.[36]

The Commission continues:

> *Deep love that reaches out to the other person respects their separate existence . . . Wants the best for them* and meets their needs . . . It seeks to avoid becoming either smothering or self controlling . . . The maturing of it is a long and difficult process that needs to recover from frequent failures and disappointment.[37]

On *time*, the Commission sees time as a gift of God, which requires patience and thought in relation to the wider temporal drama of God's dealings with the world. All this demonstrates profound moral theology which addresses the practical issues of today.

---

35 Doctrine Commission, *Being Human*, p. 85.
36 Doctrine Commission, *Being Human*, p. 86.
37 Doctrine Commission, *Being Human*, p. 99 (my italics).

5

Philosophical theology

Schleiermacher divided philosophical theology into apologetics and polemics.[1] In this broad sense, very soon after the NT era, the early Christian apologists began to engage with Greek philosophical thought, and sometimes in polemics. Justin Martyr (*c.* 100 – *c.* 165) argued that the Christian faith was not irrational, as can be shown by Christians' rejection of idolatry, and by their belief in God as Creator.[2] He also reflected an affinity with Plato. Athenagoras held together theology with philosophical and rational enquiry, and drew on the Logos concept (see Part 3, Logos). Theophilus of Antioch argued for the rationality of the doctrine of creation and the irrationality of polytheistic myths.

Clement of Alexandria (*c.* 150 – *c.* 215) had a close knowledge of pagan philosophy. He regarded Christianity as a fulfilment of both the OT and Greek philosophy, and saw Plato as speaking the words of Moses with a Greek accent. Origen (*c.* 185 – *c.* 254), his successor, drew on philosophy both in *On First Principles*, and in his apologetics, *Against Celsus*. He accuses Celsus of holding an irrational, self-contradictory philosophy.[3] Augustine (354–430) (see Introduction) had been educated in rhetoric, wrote against the Manichaeans, discussed freedom of will, considered at length the problem of evil, and wrote a philosophy of history in his *City of God*. He defended Christians against the notion that Rome fell because they had deserted the Graeco-Roman deities.[4]

In the medieval era, Anselm (*c.* 1033–1109) and Thomas Aquinas (1225–74) are the thinkers who feature most prominently in modern

---

1 Friedrich Schleiermacher, *A Brief Outline of the Study of Theology* (Eng., Edinburgh: T&T Clark, 1850), p. 113.

2 Justin, *First Apology*, 1.9 (Eng., *ANF*, vol. 1, p. 166).

3 Origen, *Against Celsus*, 4.89, 5.25 and 45 (Eng., *ANF*, vol. 4, pp. 537, 553, 559).

4 Augustine, *Enchiridion*, 3 and 4, in Albert Outler (ed.), *Augustine: Confessions and Enchiridion* (Eng., Philadelphia, Pa.: Westminster Press, 1955), pp. 341–6; and in John Hick (ed.), *Classical and Contemporary Readings in the Philosophy of Religion* (Englewood Cliffs, N.J.: Prentice Hall, 1964), pp. 19–27; and *City of God*, esp. Bks 2, 5, 8, 10, 12, and 18–19 (Eng., *NPNF*, ser. 1, vol. 2, pp. 23–42, 85–109, etc.).

philosophical theology. In Anselm's case, his formulation of the onto-logical argument for the existence of God takes a prominent place. We need not repeat the argument here (see Part 3, Ontological argument). Many modern philosophers still take his second formulation of the argu-ment as their starting point, and in many cases, are in agreement. These include J. N. Findlay, Norman Malcolm and Alvin Plantinga, often in terms of modal logic. (On Anselm, see the Introduction.)

Aquinas drew extensively on the philosophy of Aristotle, and regarded the Christian faith as wholly compatible with reason and philosophy. We discussed in the Introduction (p. 17) his arguments for the existence of God (*Summa Theologiae*, I, qu. 2–11), religious language and the use of analogy (I, qu. 12–13), and knowledge of God (I, qu. 14–18). Aquinas also saw the infinity of God in terms of his limitlessness (qu. 6), and consid-ered truth (qu. 12) and evil (qu. 47). These are all topics prominent in any modern philosophical theology.

In the early modern period John Locke (1632–1704), Jonathan Edwards (1703–58) and William Paley (1743–1805) represent notable advocates of *reasonable* Christian belief. But none could be called rationalist. Locke was an empiricist philosopher, who in Book 4 of his treatise *An Essay Concerning Human Understanding* (1690) discussed 'entitled belief'; he explored the bounds of reasonableness, and published *The Reasonableness of Christianity* (1695).[5] Edwards not only played a leading part in the Great Awakening of America, but equally critically examined its results, con-ceding that many had succumbed to self-deception and to an 'imagined' work of the Holy Spirit. Paley established a basic and classic form of the teleological argument for the existence of God. He coined the anecdotal analogy of finding a watch on the ground, which pointed to the work of a designer.[6] David Hume (1711–76), in effect, had anticipated objections to this, but Richard Swinburne and others have restored his arguments by adding suitable modifications.

In the eighteenth century outstanding philosophical theologians included Schleiermacher (1768–1834) and more especially Georg W. F. Hegel (1770–1831), whose philosophy profoundly influenced the thought of Moltmann and Pannenberg (see Introduction). Hegel introduced into philosophical theology the notion of historical reason, and also the idea

---

5 Nicholas Wolterstorff, *John Locke and the Ethics of Belief* (Cambridge: Cambridge Univeristy Press, 1996).
6 William Paley, *Natural Theology, or Evidences of the Existence and Attributes of God* (1802; Oxford: Oxford University Press, 2006), ch. 1, sect. 2.

of 'the whole' as rational and ultimate. Reality might *appear* to be non-rational. But it proved otherwise in the light of a steadily unfolding history.

Hegel built upon this foundation to argue for a particular understanding of the Holy Trinity. Some consider his doctrine to be an implication of his dialectic of logic, but this doctrine occupies more prominence in Hegel than this would suggest. He understood God the Father, God the Son and God the Holy Spirit as *an unfolding of the Ultimate* in history. Each person seemed to 'negate' or, in his language, 'to sublate' (Ger., *erheben*) the other. God the Father remains the supreme Creator and Sustainer of the universe; God the Son manifests the death of death in the cross and resurrection; finally the Holy Spirit brings life and freedom to human history. He criticizes the Roman Catholic Church for self-contradiction, because it appears to halt this process with a static crucifix, in contrast to the Protestant emphasis on the freedom of the Holy Spirit. Like Pannenberg and Moltmann in our day, he speaks of the self-differentiation of God. The doctrine of the Trinity is the 'fundamental determination' of the Christian religion.[7]

Many regard Hegel's doctrine of the Trinity as a philosophical and logical construction, rather than a theological one. Hegel would probably insist that it was both. His controlling principle was the ultimacy of *Geist*, *spirit* or *mind*. Nevertheless, he argued, religion works only with images (*Vorstellungen*); philosophy uses the critical concept (*Begriff*). Fragments of history seldom make sense; it is the *whole* that moves beyond this: a sentiment strongly opposed by Kierkegaard, yet strongly advocated later by Pannenberg.

Christian thinkers in the nineteenth century mainly adhered to the Trinitarian doctrine of biblical traditions. A minority were philosophical theologians. However, in the twentieth century Étienne Gilson (1884–1978) was a French Catholic Thomist philosopher, who was influenced by Bergson. Paul Tillich (1886–1965) was an apologist and philosophical theologian in every sense. He aimed to produce an apologetic theology and an 'answering theology'. Indeed the entire *Systematic Theology*, his major work, seeks to offer a correlation between five fundamental questions and five answers.[8]

The first volume begins with questions about human reason, and seeks answers in terms of *revelation*. Questions about being then invite an

---

7 Georg W. F. Hegel, *Lectures on the Philosophy of Religion*, 3 vols (London: Kegan Paul, Trench, 1895), vol. 1, p. 39, cf. pp. 114–5, 200; Peter C. Hodgson, 'Georg W. F. Hegel', in Ninian Smart and others (eds), *Nineteenth Century Religious Thought in the West*, 3 vols (Cambridge: Cambridge University Press, 1985), vol. 1, pp. 81–122.

8 Paul Tillich, *Systematic Theology*, 3 vols (Chicago, Ill.: University of Chicago Press and London: Nisbet, 1953, 1957, 1963).

answer in terms of symbols that point to *God*. In the second volume he asks questions about concrete *existence*, and offers answers that relate to *Jesus Christ* as the new being. In his third volume, Tillich asks questions about the *ambiguities* of life, and seeks to offer answers in terms of the action of the *Holy Spirit*, and also the meaning of *history*. Some critics have argued that the questions are simply dictated by the answers that he wishes to give. However, his genuine concern is to address Christian theology to those who are outside the Christian faith. He insists, 'The method of correlation . . . makes an analysis of the human situation . . . and demonstrates that the symbols used in the Christian message are answers to these questions.'[9] It is no accident that Tillich uses the word *symbol*. He declared, 'Symbols . . . are . . . unconditionally beyond the conceptual sphere . . . Religious symbols represent the transcendent . . . They do not make God a part of the empirical [i.e. everyday] world.'[10] In other words, the transcendence of God places him outside the *conceptual* or *cognitive* sphere, in which analogical or cognitive thought would reduce his transcendence.

Tillich draws from Jung the notion that in the use of symbol, interplay occurs between the conscious and unconscious. Symbol points beyond the self and its world. Tillich writes, 'The main function of the symbol [is] the opening up of levels of reality, which otherwise are hidden and cannot be grasped in any other way.'[11] Tillich is so concerned to emphasize the transcendence of God that he even claims that it is impossible to say that God 'exists'. On this basis some more extreme critics have described him as an atheist! But he speaks of the God who is beyond 'god', i.e. beyond the 'God' who pleases us (as Bonhoeffer also argues). He writes, 'A God whom we can easily bear, a God from whom we do not have to hide, a God whom we do not hate in moments . . . is not God at all.'[12] Tillich's work is essentially that of an apologist. He insists, '*The object of theology is what concerns us ultimately*' (his italics).[13] He presents a mixture of brilliant insights and unorthodox assumptions.

Anders Nygren (1890–1978) was a Swedish Lutheran theologian, who is more famous for his book on *Agapē and Eros* (Eng., 1957) than for

9   Tillich, *Systematic Theology*, vol. 1, p. 70.
10 Paul Tillich, 'The Religious Symbol', in S. Hook (ed.), *Religious Experience and Truth* (Edinburgh: Oliver & Boyd, 1962), p. 303.
11 Paul Tillich, *Theology of Culture* (Eng., Oxford: Oxford University Press, 1964), p. 56.
12 Paul Tillich, *The Shaking of the Foundations* (Eng., New York, N.Y.: Scribner, 1955), p. 50.
13 Tillich, *Systematic Theology*, vol. 1, p. 15.

philosophical thought. But he undertook some important philosophical theology, insisting on a 'religious *a priori*'.

Bernard Lonergan (1904–84), in Montreal, wrote two classic books on philosophical theology, *Insight*, and *Method in Theology*.[14] He rejects straightforward representational realism as unduly simplistic. Nor does the mind simply *construct* reality, as in Fichte and largely in Kant. The mind senses, perceives, imagines, enquires, understands, formulates, reflects and affirms.[15] Reasonableness is essential to knowing. He describes his own approach as that of *critical realism*. His second major work, *Method in Theology*, represents the fruit of a lifetime of study and reflection on human cognition. He applies a transcendental method, and regards the mind as operating at four levels, including observation, intellectual reflection, and judgment of value.[16] The problem of knowledge, he says, is 'embedded in the problem of hermeneutics'.[17] He rightly expounds the value of the term 'horizon'. This leads to a discussion of religious language. Lonergan is widely admired.

In keeping with Roman Catholic attitudes to philosophy, three major theologians of the Catholic tradition, Karl Rahner (1904–84), Hans Urs von Balthasar (1905–88) and Hans Küng (b. 1928), all write as philosophical theologians as well as systematic theologians. Drawing on Kant, Rahner stressed the limitations of human knowledge. God is inscrutable. Balthasar devoted his work *Theo-logic* to the question of truth. Küng fully engaged with philosophical questions. He addressed post-Freudian objections to belief, and Feuerbach's theories of God as a human projection. His book on the Incarnation explores Hegel, while several books explore Christian belief in the context of atheist objections (see Part 2, Catholicism).

In the UK a resurgence of philosophical theology emerged largely in response to logical positivism, the principle of falsification, broader issues in religious language, and the emergence of the so-called new atheism. On the first issue, many theists drew on Wittgenstein's insight that religious language depended not on a special type of language, but on *the use to which we put* ordinary language. Numerous philosophical theologians now joined battle. These included Basil Mitchell, Austin Farrer, Ian T. Ramsey, Richard Swinburne, Eric Mascall, Alvin Plantinga and

---

14 Bernard Lonergan, *Insight* (1957; New York, N.Y.: Harper & Row, 1978); Lonergan, *Method in Theology* (London: DLT, 1971).
15 Lonergan, *Insight*, p. 319.
16 Lonergan, *Method in Theology*, pp. 120–1.
17 Lonergan, *Method in Theology*, p. 155.

Nicholas Wolterstorff. Plantinga is a philosopher of religion, who is also a convinced Christian. Ian Ramsey (1915–72) is especially noteworthy for his work on models and qualifiers. God is not merely *wise* (model), he argued, but *infinitely* wise (qualifier). God is not simply *Father* (model) but *heavenly* Father (qualifier).[18]

Since David Hume, the teleological argument for the existence of God has been under fire. This was intensified by evolutionary theories, beginning with Charles Darwin and Herbert Spencer. In the early years of the twentieth century, F. R. Tennant (1866–1957) sought to reconcile religion and science, and pointed out that the theological argument depended on a *gradualness* of adaptation that was compatible with Darwin's theory.[19] A still more sophisticated 'reply' was formulated by the eminent scientist and theologian John Polkinghorne (b. 1930) in a succession of scientifically informed books.[20] Polkinghorne not only addresses the older 'evolution' debate, but also the new atheism of Richard Dawkins and others. Dawkins had attempted to raise difficulties to belief by combining evolutionary theory with contemporary theories of genetics.

In addition to all this, Richard Swinburne (b. 1934) has formulated positive material on the existence of God, the coherence of theism, miracles and a host of kindred philosophical issues.[21] Further, a number of writers approach the problem of evil and suffering. John Hick (1922–2012) is among the best known.[22] Further, the Calvinist philosophical theologians, Alvin Plantinga (b. 1932) and Nicholas Wolterstorff (b. 1932), have formulated a fresh approach to knowledge of God in what they call their 'reformed epistemology'.[23]

---

18 Ian T. Ramsey, *Religious Language: An Empirical Placing of Theological Phrases* (London: SCM Press, 1957), esp. pp. 19–89; Ramsey, *Christian Discourse* (New York, N.Y. and London: Oxford University Press, 1965).

19 F. R. Tennant, *Philosophical Theology*, 2 vols (Cambridge: Cambridge University Press, 1930), vol. 2, ch. 4.

20 John Polkinghorne, *One World: The Interaction of Science and Theology* (Princeton, N.J.: Princeton University Press, 1987); Polkinghorne, *Quarks, Chaos, and Christianity: Questions to Science and Religion* (London: SPCK, 2005); and others.

21 Richard Swinburne, *The Existence of God* (Oxford: Clarendon Press, 1979); Swinburne, *The Coherence of Theism* (Oxford: Clarendon Press, 1977).

22 John Hick, *Evil and the God of Love* (London: Macmillan, 1966; 2nd edn, 1977).

23 Alvin Plantinga and Nicholas Wolterstorff (eds), *Faith and Rationality* (Notre Dame, Ind.: University of Notre Dame Press, 1983); Alvin Plantinga, *Warranted Christian Belief* (New York, N.Y.: Oxford University Press, 2000); and many others.

6

Political theology

Some regard political theology as a twentieth- and twenty-first-century phenomenon. Others point to the Sermon on the Mount in the teaching of Jesus and to such passages as Romans 13.1–7 in Paul as pointing to NT origins of the subject. In the era of the church fathers, Eusebius was virtually a court theologian to Constantine, who was closely allied with the state, whereas Tertullian regarded the Church quite differently. He wrote, 'There is nothing more entirely foreign to us than affairs of state' (*Apology*, 38; Eng., *ANF*, vol. 3, p. 45). Thomas Aquinas urged the possibility of a just war, and Luther and Calvin believed that 'godly princes' or magistrates were appointed by God. On the other hand the radical Anabaptist Reformers opposed Luther's view.

Political theology so extensively overlaps with our discussion of moral theology, that this section requires a shorter length than other headings in Part 1. In particular we have already examined the work on politics of two outstanding thinkers in this field, Helmut Thielicke and Oliver O'Donovan. Thielicke and O'Donovan represent the dominant Christian tradition of political theology about such issues as the just war and related concepts, following Aquinas, Brunner, Niebuhr and others. Hence we shall consider especially those thinkers who propose a radically alternative world-view. The roots of this alternative view go back to the 'left-wing' Radical Reformers, Thomas Müntzer, Andreas Karlstadt (1486–1541) and Nicolas Storch, who opposed Luther. Luther and Zwingli equally opposed them as 'fanatics' (*Schwärmer*).

In the nineteenth century F. D. Maurice (1805–72) was one of the founders of Christian Socialism. He published *The Kingdom of Christ* (1838; 3rd edn, 1883) and became Professor of Theology at King's College, London (1846). He was a controversial figure. Charles Kingsley joined Maurice as a founder of Christian Socialism, and his quest for social reform was evidenced in his popular novel, *The Water Babies* (1863). Although these thinkers in effect wrote political theology, the first explicit use of the term appears to come from Carl Schmitt (1888–1985), who published a work with this title in German in 1922, which was translated into English in 1985.[1] After leaving the Catholic Church, Schmitt became Professor of Law at Bonn and Cologne, and in 1933 joined the Nazi party. He also defended fascism in Spain.

The next landmarks in the twentieth century were the publication of Reinhold Niebuhr's (1892–1971) *Moral Man and Immoral Society* (1932; Eng., 1963) and his brother H. Richard Niebuhr's (1894–1962) *Christ and Culture* (1951).[2] Both opposed liberal theology. A further phase could be associated with liberation theology and the names of J.-B. Metz and Dorothee Sölle. Arguably we might add some of Moltmann's earliest writings.

John Yoder (1927–97) was an American theologian and ethicist, whose most influential book is *The Politics of Jesus* (1972).[3] He studied at a Mennonite seminary, and then completed his ThD at Basel. Later he was a professor at the University of Notre Dame. He consistently attacked any mutual institutional support between the state and the Church. He called such mutual support 'Constantinianism', and regarded it as dangerous compromise, which was alien to the NT. Christians, he argued, must not repay evil for evil, but follow the path of renunciation followed by Jesus. He argued that the kingdom 'is a political term'.[4] He foresaw the Jubilee as 'the time when the inequities accumulated through the years are to be crossed off'.[5] The disciple, he said, is 'to share in that style of life of which the cross is the culmination'.[6] He added, 'Paul can speak of his own ministry as a sharing in the dying and rising of Jesus (2 Cor. 4.10–11)'.[7] Jesus *redefined power*, and Paul's doctrine of the powers 'reveals itself to be a very refined analysis of the problems of society and history'.[8] Contrary to the major Christian tradition, he declared, 'The authority of government is not self-justifying.'[9]

Stanley Hauerwas (b. 1940) was strongly influenced by Yoder, and is an outspoken advocate of pacifism. He is also sharply critical of liberal democracy and capitalism. At different times, he has been influenced by

1 Carl Schmitt, *Political Theology* (Eng., 1985; Chicago, Ill.: University of Chicago Press, 2004).
2 Reinhold Niebuhr, *Moral Man and Immoral Society* (London: SCM Press, 1963); H. Richard Niebuhr, *Christ and Culture* (New York, N.Y.: Harper-Collins, 1999).
3 John H. Yoder, *The Politics of Jesus* (Grand Rapids, Mich.: Eerdmans, 1972).
4 Yoder, *Politics*, p. 34.
5 Yoder, *Politics*, p. 36.
6 Yoder, *Politics*, p. 45.
7 Yoder, *Politics*, p. 95.
8 Yoder, *Politics*, p. 147.
9 Yoder, *Politics*, p. 207.

Methodists, Anglicans and Anabaptists. He holds his PhD from Yale, and his DD from Edinburgh; he has taught at Notre Dame and Duke Divinity School. He regards social ethics as part of narrative, and rejects the notion of the Church as seeking to control history. Such compromise too readily accepts liberalism as the Christian narrative. In *Resident Aliens* (1989) he rejects attempts to accommodate to secular culture.[10] Such a strategy, he says, leads to such disasters as dropping the atomic bomb on Hiroshima.

In 1998 Hauerwas gave the *Scottish Journal of Theology* lectures at Aberdeen under the title *Sanctify Them in the Truth*.[11] Truth, he says, is not separable from how we live, as Jesus declared in John 17. He comments, 'To be a Christian is to be initiated into a community with skills, not unlike learning to lay bricks that are meant to transform our lives.'[12] Bricks may look uniform, but have variations, and must be added one by one. Hauerwas has produced scores of influential books. Their titles tell us about his agenda: *A Community of Character* (1981); *Responsibility for Devalued Persons* (1982); *Unleashing the Scripture* (1993); *God, Medicine, and Suffering* (1994); *The Wisdom of the Cross* (2005); *Living Gently in a Violent World* (2008); *War and the American Difference* (2011); and many others. He is disturbed by language about 'human rights'. This regards people as strangers. He carefully considers death and suicide. As an oral speaker, he is passionate, witty, blunt, exhilarating and great fun.

---

10 Stanley Hauerwas, with William Willimon, *Resident Aliens: Life in the Christian Community* (Nashville, Tenn.: Abingdon, 2004).
11 Stanley Hauerwas, *Sanctify Them in the Truth: Holiness Exemplified* (Edinburgh: T&T Clark, 1998).
12 Hauerwas, *Sanctify Them in the Truth*, p. 236.

7

Practical theology

In his *Brief Outline of the Study of Theology* (1850), Schleiermacher (1768–1834) regarded practical theology as serving the welfare of the Church.[1] This has its roots in his controversy with Fichte in Berlin. Fichte regarded theology as simply the quest for truth, like philosophy. Schleiermacher saw theology as primarily a practical discipline, which served the training of clergy, much as the faculty of law served lawyers, and the faculty of medicine served doctors. It should be considered just as respectable as, and no less rigorous than, other faculties. It combines practical needs with 'the scientific spirit'. It presupposes philosophical and historical theology. Further, it concerns 'the organization of the Christian community'.[2] This includes the 'National Congregation' (*Landesgemeinde*) and the 'Congregational District' (*Kreisgemeinde*).[3] It further includes catechesis and mission.

Many biblical passages predate Schleiermacher's work. In the OT Job addresses the problem of suffering; Ecclesiastes addresses existential *Angst* and possible meaninglessness; Haggai addresses disappointment in the face of prophetic encouragement. In the NT Matthew is concerned about the Church; Mark addresses the cost of discipleship; the Pastoral Epistles consider the appointment of elders and deacons, and their appropriate characteristics. 1 Corinthians, Romans and Ephesians major on 'building up', on love and on unity. 1 Corinthians also considers gifts of the Spirit and ministry. After the Reformation, Richard Baxter (1615–91) produced *The Reformed Pastor* (1656), and other works of pastoral guidance, while George Herbert wrote *A Priest to the Temple* (or *The Country Parson*) (1652). However, the flowering of the discipline occurred only in the twentieth century.

Anton Boisen (1867–1966) was best known for his development of clinical pastoral education in the USA in the 1930s. He was influenced by William James. He published *The Exploration of the Inner World* (1936).

---

1 Friedrich Schleiermacher, *A Brief Outline of the Study of Theology* (Eng., Edinburgh: T&T Clark, 1850).
2 Schleiermacher, *Brief Outline*, p. 191.
3 Schleiermacher, *Brief Outline*, p. 195.

Seward Hiltner (1909–84) was Boisen's student, and advocated clinical pastoral education in the 1940s and 1950s. He became Professor of Pastoral Theology at Chicago Divinity School and then at Princeton Theological Seminary. He wrote *Pastoral Counseling* (1949). Hiltner was criticized for making too much of the image of pastor as shepherd, in spite of explicit references to this in 1 Peter. In England, the fashion of clinical counselling was carried forward by Frank Lake (1914–82). He studied medicine at Edinburgh, but did not (to my knowledge) graduate in theology. In the 1950s he trained as a psychiatrist and in 1962 he founded the Clinical Theology Association in Nottingham. This became a model for pastoral theology in at least one theological college. In 1966 he published his large book, *Clinical Theology*, which became a textbook for many. Many of Lake's assumptions, for example about memory to infancy or earlier, and about symbols in Jung and Tillich, remain open to criticism.

A new era began in the USA with Don Browning and his *Practical Theology* (1983).[4] He argued that pastoral care 'is mediated to individuals and groups in all their situational, existential, and developmental particularity'.[5] Paul Ballard adopted a similar approach in the UK in 1988.[6] Edward Farley was active in the USA. But in 1983 and 1984, two writers sharply criticized the older 'clinical' paradigm of Hiltner and Lake. Charles Gerkin (b. 1922) wrote *The Living Human Document: Re-envisioning Pastoral Counseling in a Hermeneutical Mode*, and Donald Capps published *Pastoral Care and Hermeneutics*.[7] Donald Capps (1939–2015) was Professor of Pastoral Psychology at Princeton Theological Seminary. Yolanda Dreyer reviewed his book in 2009, commenting that Capps points to a similarity between pastoral actions and texts. The article illustrates Capps' conviction that theories of pastoral care lack methodologies for understanding what makes pastoral actions meaningful. By contrast, he uses *hermeneutics* to make a contribution to the methodology of pastoral care. Further, viewing pastoral actions as texts, and exploring the hermeneutical insights of Paul Ricoeur, would contribute to understanding of the meaning of pastoral actions.[8] In similar vein, Glynn Harrison,

---

4 Don Browning, *Practical Theology* (San Francisco, Calif.: Harper & Row, 1983).
5 Browning, *Practical Theology*, p. 187.
6 Paul Ballard, 'Pastoral Theology', *Theology* 91 (1988), p. 375.
7 Charles Gerkin, *The Living Human Document: Re-envisioning Pastoral Counseling in a Hermeneutical Mode* (Nashville, Tenn.: Abingdon, 1983); David Capps, *Pastoral Care and Hermeneutics* (Philadelphia, Pa.: Fortress Press, 1984).
8 Yolanda Dreyer, 'Reflections on Donald Capps' Hermeneutical Model of Pastoral Care', *Harvard Theological Review* 70 (2005), pp. 1–37.

Emeritus Professor of Psychiatry at Bristol, warns readers against the culture of self-esteem, after the self-esteem movement took off in the 1960s.[9]

This group of recent studies carries practical theology forward in a more constructive and valid way than earlier. The concept of 'practical theology' has narrowed since Schleiermacher, to 'pastoral theology'. If we wish to return to his broader definition, there are numerous books specializing in ecclesiology, liturgy, church law, and so on. Meanwhile, in practical or pastoral theology, alongside Gerkin in the USA, British specialists include Duncan Forrester, Elaine Graham, Martyn Percy and Stephen Pattinson.

---

9 Glynn Harrison, 'The Ego-Trip Generation', Oak Hill *Commentary Magazine* (Summer 2013), p. 18.

8

Systematic theology

The earliest theologian of the Church is said to be Irenaeus (*c.* 130 – *c.* 200), Bishop of Lyons. In his treatise *Against Heresies* he affirms God as Creator, the public tradition of the rule of faith, Christ and the Spirit as 'the two hands of God', and his 'recapitulation' theology of redemption, although this can hardly be called 'systematic' theology. Origen (*c.* 185 – *c.* 254) produced more systematic work in his *On First Principles*. He begins this work by expounding a doctrine of God as light, power and without limit. He then expounds a Christology in which Christ is divine, personal, and the one through whom all things exist. The Holy Spirit was begotten, not made, and was the medium of divine revelation. He is unequivocal about the inspiration of Scripture. He has also paid attention to textual criticism and exegesis of the Bible.

Augustine (353–430) more clearly merits the title 'systematic theologian' (see Introduction, pp. 15–16). He is uncompromising on the authority of Scripture, and in his writings against the Manichaeans he affirms that God is Creator, and that evil is no dualist entity. His autobiographical *Confessions* show his developed doctrine of sin. His anti-Pelagian writings consider grace, free will, the universality and bondage of alienation from God, and human sin. He quotes Romans 5.12, that all are sinners, and in his notorious adoption of the Latin text, concludes that *in quo* means 'in whom', rather than 'because', the normal meaning of the Greek *eph' hō*.[1] He stresses the necessity of divine grace. In *The Spirit and the Letter* Augustine urges the incapacity of the law to bring salvation. It is 'the letter that kills'.[2] Pannenberg comments, 'The classical significance for the Christian doctrine of sin consists in the fact that he viewed and analyzed the Pauline link between sin and desire more deeply than Christian theology had hitherto managed to do.'[3] His treatise *The City of God* addresses Roman accusations of blame for the fall of Rome, because Christians had

---

1 Augustine, *On the Forgiveness of Sins*, Bk 1, ch. 10 (Eng., *NPNF*, ser. 1, vol. 5, p. 19).
2 Augustine, *On the Spirit and the Letter*, ch. 6, 4 (Eng., *NPNF*, ser. 1, vol. 5, p. 85).
3 Wolfhart Pannenberg, *Systematic Theology* (Eng., Edinburgh: T&T Clark, 1994), p. 241.

deserted Roman polytheism. Augustine dominated the theology of the Western medieval Church.

Through the centuries at least four outstanding systematic theologies were produced, namely those by Aquinas, Calvin, Barth and Pannenberg. Some might wish to add Schleiermacher and Rahner, but their work is not on quite the same scale and comprehensiveness, and we could then add many others.

Thomas Aquinas (1225–74) has already been discussed in our Introduction (see p. 17). It would be repetitious to consider him again. He discussed the nature of theology, and arguments for the existence of God, including his 'five ways'. The first three 'ways' constitute versions of the cosmological argument, partly in Aristotelian terms. The fifth 'way' amounts to the argument from design. His famous Part 1, question 13, concerns 'theological language'.[4] He argued, 'No word can be used literally of God' (art. 3), i.e. 'It is impossible to predicate anything univocally both of God and creatures'; they would not have the same meaning (art. 5). But they are also not 'equivocal' (ambiguous). We *need* to use language that we use of creatures, or we must remain silent about God. There is 'a certain parallelism' between God and the creature; hence we can speak metaphorically. Aquinas concludes, 'The word "God" . . . is used neither univocally nor equivocally, *but analogically*' (art. 10, my italics).

Aquinas discusses knowledge of God further in Part 1, questions 14–18 (Eng., vol. 4), and the Holy Trinity, creation, cosmogony, humankind, the image of God, divine government and the world order in questions 44–119 (Eng., vols 8–13). In question 6 he asserts, 'God alone is good by nature' (art. 3). In question 7, article 1, he declares that God is 'limitless' (Lat., *infinites*). He appeals both to Scripture and to Aristotle. More controversially today, he insists that God is unchangeable (Lat., *immutabilis*) on the basis of Malachi 3.6 (qu. 9, arts 1–2). Aquinas believes in the importance of divine revelation. He declares, 'It is impossible that any created mind should see the essence of God by its own natural powers' (qu. 12, art. 4). He quotes Psalm 3.9, 'In thy light we shall see light', and 1 Corinthians 2.8, 10, 'God has revealed to us through his Spirit . . . a wisdom which none of this world's rulers knew' (art. 13). Aquinas discusses the nature of truth. Truth is 'showing forth what is'. But in accordance with Aristotle, he added 'Truth is defined as conformity between intellect and thing' (art. 2), i.e. what today we call the correspondence theory of truth.

---

4 Aquinas, *Summa Theologiae*. On Part 1, qu. 13, see vol. 3, pp. 47–97.

On other matters Aquinas expounded the double procession of the Holy Spirit from both the Father and the Son, in accordance with the Western tradition. In question 47 he defined evil as 'an absence of good'. He declared, 'The absence of good taken deprivately is what we call evil' (art. 3). Evil also derives from 'inequalities', i.e. mountains and valleys, or what later philosophers called 'the principle of plenitude'.

The second main part of *Summa Theologiae* is divided into two parts. The first part discusses morality, love, pleasure, dispositions, virtues, sin and the effects of sin, among other topics. The second part expounded faith, hope, charity, prudence, justice and other virtues. The third main part of the *Summa Theologiae* discusses the incarnate Word, the grace of Christ, the one Mediator, the Virgin Mary, the Passion and resurrection of Christ, and the sacraments. This third part aroused most controversy at the Reformation. Aquinas utilizes Aristotle's distinction between substance and accidents to expound and explain the Catholic view of the Eucharist (see Part 3, Transubstantiation). Later Calvin and Zwingli rejected this idea; although Luther did not disagree with the broad thrust of Aquinas' argument as such, he objected to his using the extra-biblical categories of Aristotle to explain the Christian sacrament.

John Calvin (1509–64) was a second-generation Reformer. His theology constitutes a landmark because of its systematic and logical nature. He published it in the *Institutes of the Christian Religion* (1st edn, 1536; subsequent edns, in 1539, 1541 and 1559).[5] In the first part or 'Book' of the *Institutes*, Calvin expounded a doctrine of God, under the heading 'Knowledge of God the Creator'.

He argued that knowledge of God and knowledge of humankind are interdependent, and are 'bound together'.[6] He regards knowledge of God as implanted in the human mind. Nevertheless humankind retains a corrupted, distorted and neglected knowledge of God.[7]

God remains transcendent and unique.[8] Scripture is vital for understanding God and his will. Calvin uses the analogy of the need sometimes for spectacles.[9] He supports his theological claims from Scripture and from a regular appeal to Augustine. Like Luther, Calvin attacked 'enthusiasts',

---

5 Calvin, *Institutes.*
6 Calvin, *Institutes*, 1.1.1 and 3.
7 Calvin, *Institutes*, 1.4.1–3.
8 Calvin, *Institutes*, 1.10–13.
9 Calvin, *Institutes*, 1.6.1.

who make Montanist-like appeals to the Holy Spirit.[10] Calvin expounded God as a unity in three persons. In chapter 14 he turns to the doctrine of creation, arguing that in Genesis the writer stresses 'progressive steps' and the 'order of events', rather than any exact chronology.[11] Calvin also rejects the well-known distinction between the permissive and active will of God.[12]

The second 'Book' expounds his doctrine of Christ. He first recapitulates his earlier work on the sin, fall and revolt of humankind.[13] He speaks of 'the . . . corruption to which early Christian writers put the name of Original Sin, meaning by the term the deprivation of nature formally good'.[14] He expounds redemption, in which Christ is both Redeemer and Mediator. Calvin refers to many OT prophecies, including that of the Davidic king. Chapters 12–17 more explicitly expound Christ's mediation and redemption. Christ is 'very God and very man'.[15] He is 'God with us' or Emmanuel. In chapter 14 he follows the traditional 'two natures' Christology of Chalcedon. Christ is prophet, priest and king: 'By the sacrifice of his death, he wiped away our guilt, and made satisfaction for sin.'[16] This 'penal substitution' achieved reconciliation with God. He concludes, 'Christ has merited grace for us'.[17]

In Book 3 Calvin considers the application of all Christ's benefits through the Holy Spirit. He writes, 'The Holy Spirit is the bond by which Christ effectually binds us to himself.'[18] The Holy Spirit is both seal and guarantee for confirming the faith of believers. Faith depends on the Holy Spirit, and fortifies believers with the word of God.[19] The illumination of the Spirit 'is the true source of understanding'.[20] Calvin emphatically stresses the work of the Holy Spirit in sanctification and regeneration.

Book 4 concerns 'the holy Catholic church'. It includes the doctrine of the Church, sacraments and civil government. Calvin spoke of the 'communion of saints'.[21] By contrast, the papacy, he insisted, is a false

---

10 Calvin, *Institutes*, 1.9.3.
11 Calvin, *Institutes*, 1.14.2.
12 Calvin, *Institutes*, 1.18.1.
13 Calvin, *Institutes*, 2.1.1–8.
14 Calvin, *Institutes*, 2.1.5.
15 Calvin, *Institutes*, 2.12.1.
16 Calvin, *Institutes*, 2.15.6.
17 Calvin, *Institutes*, 2.17.3.
18 Calvin, *Institutes*, 3.1.1.
19 Calvin, *Institutes*, 3.2.21.
20 Calvin, *Institutes*, 3.2.36.
21 Calvin, *Institutes*, 4.21.3.

church, with a perverted government. Calvin declares, 'In place of the Lord's Supper, the foulest sacrilege has entered, the worship of God is deformed by . . . intolerable superstition.'[22] Calvin distinguished between the visible and the indivisible Church. He advocated the appointment of pastors, and asserted that the Holy Spirit and the laying on of hands constitute ordination.[23] Baptism, he urged, is the initiating sign by which we are admitted to the fellowship of the Church, being grafted into Christ and accounted children of God.[24]

In the nineteenth century Schleiermacher produced a systematic theology on a smaller scale in his *The Christian Faith* (Ger., 1821, 2nd edn, 1830; Eng., 1989). But partly because of his Romanticism, and partly because of his Pietism, he produced a theology with less balance and comprehensive scope than Aquinas, Calvin, Barth and Pannenberg.

We have already introduced Barth (see Introduction, pp. 23–5). The first English volume of his magisterial 14-volume *Church Dogmatics* concerns the revelation of the word of God.[25] The speech of God, he stated, is 'the act of God'.[26] It also takes the form of promise and judgment.[27] All revelation must be conformable to God, and lead to God. The word of God comes to us as his gift. In the same volume he insisted that the word of God has a threefold form: the word of God preached, the word written and the word revealed.[28] The second volume continued this theme. Christ is the primary mode of revelation. Jesus Christ is 'very God and very man'.[29] The phrase in the creed, 'Born of the Virgin Mary', underlines his genuine manhood.

In the second main part, Barth turned to the doctrine of God. In the German II.I (Eng., vol. 3) he wrote, 'God is known by God and by God alone'.[30] What Barth called 'the knowability of God' depends entirely on God's readiness to be known.[31] Nevertheless, he pointed out, the sin of humankind and its fall express a 'closedness' to God. We find God 'in Jesus Christ, and in him alone'.[32] The need for revelation arises because 'the hiddenness of God is the inconceivability of the Father, the Son and the Holy

---

22 Calvin, *Institutes*, 4.2.2.
23 Calvin, *Institutes*, 4.3.14.
24 Calvin, *Institutes*, 4.15.1.
25 Barth, *Church Dogmatics*, vol. 1.
26 Barth, *Church Dogmatics*, I.I, vol. 1, p. 143.
27 Barth, *Church Dogmatics*, I.I, vol. 1, p. 150.
28 Barth, *Church Dogmatics*, I.I, vol. 1, pp. 88–124.
29 Barth, *Church Dogmatics*, I.II, vol. 2, sect. 15, pp. 132–71.
30 Barth, *Church Dogmatics*, II.I, vol. 3, sect. 27, p. 179.
31 Barth, *Church Dogmatics*, II.I, vol. 3, p. 63.
32 Barth, *Church Dogmatics*, II.I, vol. 3, p. 149.

Spirit'.[33] Later in this volume, Barth considered the reality of God in terms of his *actions*: 'God is who he is in the act of his revelation. God seeks and creates fellowship between himself and us.'[34] Next, in II.II Barth considered the God who elects and commands. Barth declared, 'The election of grace is the whole of the Gospel.'[35] Jesus Christ is the elected man. He recognized that the doctrine of election is not generally valued today, but considered it self-evident from Scripture. Election is not arbitrary, but is part of our election in Christ. As a consequence, the believer 'may let go of God, but God does not let go of him'.[36]

Ideally, we could consider every volume of Barth, but we have space only to indicate the flavour and trends of Barth's theology. In Part III Barth considered creation, humankind, ethics, providence, and especially his widespread discussion of ethics. He provided thought on many themes including marriage. In Part IV he discussed reconciliation. The focus throughout the *Dogmatics* remains on *Christ* and *the Holy Trinity*.

In his *Systematic Theology* Pannenberg begins the first volume by discussing theology, doctrine, knowledge, and especially 'truth as coherence'.[37] He rejects the notion of truth as arbitrary consensus. He also rejects absolute objectivity, and appeals made solely to the testimony of the Holy Spirit. He argues, 'Words and Spirit belong together.'[38] His lengthy and detailed discussions include appraisals of many theologians. He considers the diversity of religions alongside Israel's claim that the God of Israel is exclusively God. On the subject of revelation, he stresses that the biblical accounts witness to a variety of ways of expounding this. He then considers the Holy Trinity, stressing *Jesus' self-distinction from the Father* on one side, and from *the Spirit* on the other. He especially takes up the teaching of Athanasius that the term *Father is a relational term*.[39] In spite of what many feminist theologians argue, he believes that the term *Father* must be retained, since God the Father is both the Father of Jesus and the fatherly provider for humankind. Drawing indirectly on Hegel, he stresses the *distinction and unity* of the divine persons. He concludes the first volume with a masterly exposition of the holiness, eternity, omnipotence and omnipresence of God, as well as his infinity and love. Each section is

---

33 Barth, *Church Dogmatics*, II.I, vol. 3, sect. 27, p. 197.
34 Barth, *Church Dogmatics*, II.I, vol. 3, p. 257.
35 Barth, *Church Dogmatics*, II.II, vol. 4, sect. 32, pp. 13–14.
36 Barth, *Church Dogmatics*, II.II, vol. 4, sect. 35, p. 317.
37 Pannenberg, *Systematic Theology*, vol. 1, p. 21.
38 Pannenberg, *Systematic Theology*, vol. 1, p. 33.
39 Pannenberg, *Systematic Theology*, vol. 1, p. 273.

equally informed by the biblical writings, by the history of theology, and by philosophical logic, with great sophistication.

In volume 2, Pannenberg considers creation, humanity, Christology and reconciliation. God's creation constitutes a sign of *his faithfulness*, and his conferring of *order*. He declares, 'The uniformity of events according to law is thus a condition of creaturely independence.'[40] He emphasizes God's creation of the animal world, and the advance of the sciences, in which 'we humans thus seem to be marginal phenomena in the cosmos'.[41] He continues, 'Biblical piety finds the variety and grandeur of the forms of life so fascinating', including 'the creation of the different kinds of plants and animals'.[42] Humans, however, are aware 'of their destiny of fellowship with God'.[43] The problem or barrier comes from human sin. He writes, 'Misery, then, is the lot of those who are deprived of the fellowship with God that is the destiny of human life.'[44] '*Misery*' best summarizes our detachment from God, and *alienation* represents a parallel term. He also expounds the unity of body and soul. Being with others is also a key human capacity. Concerning 'original sin', Pannenberg laments the tendency to view sin as an *individual act, rather than a corporate state*.[45] He cites biblical vocabulary for sin, and declares, 'Augustine found an autonomy of the will that puts the self in the centre, and uses everything else as a means to the self as an end'.[46]

The apostolic message of reconciliation has a constitutive function for the coming of Christ. Nevertheless, 'The Son can do nothing on his own, but only what he sees the Father doing' (John 5.19). Pannenberg observes, 'This uniqueness of Jesus rested on the unconditional subjection of his person to the lordship of God that he proclaimed.'[47] He understands the work of Christ as a *vicarious sacrifice*. Very significantly he comments:

> The fact that a later age may find it hard to understand traditional ideas is *not a sufficient reason for replacing them*. It simply shows how necessary it is to open up these ideas to later generations by interpretation, and thus to keep their meaning alive. The problems that people have with ideas like expiation and representation (or substitution) in our secularised

---

40 Pannenberg, *Systematic Theology*, vol. 2, p. 72.
41 Pannenberg, *Systematic Theology*, vol. 2, p. 74.
42 Pannenberg, *Systematic Theology*, vol. 2, p. 129.
43 Pannenberg, *Systematic Theology*, vol. 2, p. 175.
44 Pannenberg, *Systematic Theology*, vol. 2, p. 178.
45 Pannenberg, *Systematic Theology*, vol. 2, pp. 234–5.
46 Pannenberg, *Systematic Theology*, vol. 2, p. 243.
47 Pannenberg, *Systematic Theology*, vol. 2, p. 373.

age rest, less on any lack of forcefulness, . . . than on the fact that those who are competent to interpret them do not explain their content with sufficient forcefulness or clarity.[48]

In volume 3, Pannenberg considers the Holy Spirit, the kingdom of God, the Church, election and history, and the consummation of creation in the kingdom of God. He argues that the Spirit and the Son mutually indwell each other. He also declares, 'The church . . . is not identical with the kingdom of God.'[49] The Church may be sinful and fallible; the kingdom not, but it is where God rules. He stresses faith as trust, in response to God's promise. Nevertheless 'saving faith does not in any way rule out historical knowledge'.[50] Pannenberg also considers justification, adoption and the sacraments. He concludes with eschatology, arguing that 'like the reality of God himself, it transcends all our concepts'.[51] He draws on Barth and Moltmann, and the biblical concept of promise. He concludes, 'Grounding eschatology in the concept of *promise* is correct inasmuch as eschatological hope can rest only on God himself.'[52] Pannenberg constitutes a fitting climax to this brief historical survey of types of Christian systematic theology.

48 Pannenberg, *Systematic Theology*, vol. 2, p. 422 (my italics).
49 Pannenberg, *Systematic Theology*, vol. 3, p. 37.
50 Pannenberg, *Systematic Theology*, vol. 3, p. 143.
51 Pannenberg, *Systematic Theology*, vol. 3, p. 527.
52 Pannenberg, *Systematic Theology*, vol. 3, p. 539 (my italics).

9

Theology of religions

Approaches to this field vary enormously. To read Gavin D'Costa, John Hick, Ernst Troeltsch, Gerhard Ebeling and Wolfhart Pannenberg on 'theology of religion' seems like inhabiting five different worlds. Gavin D'Costa (b. 1958) is Professor in Catholic Theology in the University of Bristol, and is a well-known specialist in theology of religions and religious pluralism, as well as Catholic theology. Much of his work concerns the familiar descriptive typology of the 'exclusivist', 'inclusivist' and 'pluralist' approaches to the subject, to which he adds a fourth option, to include the Catholic notion of purgatory.[1] Ebeling (1912–2001) and Pannenberg (1928–2014) regard the term *theology* as inviting not simply phenomenological description, but descriptions of value, truth and God. Hick (1922–2012) advocates a virtually pluralistic approach, while Troeltsch remains distinctive.

D'Costa defines *pluralism* as the belief that 'all religions are equal, and that Christ represents one revelation among many equally important revelations'. He defines *exclusivity* as the belief that 'Only those who hear the gospel proclaimed and have explicitly confessed Christ are saved'. Third, *inclusiveness* suggests that 'Christ is the normative revelation of God, although salvation is possible outside the explicit Christian church, but this salvation is always from Christ'.[2] Some forms of pluralism, he argues, begin from a belief in *historical relativity*, in that all traditions are relative, and cannot claim absolute superiority. He includes John Hick among advocates of pluralism, since he argues that the Christian faith should not be Christocentric or ecclesiocentric. Hick argues that Yahweh in Judaism, Allah in Islam, and the Trinity in Christianity all represent valid traditions. Hick is also influenced by liberation theology, religious wars of conflict, and attitudes of arrogance and imperialism. D'Costa considers objections to this thesis, namely especially that D'Costa introduces a 'free-floating

---

1 Gavin D'Costa, 'Theology of Religions', in David Ford, with Rachel Muers (ed.), *The Modern Theologians* (3rd edn, Oxford: Blackwell, 2005), pp. 626–44.
2 D'Costa, 'Theology of Religions', in Ford (ed.), *Modern Theologians*, p. 627 (all three quotations).

"God". D'Costa does not underestimate the importance of historical particularity.

D'Costa associates *exclusivism* with missionary theology and evangelism. In general exclusivists regard human nature as fallen and sinful, and he suggests that Karl Barth is a representative of this approach, even though Barth's soteriology is far more complex. The logic of this theology, he argues, requires 'that salvation is an utterly gratuitous gift, entirely unmerited by us'.[3] He also distinguishes between a rigid exclusivism and a softer exclusivism. Thus George Lindbeck (b. 1923) argues that there is neither damnation nor salvation outside the Church. Joseph Di Noia (b. 1943) formulates a similar approach, with the support of a Roman Catholic doctrine of purgatory. D'Costa developed this into a fourth category in his typology. Divine grace, he argues, cannot be limited only to a conscious encounter with Christ.

Inclusiveness, according to D'Costa, does not limit divine grace to the confines of the visible Church. A number of Roman Catholics, Orthodox, and some Protestants, share this approach. A special version of this is Karl Rahner's version of 'hidden grace' and 'anonymous Christianity'. According to Rahner a response to saving grace need not necessarily be conscious, and this helps us to take account of the destiny of millions who have never heard the gospel. In criticism of this approach, D'Costa cites Hans Küng as 'accusing Rahner of creating a terminological distinction to sweep a resistant non-Christian humanity into the Christian Church through the back-door'.[4]

D'Costa cannot disprove the strongest objections to his fourth option, shared with Di Noia, namely that the whole notion of purgatory in the Catholic sense belongs to medieval speculation and is rejected by such scholars as Moltmann and many others. I have addressed these objections in both the Roman Catholic and Anglo-Catholic form in *The Last Things: A New Approach*.[5] Although he is a respected specialist in the theology of religions, we may wonder in what sense D'Costa's typology is genuinely a *theology* of religions. Like so many departments of 'religious studies', his work is largely empirical and descriptive.

On the other hand, Ebeling and Pannenberg regard theology as necessarily raising questions about truth, value and God. Pannenberg parts company from Ebeling at various points, but they also share much in

---

3 D'Costa, 'Theology of Religions', in Ford (ed.), *Modern Theologians*, p. 630.
4 Hans Küng, *On Being a Christian* (London: Collins, 1976), pp. 77–8.
5 Anthony C. Thiselton, *The Last Things: A New Approach* (London: SPCK, 2012), pp. 129–36.

common. Both thinkers approach the subject more historically and with much more evaluation than D'Costa. Pannenberg insists on the scientific study of religions as beginning in the era of the Renaissance. He shares this well-established principle in the discipline at the close of the nineteenth century. Many had pointed out that the study of other religions was a prerequisite even of biblical studies. Pannenberg describes it as an 'appropriate framework of the practice of Christian theology'.[6] Clearly OT theology has to be expounded and assessed against the background of Canaanite and other religions. Similarly the NT must be expounded against the background of Graeco-Roman religions. This does not mean however, that we should give credence to the history-of-religions speculations of Richard Reitzenstein (1861–1931) and Wilhelm Bousset (1865–1920). As Gunter Wagner (b. 1954) has shown, such approaches often confuse alleged parallels with cause and effect, and often make assumptions about dating which prove to be untenable.

Nevertheless, the proposal invites caution. As F. Heiler (1892–1967) has argued, the modern science of religion is 'for the most part making religion a human concept and eliminating the divine'.[7] Pannenberg approves of Heiler's demand that theology should take seriously religion's claim to truth. Moreover he adds, 'A theology of religions in the sense described will include first a philosophy of religion.'[8]

In his essay 'Toward a Theology of the History of Religions' Pannenberg considers that Paul Tillich (1896–1965) rejects the utter uniqueness of Christian revelation.[9] He discerns a similar problem in Ernst Troeltsch (1865–1923). Troeltsch did value history and hermeneutics, but he also belonged to the outdated history-of-religion school. He did advocate assessing the truth of other religions, but tended, like Tillich, to relativize particular traditions. Pannenberg expresses sympathy with the kerygmatic tradition that opposed him. He comments,

> Troeltsch failed to take seriously enough the fundamental Christian conviction *of the presence* of the eschaton in Jesus and in primitive Christianity. The possibility of any theology at all seemed to collapse along with the idea

---

6   Wolfhart Pannenberg, *Theology and the Philosophy of Science* (Eng., Philadelphia, Pa.: Westminster Press and London: DLT, 1976), p. 361.

7   Pannenberg quotes Heiler in *Theology and the Philosophy of Science*, p. 364.

8   Pannenberg, *Theology and the Philosophy of Science*, p. 367.

9   Wolfhart Pannenberg, 'Toward a Theology of the History of Religions', in Pannenberg, *Basic Questions in Theology*, 3 vols (Eng., London: SCM Press, 1970–3), vol. 2, p. 65.

of an eschatological revelation having occurred in Jesus. The kerygmatic reaction was certainly justified at this point.[10]

Pannenberg's major criticism of many theologies of religion is their lack of taking full account of their contexts. He observes, '[Religions are] so different within their respective concrete contexts'.[11]

Pannenberg's simultaneous affirmation of a theology of religions and serious warning about this subject may find some resolution in the approach of Ebeling.[12] He agrees with Pannenberg that religions need to be studied in biblical studies. The early Church, he argues, also defined itself in relation to Gnosticism, Manichaeism and neoplatonism. Augustine defined Christianity as 'the true religion'. He also agrees with Pannenberg that the study of religion impinges on philosophy of religion and historical questions. He observed, 'It would be an absurdity to build up a theological faculty that had no official knowledge of normative religious truth.'[13] The study of religions, he argued, should be transformed into *theology*. Meanwhile, whether the theology of religions is currently *adequate*, he seriously doubts. Our discussion seems to corroborate this.

The eminent names we have considered do not exhaust the discussion of the theology of religions. Recently Nicholas Wood (2009) has revived assessments of the respective contributions of Kenneth Cragg and Lesslie Newbigin.[14] Cragg regards the way forward as a 'theology of encounter' in relations between Christians and Muslims.[15] Wood regards Newbigin as attempting to hold together a version of 'non-provincial' pluralism with a version of mission.[16] Both Cragg and Newbigin seek a genuine *theology* of religions. Wood's bibliography lists some 21 books by Cragg, and some 16 by Newbigin. We should also note numerous other contributions of D'Costa.[17] This is a subject still in process of development.

---

10 Pannenberg, 'Toward a Theology of the History of Religions', in *Basic Questions*, vol. 2, p. 68.
11 Pannenberg, 'Toward a Theology of the History of Religions', in *Basic Questions*, vol. 2, p. 74.
12 Gerhard Ebeling, *The Study of Theology* (Eng., London: Collins, 1979), pp. 39–51.
13 Ebeling, *Study of Theology*, p. 50.
14 Nicholas J. Wood, *Faiths and Faithfulness: Pluralism, Dialogue and Mission* (Milton Keynes: Paternoster, 2009).
15 Wood, *Faiths and Faithfulness*, p. 61.
16 Wood, *Faiths and Faithfulness*, p. 204.
17 For example, Gavin D'Costa, *Theology and Religious Pluralism* (Oxford: Blackwell, 1986), and *Christianity and World Religions* (Chichester: Wiley-Blackwell, 2009).

Part 2

CONCEPTS AND ISSUES

Atonement

The atonement stands at the centre of Christian theology as a given, revealed, fact. Its *manner* of operation, however, has been contested. Virtually all Christians from the biblical and patristic era to the Reformation and the Enlightenment recognized the unique importance of the cross in the ministry of Jesus. Nevertheless there emerged some four (possibly three) main models in terms of which the life, crucifixion and resurrection of Christ was interpreted and understood.

1 Many regarded the work of Christ as a *ransom* from sin or bondage. In accordance with the nature of redemption, they saw the atonement as (a) deliverance *from*, e.g. oppression, bondage or the consequences of sin; (b) redemption *by* a mighty act of God; (c) restoration *to* a state of safety, security and blessing. The classic model or paradigm case was Israel's redemption *from* Egypt, *by* God's saving act at the Red Sea, *to* a new life of safety in the Promised Land. On the whole this featured as a dominant model in the church fathers, although not exclusively so.

2 Many regarded the work of Christ as the supreme *example* of sacrificial love. Neither before nor since has the generosity of such love been seen. Peter Abelard represents the classic example of such an interpretation, which has often been called the 'exemplarist' or 'moral influence' approach. In particular he opposed Anselm's claim that this account of the atonement would be woefully insufficient, especially without a 'Godward' dimension.

3 A more specific model regards the atonement as concerned with God's governance of the world, and with God's justice as well as his love. This model takes two forms. The earlier is Anselm's interpretation of the atonement as offering '*satisfaction*' to God's honour. The better-known version is John Calvin's interpretation of the *penal substitution*. Christ lived and died in our place. He did this to bear the punishment for sin which we deserved, so that we might also be raised with Christ free from sin. This model, like the others, need not be exclusive of other interpretations.

4 Some regard the model of penal substitution as distinct from the 'satisfaction' model of Anselm, although others regard them as basically sharing the same approach. For some today it constitutes the key model of the atonement. In English scholarship Colin Gunton has defended it as a defining metaphor, but not as an exclusive one.

Each of these four models has biblical support. We shall consider each model in turn.

1 The ransom model

In Mark Jesus says, 'The Son of Man came . . . to give his life a ransom (Gk, *lutron*) for many' (10.45). In 1 Corinthians 6.20 Paul asserts, 'You were bought (Gk, *ēgorasthēte*) with a price'. In Galatians 3.13 Paul declares, 'Christ redeemed us from the curse of the law'. In Romans 3.24 Paul writes that Christians 'are justified . . . through the redemption (Gk, *dia tēs apo-lutrōseōs*) that is in Christ'. These are all from 'pillar' epistles, of which Pauline authorship is not disputed. The anonymous author of the Epistle to the Hebrews likewise speaks of Christians' receiving 'eternal redemption' through the shed blood of Christ (9.2). Further, we have also noted the classic model in the OT of God's redemption from Egypt. In Exodus 6.6 God promises, 'I will *redeem* you (Heb. verb *gā'al*) with an outstretched arm and with mighty acts' (see Part 3, Redemption).

The patristic writers are no less clear. Clement of Rome speaks of 'redemption through His blood' (*1 Clem.*, 12.7; *c.* AD 96). Justin Martyr (*c.* 100 – *c.* 165) declares that Christ 'has redeemed us' (*Dialogue*, 86). Irenaeus of Lyons (*c.* 130 – *c.* 200) argued that Christ came 'That he might destroy sin, overcome death, and give life to humankind' (*Against Heresies*, Bk 3, 18.7). He also writes, 'Redeeming us with his blood, he gave himself as a ransom for those who had been led into captivity' (Bk 4, 1.1). Gustaf Aulén cites many other passages in Irenaeus, although not all of them are relevant to this ransom model.[1] Tertullian (*c.* 150 – *c.* 225) follows Irenaeus closely. Origen (*c.* 185 – *c.* 254) mainly expounds the exemplarist model, but also speaks of the atonement as a victory in which Christ overcomes the demons, who have seduced humankind and led people astray. He explicitly discusses 1 Corinthians 2.8, and asks,

> To whom did he [Jesus] give his soul as a ransom for many? Certainly not to God: why not then to the devil? For he had possession of us until there should be given to him the ransom for us, the soul of Jesus; though he was deceived by thinking that he could have dominion over it and did not see that he could not bear the torture caused by holding it.
>
> (*On First Principles*, Bk 3.3.3; 5.6–7)

After Nicaea, more critical discussion of this model comes in Athanasius and especially in the Cappadocian Fathers. In his classic book *On the*

---

1 Gustaf Aulén, *Christus Victor* (London: SPCK, 1931), pp. 34–44, 50–1.

Incarnation, Athanasius (*c.* 296–373) integrated his view of the work of Christ with the person of Christ as both God and man. Certainly he also argued that the death of Christ was to 'free humankind from the primal transgression' (*On the Incarnation*, 20).[2] He wrote, 'He [Christ] died to ransom all' (21). He also wrote, 'Christ accepted death at the hands of men, thereby completely to destroy death in his own body' (23), and declared, 'The death of the Lord is the ransom of all, and by it "the middle wall of partition" is broken down, and the call of the Gentiles came about' (25). On Christ's resurrection he added, 'Death has become like a tyrant who has been completely conquered by the legitimate monarch' (27).

A more precise exposition of the ransom model occurs in Gregory of Nyssa (*c.* 330–95), and a more precise *critique* of it in Gregory of Nazianzus (*c.* 330–90). Gregory of Nyssa discusses Paul's 'the rulers of this age' (1 Cor. 2.8), and writes,

> In order to secure the ransom on our behalf . . . The Deity was hidden under the veil of our nature so that, as with ravenous fish, the hook of the Deity might be gulped down along with the bait of flesh, and thus, life being introduced into the house of death . . . that which is diametrically opposed to light and life might vanish.
>
> (*Catechism*, 24; Eng., *NPNF*, ser. 2, vol. 5, p. 494)

However, Gregory of Nazianzus is said to have regarded this analogy as *grotesque*. He firmly rejected any notion that the ransom could somehow be 'paid' either to the devil or to God. He asks, 'To whom was that blood offered that was shed for us and why was it shed? . . . If it is to the Evil One, fie upon the outrage! (Gk, *pheu tēs hubreōs*).'[3] Gregory thus shows that the metaphor should not be overpressed.

In the modern era the best-known exponent of the ransom model has been Gustaf Aulén in *Christus Victor* (1931). He describes it as the 'classic' view of the atonement.[4] He writes, 'Its central theme is the idea of the Atonement as a Divine conflict and victory . . . Christus Victor triumphs over evil powers . . .'[5] He describes this as a dramatic account of the atonement, in contrast to the so-called objective model. This has become a seminal work. However, some of its details may be questioned.

---

2 Athanasius, *On the Incarnation* (London: Mowbray, 1963), p. 49; sections 20–7 are translated on pp. 49–57.

3 Gregory of Nazianzus, *Oration, 45: The Second Oration on Easter*, 22; Eng., *NPNF*, ser. 2, vol. 7, p. 431.

4 Aulén, *Christus Victor*, pp. 20–3.

5 Aulén, *Christus Victor*, p. 20.

In particular he claims that this is the view of Anselm of Canterbury, whereas, although he takes account of it, Anselm also has other ways of interpreting the atonement. More especially he claims that this view stands at the heart of Luther's understanding of the atonement.[6] But both Anselm and Luther hold a broader view, in which the ransom theory plays one part among others.

2 The *exemplarist* or '*moral influence*' model

Clearly the NT provides evidence for this, and in the history of thought Peter Abelard (1079–1142) expounded this interpretation. He defended it against Anselm's approach. The NT certainly sees the atonement as springing from the love of God in Christ. The question is whether the atonement must be understood *exclusively* as this. John records, for example, 'No one has greater love than this, to lay down one's life for one's friends' (15.13). Paul is even more emphatic. He declares,

> God proves his love for us in that while we were still sinners Christ died for us . . . For if while we were enemies, we were reconciled to God through the death of his Son, much more surely, having been reconciled, will we be saved by his life.   (Rom. 5.8, 10)

R. S. Franks, a classic critical expositor of the historical thought on the atonement, comments concerning Abelard: 'He has reduced the whole process of redemption to one single, clear, principle, namely the manifestation of God's love to us in Christ, which awakens an answering love in us. Out of this principle Abelard endeavours to explain all other points of view.'[7] Abelard expounded his view in his commentary on Romans. He interpreted the passage about showing *God's justice* as showing forth God's *love*. He explicitly declares, 'He [Paul] clearly intimates how he first understood this righteousness to be love, which perfectly meets the needs of the men of our time.'[8] He adds: 'How cruel and wicked it seems that anyone should demand the blood of an innocent person as the price for anything!'[9] Some suggest that his love affair with Héloise, which so dominated his life, may well have influenced his emphasis on the primacy

---

6 Aulén, *Christus Victor*, pp. 119–38.

7 R. S. Franks, *The Work of Christ: A Historical Study of Christian Doctrine* (London: Nelson, 1962), p. 146.

8 Peter Abelard, *Exposition of the Epistle to the Romans*, in E. R. Fairweather (ed.), *A Scholastic Miscellany* (Philadelphia, Pa.: Westminster Press and London: SCM Press, 1956), p. 279; cf. pp. 276–87.

9 Abelard, *Romans*, in Fairweather (ed.), *Scholastic Miscellany*, p. 283.

of love to the exclusion of other factors. Abelard had also thought more widely about the atonement than this one section of Romans.

In spite of its inadequacies, Abelard's approach influenced many other thinkers. These included Faustus Socinus (1509–1604), Friedrich Schleiermacher (1768–1834), Albrecht Ritschl (1822–89) and Adolf von Harnack (1851–1930). The persuasiveness of the argument depends on our view of the seriousness of human sin, and on whether the atonement relates to God's governance of the world.

3 The satisfaction model

This model also finds support in the biblical writings, but extensively overlaps with the model of substitutionary sacrifice. It is clear from the Gospels that the death of Jesus is intimately related to his resurrection, and that this is an act of God. For example, in Mark 12.10–11 we read, 'The stone that the builders rejected has become the cornerstone; this was the Lord's doing'. In Luke 17.25, we read that the Son of Man 'must endure much suffering and be rejected by this generation'. Mark declares, 'The Son of Man is to be betrayed into human hands, and they will kill him, and three days after being killed he will rise again' (9.31). Mark 14.36 is clear: 'Remove this cup from me; yet, not what I want, but what you want.'

Many of the references in the Pauline epistles go back to a pre-Pauline tradition which is early. It applies to the words of institution of the Lord's Supper in 1 Corinthians 11.25–26, 'This cup is the new covenant in my blood. Do this, as often as you drink it, in remembrance of me. For as often as you eat this bread and drink the cup, you proclaim the Lord's death until he comes.' The other firm example of pre-Pauline tradition comes in 1 Corinthians 15.3–4, where Paul repeats the common apostolic doctrine, 'that Christ died for our sins in accordance with the scriptures, and that he was buried, and that he was raised on the third day in accordance with the scriptures'.

The interpretation of Romans 3.25 is controversial. Paul speaks of Christ Jesus

> whom God put forward as a sacrifice of atonement by his blood, effective through faith. He did this to show his righteousness, because in his divine forbearance he had passed over the sins previously committed; it was to prove at the present time that he himself is righteous, and that he justifies the one who has faith in Jesus. (vv. 25–26)

91

Older versions, including the AV, used the term *propitiation* to translate the phrase which the NRSV renders 'a sacrifice of atonement'. More modern versions usually render the phrase as *expiation*. Some have suggested the translation 'mercy seat', or 'place of meeting', because of its reference to Jewish sacrificial ceremony, to avoid this sharp polarization. Respected scholars defend both interpretations, and if this means *propitiation*, it points in a Godward direction.[10] *Both terms say something useful: expiation* avoids the primitive notion that God is persuaded to be merciful in response to some human gift; *propitiation* avoids a merely *impersonal or mechanical* notion of the process that is involved.[11]

Anselm of Canterbury (*c.* 1033–1109) was the classic advocate of the 'satisfaction' model. In the first part of his book, *Why God Became Man*, Anselm argued that *only God* can put right the damage that sin has done.[12] Sin is not simply an internal matter, but concerns our entire relationship with God, and *God's governance of the world*. Humankind stands under bondage and is in need of redemption. Sin, meanwhile, constitutes 'an infinite debt' to God.[13] Anselm wrote:

> To sin is . . . not to render his due to God . . . It is not enough for someone who violates another's honour to restore the honour, unless he makes some kind of restitution, according to the extent of the injury and dishonour . . . Everyone who sins must repay to God the honour that he has taken away.[14]

The notion of a person's rank or 'honour' belongs distinctively to the feudal culture of medieval society, in which the greater or more esteemed the person injured, the greater should be a compensation or satisfaction. Critics have suggested that Anselm's model owes too much to the conventions of feudal society.

Anselm also examines the NT passages which use 'must' of Christ's suffering and death. He clarifies the notion *of necessity*. He explains, 'If it is not fitting for God to do anything unjustly or without due order, hence it does not belong to his freedom . . . to forgive unpunished a sinner who

---

10 David Hill, *Greek Words and Hebrew Meanings* (Cambridge: Cambridge University Press, 1967), pp. 23, 37; C. E. B. Cranfield, *The Epistle to the Romans*, 2 vols (Edinburgh: T&T Clark, 1975–9), vol. 1, pp. 214–18.

11 Joseph Fitzmyer, *Romans* (New York: Doubleday, 1992), pp. 348–50.

12 Anselm, *Why God Became Man*, chs 1–25; Eng. in Fairweather (ed.), *A Scholastic Miscellany*, pp. 101–46.

13 Anselm, *Why God Became Man*, chs 6, 7 and 11–15, in Fairweather (ed.), *A Scholastic Miscellany*, pp. 118–24.

14 Anselm, *Why God Became Man*, ch. 11, in Fairweather (ed.), *A Scholastic Miscellany*, p. 119.

does not repay to God what he owes.'[15] Thus 'necessity' comes to mean 'fitting' in relation to God's nature.

4 The (penal) substitution model

This explores the notion that, in a child's language, Christ died *in our place*, i.e. through substitution. A further step, adopted by Calvin, is the notion that Christ bore the punishment for sin in our place. This approach is strictly that of penal substitution. In modern theology a number of scholars accept the model of substitution, but not of *penal* substitution. One classic verse in Paul is Galatians 3.13:

> Christ redeemed us from the curse of the law by becoming a curse for us – for it is written, 'Cursed is everyone who hangs on a tree' – in order that in Christ Jesus the blessing of Abraham might come to the Gentiles.

There is also good evidence that some NT writers thought of Isaiah 53.4–5 as prefiguring the sacrifice of Christ: 'Surely he has borne our infirmities and carried our diseases . . . he was wounded for our transgressions, crushed for our iniquities; upon him was the punishment that has made us whole, and by his bruises we are healed.' The second classic Pauline text, which is often cited to support this view, is 2 Corinthians 5.21: 'For our sake he [God] made him [Christ] to be sin, who knew no sin, so that in him we might become the righteousness of God.' Some interpret *sin* in this verse to mean sin offering. D. E. H. Whiteley opposed the traditional interpretation emphatically.[16] But many see Whiteley's argument as strained.

Paul frequently uses the term *sacrifice*. He writes, for example, 'our paschal lamb, Christ, has been sacrificed' (Gk, *etuthē*; 1 Cor. 5.7). In Hebrews 9.26. 'He [Christ] has appeared once for all at the end of the age to remove sin by the sacrifice of himself' (Gk, *ephapax . . . dia tēs thusias autou*). Hebrews further declares, 'Christ . . . offered for all time a single sacrifice for sins' (10.12). If the Greek word *sacrifice* translates the Hebrew word *'āshām* (guilt (or sin) offering), this would strengthen this argument.

J. K. S. Reid observes that in the NT there is sometimes 'a rule of correspondence', for example 'because he lives, we shall live also'; but also 'a rule of contrariety: Christ wins those benefits for us who had himself no need of them'.[17] The second principle strongly implies the principle of substitution. The most explicit advocate of this approach in history,

---

15 Anselm, *Why God Became Man*, ch. 12, in Fairweather (ed.), *A Scholastic Miscellany*, p. 121.
16 D. E. H. Whiteley, *The Theology of St Paul* (Oxford: Blackwell, 1971), pp. 135–7.
17 J. K. S. Reid, *Our Life in Christ* (London: SCM Press, 1963), pp. 89–91.

however, was John Calvin (1509–64). Calvin explicitly calls Christ 'our *substitute-ransom and propitiation*' (his italics).[18] Jesus Christ, he says, is 'a propitiatory victim for sin (. . . Isa. 53.5, 10) on which guilt and penalty being in a manner laid, ceases to be imputed to us'. Calvin also cites 2 Corinthians 5.21, and the Hebrew term *āshām*, sin (or guilt) offering. In pastoral vein, Calvin continues: 'We must especially remember this substitution in order that we may not be all our lives in trepidation and anxiety'.[19] This approach grants the Christian full assurance of faith.

In the modern era, many have misunderstood this approach. Even Leon Morris, otherwise an advocate of this view, comments that some conservatives 'have unwittingly introduced a division into the Godhead', as if Christ sought to change the mind of an unwilling God.[20] Further, Jürgen Moltmann (b. 1926) and Donald Baillie rightly insist that God was gracious in *initiating* the atonement, and in no way had to be rendered gracious. In the third place, Colin Gunton (1941–2003) has insisted that this approach is complementary, not exclusive, to others, and that it is a valid metaphor among images of the atonement. He laments the fact that 'the intellectual and cultural poverty' of our age makes this model readily misunderstood.[21] Many popular writers have disparaged this model, but this is mainly through misunderstanding its main point. Gunton largely blames the legacy of Kant, Schleiermacher and Hegel for the misunderstanding and distortion of this model. By contrast, he describes it as 'an indispensable means for advance of cognitive knowledge and understanding'.[22] Each model serves, in Ian Ramsey's phrase, as a *model* which other approaches *qualify*, in order to reach a holistic understanding of such a decisive act of God.

Authority of the Bible

The authority of the Bible was universally taken for granted among Catholic, Protestant and Orthodox Christians until the Enlightenment. To quote biblical texts on this subject often becomes a circular argument. For except in very late books, the NT itself was barely formed. Such passages

---

18 Calvin, *Institutes*, 2.16.6, p. 440.
19 Calvin, *Institutes*, 2.16.5, p. 439.
20 Leon Morris, *Glory in the Cross* (London: Hodder & Stoughton, 1966), p. 46.
21 Colin Gunton, *The Actuality of Atonement: A Study of Metaphor, Rationality, and the Christian Tradition* (Edinburgh: T&T Clark, 1988), p. 1.
22 Gunton, *The Actuality of Atonement*, p. 17.

indicate the authority of the word of God, but for those who dispute whether we can equate the Bible with the word of God, this argument cuts no ice. However, the passage in 2 Timothy, which is late, refers to the sacred writings, and its reference to 'Scripture' refers at minimum to the OT. The passage reads:

> From childhood you have known the sacred writings (Gk, *hiera grammata*) that are able to instruct you for salvation through faith in Christ Jesus. All Scripture is inspired by God (Gk, *pāsa graphē theopneustos*; some translate 'God-breathed'), and is useful for teaching, for reproof, for correction, and for training in righteousness, so that everyone who belongs to God may be proficient, equipped for every good work. (2 Tim. 3.15–17)

Danker's acknowledged major Greek lexicon retains 'inspired by God'.[23] 'Sacred writings' was the regular word for the OT for Jews, as used also by Jesus.[24] The author of 2 Peter 1.21, which is also late, writes: 'No prophecy ever came from human will, but men and women, moved by the Holy Spirit, spoke from God.'

The authority of the word of God is a different matter. In 1 Thessalonians 2.13, Paul writes, 'We . . . give thanks to God . . . that when you received the word of God . . . you accepted it not as a human word but as what it really is, God's word.' Similarly Hebrews 4.12 declares that 'the word of God is living and active, sharper than any two-edged sword, piercing until it divides soul from spirit . . . ; it is able to judge the thoughts and intentions of the heart.' Such passages could be multiplied, including OT references to true and false prophecy. Deuteronomy expresses the warning: 'Any prophet . . . who presumes to speak in my name a word that I have not commanded the prophet to speak – that prophet shall die' (18.20).

From earliest times, the patristic writers affirm the inspiration of the Scriptures by the Holy Spirit. Irenaeus (*c.* 130 – *c.* 200) speaks of heretics who 'disregard the order and connection of the scriptures, and destroy the truth' (*Against Heresies*, 1.8.1; Eng., *ANF*, vol. 1, p. 326). Clement of Alexandria (*c.* 150 – *c.* 215) cites 2 Timothy 3.15–17 to the same effect. Origen (*c.* 185 – *c.* 254) declares, 'The Scriptures themselves are divine, namely inspired by the Spirit of God' (*On First Principles*, 4.1.1; Eng., *ANF*, vol. 4, p. 349). Cyril of Jerusalem (315–68) speaks of 'the inspired scriptures of the Old and New Testaments' (*Catechetical Lectures*, 4.33;

---

23 Frederick W. Danker *et al.*, *A Greek-English Lexicon of the New Testament* (3rd edn, Chicago, Ill.: University of Chicago Press, 2000), pp. 449–50.

24 George W. Knight, *The Pastoral Epistles* (Grand Rapids, Mich.: Eerdmans, 1992), pp. 443–4.

Eng., *NPNF*, ser. 2, vol. 7, p. 26). Basil of Caesarea (*c.* 330–79) regularly speaks of Scripture as inspired by the Holy Spirit (*Letter* 22.1; Eng., *NPNF*, ser. 2, vol. 8, p. 128).

In the medieval period, Thomas Aquinas (1225–74) regarded the Scriptures as divine revelation, not merely human thoughts.[25] In the pre-Reformation era, John Wycliffe (*c.* 1333–84) declared, 'A Christian should speak Scripture's words on Scripture's authority in the form that Scripture displays.'[26] In the Reformation, Martin Luther (1483–1546) regarded the Bible as God's address to humankind, especially through his promises.[27] Luther, however, also wrote critically of James, and suggested that 1 and 2 Kings were more historically accurate than 1 and 2 Chronicles. William Tyndale (*c.* 1494–1536) endorsed Luther's emphasis on promise. This led him to expound an anticipatory version of speech-acts. A promise did not inform, but changed a state of affairs by bestowing a new task, a new identity or a new status. Scripture may heal, name, assess or perform a number of practical acts which produce effects in life. Hugh Latimer (1485–1555) regarded the Bible as 'producing a right faith'.[28] John Calvin (1509–64) wrote, 'Aided by glasses [people] begin to read distinctly, so Scripture dissipates the darkness, and shows us the true God clearly.'[29] He added that Scripture 'harmonizes all its parts, needs no rhetorical art, and provides saving knowledge of God'.[30]

In the modern era J. K. S. Reid, Paul Achtemeier and A. M. Hunter stress that Calvin 'does not delegate it [inspiration] to the *words* of Scripture, but rather uses these words to convince people of the *content* of the message to which Scripture bears witness'.[31] This finds an echo in the nineteenth-century work of James Orr (1844–1913) and P. T. Forsyth (1848–1921), who stressed the authority of its *content*, in contrast to Charles Hodge (1797–1878) and B. B. Warfield (1851–1921), who stressed the infallibility of *words*. The Roman Catholic Douai Bible (*c.* 1590) asserted, 'All the books which the church receives as sacred and canonical are written

---

25 Aquinas, *Summa Theologiae*, I, qu. 1, art. 1.

26 John Wycliffe, *De Veritate Sacrae Scripturae*, 1.2 (Eng., London: Wycliffe Society and Trubner, 1907).

27 Martin Luther, *Luther's Works*, 55 vols (Eng., St Louis, Mo.: Concordia), vol. 31, p. 357.

28 Hugh Latimer, *Sermons* (Cambridge: Cambridge University Press, 1844), p. 70.

29 Calvin, *Institutes*, 1.6.1.

30 Calvin, *Institutes*, 1.8.1 and 8.11.

31 J. K. S. Reid, *The Authority of Scripture* (London: Methuen, 1957), pp. 48–9; cf. Paul Achtemeier, *The Inspiration of Scripture* (Philadelphia, Pa.: Fortress Press, 1980), p. 140; A. M. Hunter, *The Teaching of Calvin* (London: James Clarke, 1950), p. 75.

wholly and entirely . . . at the dictation of the Holy Ghost . . . [They are] essentially incompatible with error.'[32]

A profound change came with the Enlightenment, deism, and the foundation of early types of biblical criticism. First, the founder of biblical criticism was arguably J. S. Semler, notably through his book *A Treatise on the Free Investigation of the Canon* (1771–5). He separated the *purely historical* investigation of the Bible from *theological* enquiry. At the time, this seemed reasonable. But it emerged that it would exclude much moderate and theological criticism of the kind exemplified by B. F. Westcott, J. B. Lightfoot, and F. J. Hort in the late nineteenth century. Second, the Enlightenment gave privilege to a *wholly rationalist* approach to the Bible. Third, Henning Graf Reventlow (1929–2010) argued that the advent of deism played a decisive part in promoting an extreme kind of biblical criticism, which undermined the faith of the Church.[33]

In the twentieth century Gerhard Ebeling (1912–2001) revived Luther's point that the Bible often functions as our adversary, not merely to confirm what we want. Barth and Bonhoeffer have made precisely this point. Similarly James Smart writes, 'Let the scriptures cease to be heard, and soon the remembered Christ becomes an imagined Christ, shaped by the religiosity and unconscious desires of the worshippers.'[34] On a general attitude to authority, Hans-Georg Gadamer (1900–2002) writes, 'Authority . . . rests on an acknowledgement, and hence on an act of reason itself, which, aware of its limitations, trusts the better insight of others.'[35] He attacks the illusion of the Enlightenment concerning supposed autonomy and freedom. Mikhail Bakhtin insisted that polyphonic discourse studies exposed a false assumption about alleged 'contradictions', while such narrative theorists as Gerard Genette and Paul Ricoeur (1913–2005) have replaced misguided objections about alleged chronological inaccuracies by narrative plot and narrative time (see Part 3, Time).

In the twenty-first century Richard Bauckham has undertaken fresh research on the value of eyewitness traditions of the Gospels, and in effect turned some form-critical assumptions on their head.[36] Similarly, N. T. Wright insists that the Bible remains 'essential to devotion and discipleship

---

32 Douai, *Providentissimus Deus*, 23.

33 Henning Graf Reventlow, *The Authority of the Bible and the Rise of the Modern World* (London: SCM Press, 1984).

34 James Smart, *The Strange Silence of the Bible in the Church* (London: SCM Press, 1970), p. 25.

35 Hans-Georg Gadamer, *Truth and Method* (Eng., London: Sheed & Ward, 1989), p. 279.

36 Richard Bauckham, *Jesus and the Eyewitnesses: The Gospels as Eyewitness Testimony* (Grand Rapids, Mich.: Eerdmans, 2006).

as well as to doctrine'.[37] Joel Green, James Dunn and John Webster make similar comments.[38] Meanwhile, the Roman Catholic Vatican document *The Interpretation of the Bible in the Church*, with papal approval, broadly continues this tradition.[39]

Catholicism

Catholicism has at least two meanings. (1) When churchgoers recite the creed, 'I believe in one, holy, catholic and apostolic church', it refers to its *universality*, alongside its being *apostolic* (i.e. based on apostolic doctrine and practice), *holy* (i.e. belonging to God) and *one* (i.e. as God's one people). These are usually called 'the marks of the Church'. During the first millennium the 'Catholic' Church, or Catholicism, often stood in contrast to Gnosticism, Montanism, or to some independent or new sects. (2) The term, however, usually denotes specifically the *Roman Catholic Church*, in contrast to the Eastern Orthodox Church and the Protestant churches. There have been two or three eras in the development of Catholic theology.

First, mainstream Roman Catholicism is represented formally in the theology of Thomas Aquinas, which we examined in the Introduction (see p. 17). This is virtually official Catholic theology. Some may cite a second era before Vatican II when liberal Catholicism was represented by Alfred Loisy (1857–1940), progressive Catholicism by John Henry Newman (1801–90); and conservative Catholicism by the ultra-Montanists. Nevertheless the most important era for most people is the post-Vatican II era, led by the distinguished theologians, Rahner, Congar, Balthasar and Küng (see Part 3, Vatican II).

Karl Rahner (1904–84) was a Jesuit, thoroughly grounded in patristic thought and Aquinas. He also drew on Kant. In 1962 Pope John XXIII appointed him as an expert adviser on Vatican II, especially on the Church. From 1954 onwards he published 23 volumes of *Theological Investigations*, and in 1976 his *Foundations of the Christian Faith*.[40]

Drawing on Kant, Rahner stressed the limitations of human knowledge. God is inscrutable. He cited Romans 11.33, and Isaiah 55.8. Revelation

---

37 N. T. Wright, *Scripture and the Authority of God* (London: SPCK, 2005).

38 John Webster, *The Domain of the Word: Scripture and Theological Reason* (New York, N.Y. and London: T&T Clark, 2012).

39 Pontifical Biblical Commission, *The Interpretation of the Bible in the Church* (Collegeville, Minn.: The Liturgical Press, 1994).

40 Karl Rahner, *Theological Investigations*, 23 vols (Eng., London: DLT, 1961–92); and Rahner, *Foundations of the Christian Faith* (London: DLT, 1978).

'reaches its climax and goal in Jesus Christ'.[41] Nevertheless, he argued, grace does not always entail consciousness of it; hence he expounded his distinctive notion of 'anonymous grace'. The faith of Jesus is seen in his utter surrender to the incomprehensibility of God on the cross. Christian faith and hope are also a 'letting go of the self'.[42] In theology, he argued, we need 'the courage to think'.[43] Rahner believed that the word genuinely became flesh, and that Jesus performed 'mighty deeds, signs and wonders', and that he saw himself 'not merely as one of many prophets . . . but as the *eschatological* prophet' (his italics).[44] He also affirmed the full divinity of Jesus Christ. On the other hand, he argued that the formula of Chalcedon must be understood within the framework of Kant's *transcendental philosophy*. He accepted Augustine's traditional distinction between the visible and invisible Church. His notion of 'anonymous Christianity' formed part of his answer to a pluralistic world. But Rahner also insisted that he is not suggesting a liberal agenda in the sense of trimming or changing the gospel. On the office of the pope, he asserted, 'The power of primacy and the power of leadership in the church . . . do not really contradict the essence of Christianity'.[45] Like Tillich, Rahner distinguished between a sign and a symbol; he considered the sacraments as examples of the latter, and endorsed the notion of the sacrament as a tangible word.[46]

Yves Congar (1904–95) also greatly influenced Vatican II. Like Rahner, he was appointed as a special adviser in 1962. He worked especially on the theology of the Holy Spirit, ecumenism, and the doctrine of the Church and tradition. He was influenced by the Catholic Thomist philosopher Jacques Maritain. He became attracted to Barth's theology, as Balthasar was, especially on the sovereignty of God, divine grace, and his attack on liberalism. Congar advocated ordaining laypeople as priests, where there was real need. He published *Tradition and Traditions* in 1960 (and 1963).[47] Tradition, he argued, is a living self-communication of God, and not a mere collection of conventions and customs. He also produced a remarkable three-volume work, *I Believe in the Holy Spirit*.[48] The first volume

41 Rahner, *Foundations of Christian Faith*, p. 176.

42 Rahner, *Theological Investigations*, vol. 10, p. 250.

43 Rahner, *Theological Investigations*, vol. 9, p. 63.

44 Rahner, *Foundations of Christian Faith*, pp. 245–6.

45 Karl Rahner, *The Shape of the Church to Come* (Ger., 1972; Eng., London: SPCK, 1974), p. 387.

46 Rahner, *Foundations of Christian Faith*, p. 427.

47 Yves Congar, *Tradition and Traditions* (Eng., New York, N.Y.: Macmillan, 1966).

48 Yves Congar, *I Believe in the Holy Spirit*, 3 vols (Eng., New York, N.Y.: Seabury Press and London: Chapman, 1983).

provided solid theology; the second discussed the Spirit in everyday life, avoiding the dualism between institutional and charismatic. He is very supportive of the renewal movement, although he recognized that 'the style of . . . meetings is not acceptable to everyone'.[49] In *The Mystery of the Church* (Fr., 1941; Eng., 1960), he stressed the continuity between Aquinas and the church fathers, and drew on Aquinas for a theology of mission. In his further volume, *Lay People in the Church* (Eng., 1959), Congar sought to produce a theology for the laity.

Hans Urs von Balthasar (1905–88) has enjoyed varied esteem in the Catholic Church. In the late 1960s he tended to be marginalized, and was not invited to participate in Vatican II. But thereafter he gained esteem, especially under Pope John Paul II. He produced a vast quantity of theological literature. The most famous of his illustrious published works is his multi-volume *The Glory of the Lord* (7 vols, between 1961 and 1969).[50] He then produced *Theo-drama: Theological Dramatic Theory* (5 vols, between 1973 and 1983), and *Theo-logic* on truth (3 vols, between 1985 and 1987). Balthasar held no teaching position in a university, but he attended the seminars led by Karl Barth. He admired various themes in his theology, publishing *The Theology of Karl Barth* in 1951.[51]

In volume 1 of *The Glory of the Lord*, Balthasar insisted on the primacy of the revelation of the living God. He expounded God's ineffable beauty. The second volume reconsidered the theology of the fathers and the medieval Church, including Dionysius and Anselm. He declared, 'To think means to make something visible spiritually.'[52] In volume 3, he considered lay theologians, who include Dante, John of the Cross, Pascal and others. Volumes 4 and 5 addressed metaphysics, while volumes 6 and 7 addressed *glory* as a biblical theme expressing 'the luminous splendour' of God's glory.[53] Volume 6 explored the graciousness of God and the covenant. *Theo-drama* as a whole explored God's purposive and dynamic action through the grand theatre of history from creation to the end. Balthasar shared Barth's Trinitarian and Christological perspective. He commented, 'All see theology stuck fast on the sandbank of

49 Congar, *I Believe in the Holy Spirit*, vol. 2, p. 156.

50 Hans Urs von Balthasar, *The Glory of the Lord: A Theological Aesthetics*, 7 vols (Eng., Edinburgh: T&T Clark, 1982–9).

51 Hans Urs von Balthasar, *The Theology of Karl Barth* (Eng., San Francisco, Calif.: Ignatius Press, 1992).

52 Balthasar, *The Glory of the Lord*, vol. 2, p. 220.

53 Balthasar, *The Glory of the Lord*, vol. 6, p. 18.

rational abstraction, and want to get it moving again.'[54] He also argued in volume 2, 'All theology is interpretation of divine revelation ... It can only be hermeneutics.'[55]

Hans Küng (b. 1928), Swiss Catholic theologian, studied at the Sorbonne and elsewhere, and completed his doctoral thesis on justification. Like Balthasar, he was influenced by Karl Barth, but unlike Balthasar came under the influence of more open than moderate Catholic scholars. He attended Barth's seminars in Basel, and concluded, 'On the whole there is fundamental agreement between a theology of Barth and that of the Catholic Church.'[56] In 1962 Pope John XXIII invited him to be a special theological adviser for Vatican II. In his book *The Living Church* he commented, 'The reunion of separated Christians is bound up with the renewal of the Catholic Church.'[57] In his book *Infallible?* Küng then discussed the infallibility of the pope, arguing that this was problematic for Catholics, as well as for Protestants. He declared, 'The case for the dogma of infallibility based on Scripture and tradition is plainly as meagre as it is brittle.'[58] In 1979, the Vatican declared him to be no longer a bona fide Catholic teacher and theologian, and Rome's Sacred Congregation for the Doctrine of the Faith deprived him of his Catholic chair. Demonstrations at the University of Tübingen led to his being appointed to an ecumenical chair of theology there.

Perhaps Küng's greatest book was *The Incarnation of God*, published in Germany in 1970.[59] He maintained that Hegel's thought is seminal for theology, as Pannenberg and Moltmann do. Before Hegel, he argued, Christology was mainly static. But Hegel introduced a more dynamic concept, together with a stronger emphasis on divine transcendence. In Hegel, he argued, the cross of Jesus Christ is 'infinite pain' and 'the death of God'; in the resurrection of Christ, we see 'the true nature of God', and the movement of the Holy Spirit.[60] Two more popular books were *On Being a Christian* (Eng., 1977) and *Does God Exist?* (Eng., 1980). In many ways Küng is the most adventuresome and innovative of all the four major

---

54 Balthasar, *Theo-drama: Theological Dramatic Theory*, 5 vols (Eng., Edinburgh: T&T Clark, 1988–98), vol. 1, p. 25.
55 Balthasar, *Theo-drama*, vol. 2, p. 91.
56 Hans Küng, *Justification: The Doctrine of Karl Barth and a Catholic Reflection* (Eng., New York, N.Y.: Nelson, 1964), p. 282.
57 Hans Küng, *The Living Church* (Eng., London: Sheed & Ward, 1963), p. 24.
58 Hans Küng, *Infallible? An Unresolved Enquiry* (Eng., London: SCM Press, 1994), p. 99.
59 Hans Küng, *The Incarnation of God: An Introduction to Hegel's Theological Thought as Prologue to a Future Christology* (Eng., Edinburgh: T&T Clark, 1987).
60 Küng, *The Incarnation of God*, pp. 162, 209.

101

recent theologians. Other Catholic theologians deserve mention, including especially Edward Schillebeeckx (1914–2009).

We have concentrated on the *theology* of Catholicism. Entries elsewhere discuss such practical issues as transubstantiation (see Part 3, Eucharist; Transubstantiation).

Christology

Nowadays the reconstruction of the earthly life of Jesus has at last become freed from the errors of what is conventionally called 'the quest of the historical Jesus'. The latest stage includes such scholars as George Caird, Ben Witherington, N. T. Wright, James Dunn and Richard Bauckham, all of whom have worked to convey a scholarly but common-sense approach. Originally *The Quest of the Historical Jesus* constituted the title of the English translation of Albert Schweitzer's book *From Reimarus to Wrede* (Ger., *Von Reimarus zu Wrede: eine Geschichte der Leben-Jesu-Forschung* (Tübingen, 1906). The work of Reimarus (1694–1768), Schweitzer argued, was the first of the 'historical' lives of Jesus to be attempted. It had defended deism, natural religion, rationalism, and the exclusion of all supernatural miracles and the resurrection. Schweitzer attacked its conclusions, together with a number of rationalist 'lives'. Schweitzer concluded, for instance, that David Strauss had written 'A dead book . . . Scarcely ever has a book let loose such a storm of controversy, and scarcely ever has a controversy been so barren'.[61]

Schweitzer considered the research of Bruno Bauer, Ernest Renan and Wilhelm Wrede. Bauer seemed to continue the work of Strauss; Renan owed far too much to 'artistic imagination'.[62] Wrede had published his theory of the 'Messianic Secret' in 1901, in which he dismissed Mark's account of Jesus' instructions, 'Tell no one', as no more than a theological construction without historical basis (e.g. Mark 1.23–25, 43–45). Schweitzer argued that Wrede had side-stepped much of the work of J. Weiss. He concluded,

> Jesus comes to us as One unknown, without a name . . . To those who obey Him, whether they be wise or simple, He will reveal Himself in the toils, the conflicts, the suffering which they shall pass through in His fellowship . . . They shall learn in their own experience Who He Is.[63]

---

61 Albert Schweitzer, *The Quest of the Historical Jesus* (London: Black, 1910 and 1954), pp. 76, 97; David F. Strauss, *Life of Jesus, Critically Examined* (Eng., New York, N.Y.: Blanchard, 1860).

62 Schweitzer, *Quest*, p. 181.

63 Schweitzer, *Quest*, p. 401.

In spite of considerable support, especially in Germany in the early and mid twentieth century, it is generally agreed today that the 'first quest', as it is called, was a failure. Schweitzer's conclusion encourages the notion that history and theology were exclusive alternatives.

The so-called 'new quest' emerged from Bultmann's former pupils. These included Ernst Käsemann (1906–98), Günther Bornkamm (1905–90) and Ernst Fuchs (1903–83). Käsemann began the movement in 1954, with the publication of his article 'The Problem of the Historical Jesus'. He concluded that we cannot deny the identification of the exalted Lord with the incarnate Lord. Indeed he is 'Bearer of the Word'. James Robinson has chronicled this movement.[64] Bornkamm and Fuchs regarded the identity of Jesus as revealed in both his words and deeds.[65] We can see Jesus' conduct as God's conduct. Nevertheless, their perspective remains existentialist, and, in the case of Fuchs, intra-linguistic. Thus many believed that the new quest did not go far enough in positive or historical directions.

In 1985 Robert Funk founded the 'Jesus Seminar' of the Society of Biblical Literature. But this raised at least two problems. First, its members called partly on the *Gospel of Thomas* to establish criteria of authenticity for the life of Jesus, and these were far too reductive and negative. Second, they often called on postmodern criteria to supplement this approach. To many, the conclusions of J. D. Crossan and Burton Mack seemed bizarre.[66] Since the dawn of the twenty-first century, NT scholarship has tended to settle down with more positive and sane contributions, at least in the UK, with assessments from James Dunn, N. T. Wright, Richard Bauckham and others. Some call this the 'third quest', but writers diverge in their conclusions so much that a common label achieves little. This reaction is emphatically not simply a recent one. Wright rightly looks back to the work of George Caird. Martin Hengel has published a number of positive, careful books, and Larry Hurtado, Raymond Brown and Graham Stanton have also shaped the thought of many as scholars of eminent common sense, good judgment and learning.[67]

In contrast to NT studies alone, Jürgen Moltmann (b. 1926), Wolfhart Pannenberg (1928–2014), Donald Baillie, Karl Barth (1886–1968), Emil

---

64 James Robinson, *A New Quest of the Historical Jesus* (London: SCM Press, 1959).

65 Günther Bornkamm, *Jesus of Nazareth* (Minneapolis, Minn.: Fortress Press, 1959).

66 John Dominic Crossan, *The Historical Jesus: The Life of a Mediterranean Jewish Peasant* (San Francisco, Calif.: Harper-Collins, 1991); as against N. T. Wright, *Jesus and the Victory of God* (London: SPCK, 1996), esp. pp. 31–5.

67 Graham Stanton, *Jesus of Nazareth in New Testament Preaching* (Cambridge: Cambridge University Press, 1974).

Brunner, John Macquarrie, Walther Kasper and Karl Rahner (1904–84) provide more positive answers to today's questions in Christology.[68] Dunn, Hurtado, Jeremias, Cullmann, and (earlier) Alan Richardson, John A. T. Robinson and Vincent Taylor, combine work in both fields.[69] Robinson urges an emphasis on the genuine humanness of Jesus in *The Human Face of God*, alongside Jesus' acting in the place of God.[70] Admittedly in *Christ, Faith and History*, together with Maurice Wiles, he had opposed the notion that 'Jesus was a hybrid . . . a God-Man . . . a sort of bat-man or centaur', as in Chalcedon.[71] But in *The Human Face of God*, he wishes to emphasize that the humanness of Jesus made him 'like one of us', fully human in every respect, except sin. The Alexandrian theologians were a special target for attack, because they stressed his deity one-sidedly. Cyril of Alexandria claimed that Jesus was 'timeless and incapable of grief'.[72] By contrast Robinson asserted, 'The nexus of theological, historical, and social relationships' are part of his humanness.[73] Too often, Robinson argued, Jesus 'became an unreal figure with the static perfection of flawless porcelain, rather than a man of flesh and blood'.[74] Jesus, he urged, was not a sexless, cardboard, Christ.

The value of systematic theology for Christology is especially true with reference to the resurrection of Christ. The most outstanding example is Pannenberg. He writes, 'If Jesus had been raised, this for a Jew can only mean that God himself has confirmed the pre-Easter activity of Jesus.'[75] He explains what the experience of resurrection might mean. He writes, 'The familiar experience of being awakened and rising from sleep serves as a parable for the completely unknown destiny expected for the dead.'[76] Pannenberg takes with historical seriousness the appearances of the raised Jesus to Peter, to the Twelve, to 500 Christian brothers and to Paul.[77] He also understands the tradition of the empty tomb as 'historical fact'.[78]

---

68 John Macquarrie, *Jesus Christ in Modern Thought* (London: SCM Press, 1990).

69 Oscar Cullmann, *The Christology of the New Testament* (Eng., London: SCM Press, 1963); Joachim Jeremias, *New Testament Theology* (London: SCM Press, 1971).

70 John A. T. Robinson, *The Human Face of God* (London: SCM Press, 1973).

71 John A. T. Robinson, 'Need Jesus Have Been Perfect?', in Stephen Sykes and J. P. Clayton (eds), *Christ, Faith and History* (Cambridge: Cambridge University Press, 1972), p. 39.

72 Cyril of Alexandria, *Commentary on John 7*; Robinson, *Human Face*, p. 39.

73 Robinson, *Human Face*, p. 41.

74 Robinson, *Human Face*, p. 68.

75 Wolfhart Pannenberg, *Jesus – God and Man* (Eng., Philadelphia, Pa.: Westminster Press and London: SCM Press, 1968), p. 67.

76 Pannenberg, *Jesus – God and Man*, p. 74.

77 Pannenberg, *Jesus – God and Man*, p. 89.

78 Pannenberg, *Jesus – God and Man*, p. 100.

He comments that as Paul Althaus said, 'The resurrection Kerygma "could not have been maintained in Jerusalem for a single day, for a single hour, if the emptiness of the tomb had not been established as a fact for all concerned".'[79] It is self-contradictory, he urges, to begin with the positivist assumption that 'dead men do not rise'.[80]

Jürgen Moltmann also argues that Jesus is Lord because God raised him from the dead.[81] For him, it is 'the inbreaking of the eschatological hope'.[82] Karl Rahner has a place in his theology 'for Christ's death and resurrection'.[83] Earlier, Walter Künneth had urged that the action of God raised Jesus from the tomb in a visible way.[84] In the Pauline epistles the confession 'Jesus is Lord' presupposes God's raising him from the dead (Rom. 1.4 and 8.8–11). Bultmann portrays Christ as Lord through the Christian's experience of 'belonging' to Christ as Lord; but he derives this from existential experience, whereas it is based on ontological reality. God is the basis of Christ's resurrection and lordship, as Barth and others insist.

Many other aspects of Christology demand mention. Cullmann draws attention to the status of Jesus as eschatological prophet, his vocation as Suffering Servant, his ministry as our great High Priest, his Messiahship, his status as Saviour, his identity as the Word of God or Logos, and his title 'Son of God'.[85] These are not less important because to approach Christology in terms of 'titles' has become no longer fashionable. On the high priesthood of Christ he writes, 'Jesus intercedes for us no longer simply in a collective sense . . . ; now he intercedes . . . for each individual' (Heb. 7.25).[86]

Ecclesiology

The community (Heb., *qāhāl*, assembly; Gk, *ekklēsia*, church) of God's people owes its origin to God's call not simply to an individual (Abraham), but also primarily to a people (Israel and the Church). At the Jewish

---

79 Pannenberg, *Jesus – God and Man*, p. 100.
80 Pannenberg, *Jesus – God and Man*, p. 109.
81 Jürgen Moltmann, *The Way of Jesus: Christology in Messianic Dimensions* (Eng. London: SCM Press, 1989), pp. 41–3.
82 Moltmann, *Way of Jesus*, p. 109.
83 Karl Rahner, *Foundations of Christian Faith* (Eng., New York, N.Y.: Seabury Press and London: DLT, 1978), p. 253.
84 Walter Künneth, *The Theology of the Resurrection* (Eng., London: SCM Press, 1965), pp. 117, 111–49.
85 Cullmann, *Christology*, throughout.
86 Cullmann, *Christology*, p. 102.

Passover meal, when the son asks the host, 'What do these testimonies mean?', the reply is: '*We* were Pharaoh's slaves in Egypt, and the Lord brought *us* out of Egypt.' Pentecost, the birthday of the Church, was a *communal* affair.

Individualism took its rise from Descartes (1596–1650) in philosophy, from the marketplace in consumer society, and from the industrial revolution in economies. The biblical, ancient and medieval worlds regarded the community as more significant than the lone individual. In philosophy John Locke (1632–1704), David Hume (1711–76) and Immanuel Kant (1724–1804) continued the new individualist tradition. Hans-Georg Gadamer (1908–2002) shows how the individualism of the Enlightenment and Descartes was challenged by the more historical and communal perspective of Giambattista Vico (1668–1744) and the hermeneutical tradition.

Lionel Thornton (1884–1960) explores this communal perspective in *The Common Life in the Body of Christ*. He traces the corporate identity of God's people, culminating in the imagery of the vine in John 15, and of the body of Christ in Paul. He writes, for example:

> The hope of Israel went down into the grave, and their hopes went too . . . There is no Israel apart from the Messiah. So also, finally when he [Christ] rose from the tomb, they rose . . . When Christ rose, the Church rose from the dead.[87]

In 1 Corinthians 12.12–26, Paul sets out his concept of the Church as the body of Christ. He declares in verse 12: 'Just as the body is one and has many members . . . all the members of the body, though many, are one.' He adds: 'The body does not consist of one member but of many . . . If the whole body were an eye, where would the hearing be? . . . If all were a single member, where would the body be?' (12.14, 17, 19). John Robinson explains that 'being a member' of the body of Christ is not like being a member of a golf club or a motoring association. It is more like being a 'limb' or 'membrane' of Christ's body.[88]

From the day of Pentecost onwards, the common life of the Christian community emerges. Acts 2.46 concludes, 'Day by day . . . they spent much time together in the temple'. In Acts 6.5 'the whole community' chose Stephen and the Seven. When Paul speaks of 'the *koinōnia* (fellowship) of

---

87 Lionel S. Thornton, *The Common Life in the Body of Christ* (3rd edn, London: Dacre Press, 1950), p. 282.
88 John A. T. Robinson, *The Body: A Study in Pauline Theology* (London: SCM Press, 1952), p. 51.

the Holy Spirit', Thornton translates this as the Holy Spirit in whom we all participate or 'all share'; it involves 'common and mutual interest, and participation in a common object'.[89] A solitary Christian in principle constitutes a self-contradiction. We stand in solidarity with other Christians to learn together, to worship and pray together, and to build up one another's faith and discipleship.

The Greek Orthodox theologian John Zizioulas (b. 1931) writes, 'There is no being without communion. Nothing exists as an "individual", conceivable in itself.'[90] Paul Ricoeur (1913–2005) writes, 'Otherness is not added to selfhood from outside . . . [It belongs] to the ontological constitution of selfhood.'[91] In this sense 'going to church' becomes an odd phrase. It sees 'church' primarily as a building to be visited, which in biblical and theological terms is entirely secondary and even optional. Paul also wrote, 'You [plural] are God's field, God's building and God's temple' (1 Cor. 3.9, 16–17). Jesus in John called his disciples a flock (John 10.1–18).

'Ecclesiology', however, denotes not only the existence of the Church, but also its constitution and how it governs its affairs. Is it primarily local, national or universal? Is it visible or invisible? Are the ministry and sacraments an essential part of it? Wolfhart Pannenberg (1928–2014) points out that the concept of the local church is more complex than we often realize. He asks,

> What is precisely the meaning of the term 'local church'? . . . Are we speaking of the congregation assembled locally for the preaching of the Word and the Eucharist, or is 'local church' a term for the diocese subject to a bishop?[92]

There are at least three traditions of church government and the nature of the ministry. It is clear from Paul that he ministered collaboratively, with colleagues or fellow-workers. These included Barnabas, Silvanus, Apollos, Timothy, Titus, Epaphras, Mark, Luke, Priscilla, Aquila and Philemon. It is now well established that Junia (rather than the masculine form Junias) is named among a plurality of apostles (Rom. 16.3, 7, 9, 21). Paul often describes himself as a steward or manager of a household (Gk, *oikonomos*; 1 Cor. 4.1–2). Today we may distinguish: (1) Congregationalists and Baptists, who in principle regard the Church as a network of independent

---

89 Thornton, *Common Life*, p. 74; cf. pp. 70–5.

90 John Zizioulas, *Being as Communion: Studies in Personhood and the Church* (New York, N.Y.: St Vladimir's Seminary Press, 1985 and 1997), pp. 103, 118.

91 Paul Ricoeur, *Oneself as Another* (Chicago, Ill.: University of Chicago Press, 1992), p. 317.

92 Wolfhart Pannenberg, *Systematic Theology*, 3 vols (Eng., Edinburgh: T&T Clark, 1991–8), vol. 3, p. 109.

autonomous congregations; (2) Presbyterians, who allot oversight to presbyters or elders, whether or not they carry the formal title of *bishop*; and (3) episcopal churches, who believe in the three 'orders' of bishops, priests (or presbyters) and deacons. The diocesan bishop has jurisdiction within his diocese, and ordains priests and deacons, and confirms committed laypeople (see in Part 3, Anglicanism). The Roman Catholic Church also in principle submits to the authority of the pope. The Eastern Orthodox Church sometimes calls senior bishops patriarchs. In addition to these three categories, (4) Lutherans and Methodists sometimes accept the supervision of bishops, as in the USA, but not in England. The constitution of Lutherans differs in Germany and Scandinavia.

The office or role of *deacon* is currently under discussion. Traditionally deacons minister financial and practical needs, but recently it has been argued that they function as deputies to bishops or priests.[93] The qualities normally expected of bishops (or perhaps elders) are listed in 1 Timothy 3.1–7 and Titus 1.5–9, and are fully assessed with comparative lists for elders and deacons by W. D. Mounce.[94] In 1 Timothy, being skilled in teaching is mentioned first, then being level-headed, then disliking conflict, and being disciplined. Other qualities follow.

The most significant difference between Christian traditions, some argue, concerns divisions arising from different views of the sacraments (see Part 3, Transubstantiation). *Sacrament* is not a biblical term (see Part 3, Sacrament, where three meanings are distinguished: (1) the two sacraments of baptism and the Lord's Supper; (2) the seven sacraments of the Roman Catholic Church and the Eastern Orthodox churches; and (3) an unlimited number in which the visible appearance represents an invisible grace). The Reformers Luther, Tyndale, Calvin and Zwingli regarded the sacraments as at minimum covenantal signs. Calvin defined a sacrament as 'an external sign by which the Lord seals in our consciences his promise of goodwill towards us, in order to sustain the weakness of our faith'.[95]

Paul's main section which expounds a theology of baptism is in Romans 6.1–11. It frequently means incorporation into the body of Christ through identification with his death and resurrection. Contrary to popular belief, the notion of cleansing does not form a primary or prominent theme in Paul, and the theology of baptism is brilliantly expounded

93 John N. Collins, *Diakonia: Re-interpreting the Sources* (Oxford: Oxford University Press, 1990).

94 William D. Mounce, *Pastoral Epistles* (Nashville: Nelson, 2000), pp. 168–90.

95 Calvin, *Institutes*, 4.14.1.

by Rudolf Schnackenburg.[96] Paul expounds his theology of the Holy Communion, Eucharist, or Lord's Supper, mainly in 1 Corinthians 11.23–32. Joachim Jeremias and F. J. Leenhardt show convincingly that the Last Supper dovetails with the observance of the Passover, and that there are close parallels between the *Seder* or Jewish *Haggadah* and the words of institution of the Lord's Supper.[97] Hans Urs von Balthasar (1905–88) and Kevin Vanhoozer regard the Eucharist as a dramatic event, in which Christ's once-for-all death and resurrection become contemporary. This reflects the black spiritual, 'Were you there when they crucified my Lord?'

Thomas Aquinas' theory of transubstantiation is still controversial (see Part 3, Transubstantiation). Luther rejected the theory on the basis of its dependence on Aristotle's philosophical categories. Although he rejected transubstantiation as 'unbiblical', Luther held a view of the 'real presence' of Christ in the elements. Calvin insisted on the parity of word and sacrament. Zwingli rejected every 'literalistic' interpretation of the Lord's Supper, seeing it as purely metaphorical or symbolic. In Anglican theology 'High Church' traditions are close to Luther; other Anglican traditions follow Calvin or sometimes Zwingli. It is perhaps unfortunate that while the Anglican–Roman Catholic Commission (ARCIC) of 1971 found points of agreement between Catholic and Anglican views, Vatican II still adhered to the Thomist view of transubstantiation.

Eschatology

Eschatology (from Gk, *eschatos*, last) traditionally denotes the three last things of the Parousia (or public return) of Jesus Christ, the Last Judgment and the resurrection of the dead. But recently death has been added as demanding special comment. Additionally there have always been a number of related issues: the nature of time and eternity, heaven and hell, future hope, the intermediate state, the fate of those who are not believers, the imminence of the end, and the validity or otherwise of purgatory.

The term *Parousia* may denote *coming or presence*, as in the coming or presence of an emperor. The background relates to apocalyptic Judaism. The teaching of Jesus regularly manifests a contrast between

---

96 Rudolf Schnackenburg, *Baptism in the Thought of St. Paul: A Study in Pauline Theology* (Oxford: Blackwell, 1964), pp. 3–61.
97 Joachim Jeremias, *The Eucharistic Words of Jesus* (London: SCM Press, 1966), pp. 41–9; F. J. Leenhardt, 'This Is My Body', in Oscar Cullmann and F. J. Leenhardt (eds), *Essays on the Lord's Supper* (London: Lutterworth Press, 1958), pp. 39–40.

the present and the future. Thus in the future the hidden will become revealed (Matt. 10.26); the poor will become rich (Luke 6.20); the blind will see (Matt. 11.5), and so on. Jeremias shows how many parables of Jesus corroborate this.[98] 'Apocalyptic' passages occur in Mark 13, Matthew 24 and Luke 21. Some insist that Jesus addressed the timing of the fall of Jerusalem, to which apocalyptic material has been added. But George Caird, George Beasley-Murray and R. T. France show how Mark 13 constitutes a coherent and authentic account.[99] On the imminence or dating of the Parousia, Jesus warned, 'Of that day or hour no one knows, neither the angels in heaven, nor the Son, but only the Father' (Mark 13.32). Christians must 'keep alert; for you do not know when the time will come' (13.33).

The Parousia will be public and visible to all. The earliest NT passage, apart from the teaching of Jesus himself, comes in 1 Thessalonians 4, where Paul declares,

> The Lord himself, with a cry of command, with the archangel's call and with the sound of God's trumpet, will descend from heaven, and the dead in Christ will rise first. Then we who are alive, who are left, will be caught up in the clouds together with them to meet the Lord in the air; and so we will be with the Lord for ever. (vv. 16–17)

Some scholars, including Rudolf Bultmann, are caustic about some of this imagery. Even George Caird and N. T. Wright insist on the metaphorical status of this eschatological language. Wright describes this passage as 'the tricky verses' of 1 Thessalonians 4, and insists, 'They are not to be taken as a literal description of what Paul thinks will happen. They are simply a different way of saying what he [Paul] is saying in 1 Cor. 15.23–27 and 51–54, and in Phil. 3.20–21.'[100] Caird insists, 'Luke and Paul did not expect their language about life after death to be taken with flat-footed literalness.'[101] Yet both believe that, in accordance with the teaching of Jesus, the Parousia, or Second Coming, will be public and visible to all. This language provides an extension from the idea of the eventful arrival of the emperor, king or dignitary, to the arrival of the King of kings in visible and final glory. His coming will put to rights everything that has been wrong about the world.

---

98 Joachim Jeremias, *The Parables of Jesus* (London: SCM Press, 1963), pp. 221–2, 224–7.

99 George Caird, *The Language and Imagery of the Bible* (London: Duckworth, 1980), pp. 265–8; George Beasley-Murray, *Jesus and the Last Days* (Peabody, Mass.: Hendrickson, 1995), throughout; R. T. France, *The Gospel of Mark: A Commentary on the Greek Text* (Grand Rapids, Mich.: Eerdmans, 2002), pp. 497–546.

100 N. T. Wright, *Surprised by Hope* (London: SPCK, 2007), p. 143.

101 Caird, *Language and Imagery*, p. 246.

The phrase, 'we who are alive and remain', raises another controversial point. Does Paul expect the Parousia to occur *in his own lifetime?* Probably the majority of specialist scholars claim that he does, but Arthur Moore, Beda Rigaux, Ben Witherington and Joost Holleman, among others, have brought forward strong arguments to the contrary.[102] One important point is the difference between *statements* and *presupposition*, as the philosopher P. F. Strawson has expounded it. If he had simply said *'those* who are alive and remain', Paul would have been distancing himself from his readers. He merely leaves the possibility *open*, although he realizes that an imminent state is a distinct possibility. After all, he would scarcely have claimed to know more than Jesus Christ about the timing of the event.

The Last Judgment confronts everyone, including Christians. Paul writes, 'All of us must appear before the judgement seat of Christ, so that each may receive recompense for what has been done in the body, whether good or evil' (2 Cor. 5.10). At first sight this suggests that most people would fear this prospect. Yet the OT shows how frequently the prospect is greeted with joy, not fear. The psalmist writes, 'He [God] will judge the peoples with equity. Let the heavens be glad, and let the earth rejoice . . . Then shall all the trees of the forest sing for joy before the LORD; for he is coming, for he is coming to judge the earth. He will judge the world with righteousness' (Ps. 96.10–13). Similarly we read: 'Let the nations be glad and sing for joy, for you [God] judge the peoples with equity, and guide the nations upon earth' (Ps. 67.4). The reason for joy in the face of the judgment is clear. First, the disclosure of God's righteousness and truth puts an end to all *deception and delusion.* Second, God will publicly and definitively *vindicate the oppressed.* Hidden faith will be vindicated in plain sight. The theme of 'putting things right' constitutes a key connecting thread between justification by grace and the Last Judgment.

It would be false to claim that the teaching of Jesus is somehow 'softer' than that of Paul or the OT. For example, Jesus tells the parable of the weeds and wheat, when the angels will discern the difference between each harvest at the end time (Matt. 13.24–30, 37–43). Jeremias comments, 'Conditions are reversed; what is hidden becomes manifest (Matthew 10.26); the poor become rich (Luke 6.20); the last are first (Mark 10.31);

---

102 Arthur L. Moore, *The Parousia in the New Testament* (Leiden: Brill, 1966; NovT Supp. 13), pp. 108–10; Moore, *1 and 2 Thessalonians* (London: Nelson, 1969), pp. 69–71; Joost Holleman, *Resurrection and the Parousia* (Leiden: Brill, 1996; NovT Supp. 84), p. 24; Ben Witherington III, *1 and 2 Thessalonians: A Socio-rhetorical Commentary* (Grand Rapids, Mich.: Eerdmans, 2006), pp. 133–4.

the hungry are filled (Luke 6.21); and so on.'[103] God will reach a verdict which will definitively end all ambiguity and hiddenness, and will reveal reality as what it is.

It is clear that the resurrection of the dead is a *gift* of *the grace and sovereign power of God*. Paul's argument appears in 1 Corinthians 15; Romans 4.16–25; 2 Corinthians 1.9; 5.1–10; and 1 Thessalonians 4.14–17. In all these passages resurrection constitutes a sheer gift of God's sovereign, creative grace, and never the fruit of latent capacities in the human soul. Moltmann corroborates this understanding.[104] The latter view stems only from Plato and other Greeks, not from the NT (see Part 2, Resurrection of the dead).

We must not allow detailed questions about this subject to distract us from the three key events of the Parousia, the Last Judgment, and the resurrection. But we must say a word about death, even though the biblical emphasis is more upon cosmic transpersonal events than individual dying. Certainly Scripture as a whole witnesses to the importance of mourning and grieving. These were serious events in biblical culture, and even Jesus was deeply moved and shed tears at the death of Lazarus (John 11.34–35). The notion of an almost hole-in-the-corner mourning, death and burial, constitutes a wholly modern Western phenomenon which is entirely foreign to biblical expectations. It is harmful to suppress mourning, and in the Bible it is a shared event. The individualism which followed modern Western philosophy and the industrial revolution does no favours to anyone. Yet grief must not become overlong and obsessive. Paul writes to Christian believers not to grieve 'as others do who have no hope' (1 Thess. 4.13). They will meet those who have passed on at the resurrection. On mourning for others, Moltmann writes, 'the greater the love, the deeper the grief'.[105]

Much time has been spent on the supposed problem of 'the intermediate state'. Admittedly Paul writes that he can desire 'to depart and to be with Christ, for that is far better' (Phil. 1.23). On the other hand he envisages events which culminate in a trumpet sounding, 'and the dead will be raised imperishable, and we will be changed' (1 Cor. 15.52). It is as if the dead have to wait for the final moment of resurrection and judgment. In fact there is no contradiction between these two things. The philosopher Gilbert Ryle has demonstrated how a participant perspective

---

103 Jeremias, *Parables*, pp. 221–2.
104 Jürgen Moltmann, *Theology of Hope* (London: SCM Press, 1967), pp. 165–72, 190–216;
    Moltmann, *The Coming of God: Christian Eschatology* (London: SCM Press, 1996), pp. 25–9.
105 Moltmann, *The Coming of God*, p. 119.

may differ from an observer perspective.[106] I have suggested the analogy of a child falling asleep on Christmas Eve, but waiting for the morning of Christmas. From a participant's perspective, we may tell the child, 'The sooner you fall asleep, the sooner Christmas will come.' But from an observer perspective the adults of the household need to do many things, including preparing meals, wrapping up presents, and so forth. The analogy exactly matches the experience of the participant in death and transformation, and the observer of the eschatological drama. It is true in both cases: the departed are with Christ, but certain events must take place before the end (see Part 3, Intermediate state).

Another fruitless discussion concerns the Roman Catholic and Anglo-Catholic views of purgatory. This is traditionally seen as a time of purification, and worse still, the notion of somehow supplementing the work of Christ in atoning for sin (see Part 3, Purgatory). However, Paul insists that the resurrection is inconceivable without the transforming power of the Holy Spirit (Rom. 8.9–11). Hence part of that transforming power will be the gift of holiness at the resurrection, which entirely matches the Christian doctrine of justification by grace through faith.

Time and eternity are considered in Part 3 under 'Time'. There we refer to different concepts of time in physics, in philosophy and in narrative theory. On the fate of unbelievers, many follow a consensus of opinion that we simply cannot know the fate of unbelievers in general, and certainly not know the fate of this or that person, whose heart is known only to God. All that can be said is that we cannot offer such people the positive certainty and assurance of eternal life, since this is promised in the Bible only to believers in Christ. The issue must be left in the hands of a loving God (see Part 3, Hell; Universalism).

Something must be said about heaven and hell. The notion that hell entails everlasting punishment constitutes only one of three possible views held by theologians. There is no justification for calling it the 'orthodox' view (see Part 3, Hell; Universalism). Some believe that since hell entails separation from God, and since God is the source of life, this implies that an existence in hell cannot be sustained without the source of life. The whole subject is shrouded in controversy and mystery.

'Heaven' cannot be a static condition, like 'flawless porcelain' or eternal perfection. Apart from other factors, this could be in danger of becoming monotonous. The Holy Spirit will do *new* things, and is *ever-fresh*

---

106 Gilbert Ryle, *Dilemmas* (Cambridge: Cambridge University Press, 1966), pp. 36–53.

and *ever-new*. Those in Christ will grow, as it were, from glory to glory. Believers will be face-to-face with God (1 Cor. 13.12). God's gifts will be inexhaustible. God will make us 'stand without blemish in the presence of his glory with rejoicing' (Jude 24). The redeemed will acknowledge: 'Just and true are your ways' (Rev. 15.3). Isaiah declares, 'The glory of the LORD shall be revealed, and all people shall see it together' (40.5). The book of Revelation uses symbolic language because the glories of heaven surpass literal human language. It is purposed by God; heaven will praise the slaughtered Lamb (Rev. 5.9); and the Holy Spirit will animate and characterize the raised 'body' (1 Cor. 15.44). (See also Part 3, Heaven.)

Feminist theology

Feminist theology may be said to have begun in modern times with Elizabeth Cady Stanton (1815–1902) and the publication of *The Woman's Bible* (1895 and 1898). But a decisive landmark in the 1940s was Simone de Beauvoir's book *The Second Sex* (Fr., 1949).[107] This raised questions about the relation between symbolic and conceptual perceptions of women, and questioned and attacked conventional roles for women in society. Her words, 'humanity is male, and man defines woman not in herself but as relative to him . . . He is the subject . . . She is the Other', became a key theme.

Before the modern era, in the NT Paul refers to Junia as 'prominent among the apostles' (Rom. 16.7). Eldon Epp's recent research as an eminent textual critic has revealed that the masculine name Junias was a later alteration to the feminine name Junia.[108] Junia was therefore a woman apostle. Recent research also stresses that Mary Magdalene was a key witness to the resurrection of Christ, and that Priscilla and Phoebe held key leadership roles.[109] The uncovering of these phenomena forms part of a more recent feminist endeavour to 'retrieve' a largely 'lost' past in the NT and patristic era.

Serious feminism began to emerge in the late 1960s and early 1970s. Kate Millett's *Sexual Politics* (1969) unmasked a network of social power-structures in which roles were determined more by gender identity than by

---

107 Elaine Marks and Isabelle de Courtivron (eds), *New French Feminisms: An Anthology* (Englewood Cliffs, N.J.: Prentice Hall, 1981), p. 44.

108 Eldon Jay Epp, *Junia: The First Woman Apostle* (Minneapolis, Minn.: Fortress Press, 2005), pp. 23–48, and throughout.

109 Elisabeth Schüssler Fiorenza, *In Memory of Her: A Feminist Theological Reconstruction of Christian Origins* (New York, N.Y.: Crossroad and London: SCM Press, 1983).

merit. Millett particularly attacked so-called patriarchal power-structures within the family. Similarly, in her book *The Female Eunuch* (1970) Germaine Greer re-enforced the argument that social roles were simply imposed on women by the constraints of education, the family, work and capitalist market-forces. The effect of this was 'to reduce' women as people, for which her term was the 'castration' of women. Feminist *theology* and feminist *hermeneutics* emerged mainly in the 1970s in studies by Phyllis Trible, Letty Russell, Rosemary Ruether and Mary Daly.[110] These contributed to the 'first wave', and would shortly be followed by another, in the 1980s and 1990s.

In *God and the Rhetoric of Sexuality* Phyllis Trible argued that the hermeneutics of tradition must be supplemented by a hermeneutics of enquiry to question tradition. One of her influential conclusions was that not only 'man' was created in the image of God, but man-and-woman. It is often forgotten that earlier Barth had insisted on this. God, she argued, is neither male nor female. Phyllis Bird also urged that the image of God referred to both sexes. Rosemary Ruether and Eleanor McLaughlin aimed at re-capturing leadership roles among women from the first to the third century. Elisabeth Schüssler Fiorenza similarly claimed that 'only a fraction of such traditions about significant women' passed through the filter of 'patriarchal' tradition.[111]

Mary Daly and Rosemary Radford Ruether (b. 1936) effectively founded the 'women's caucus' in the American Association of Religion in 1971. From this caucus Letty Russell published her moderate book *The Liberating Word*. In this she again warned against stereotyping each gender. Ruether, however, proposed that 'women's experience' should promote the basis for an ideological critique in hermeneutics. She declared, 'Women's experience explodes as a critical force, exposing classical theology, including its foundational tradition in scripture as shaped by male experience rather than the human experience.'[112] Daly offered a still more 'radical' feminism, which would eventually become *post-Christian* feminism.

---

110 Phyllis Trible, 'Depatriarchalizing in Biblical Tradition', *Journal of the American Academy of Religion* 41 (1973), pp. 35–42; Trible, *God and the Rhetoric of Sexuality* (Philadelphia, Pa.: Fortress Press, 1978); Letty Russell, *The Liberating Word* (Philadelphia, Pa.: Westminster Press, 1976); Rosemary Ruether and Eleanor McLaughlin (eds), *Women of Spirit: Female Leadership in the Jewish and Christian Traditions* (New York, N.Y.: Simon & Schuster, 1979); Mary Daly, *Beyond God the Father* (Boston, Mass.: Beacon Press, 1973).

111 Ruether and McLaughlin (eds), *Women of Spirit*, p. 57.

112 Daly, in Russell, *Liberating Word*, pp. 112–13.

The high point of feminist theology emerged in the 1980s and 1990s, with a flood of literature. The most influential was Schüssler Fiorenza's *In Memory of Her*.[113] She argued for 'women's self-affirmation, power and liberation from all patriarchal alienation, marginalization, and oppression'.[114] Her 'ecclesia of women' or 'women-church' has, she claimed, 'authority' to choose and reject 'biblical texts'.[115] She argued that the Bible was written in androcentric language, and reflects male experience. From a hermeneutical viewpoint, it is a self-fulfilling hermeneutic, with many subjective elements and selections of texts, as in much liberation theology. But among the polemics there is solid historical research. In the Johannine tradition, Fiorenza argued, Mary became the *apostola apostolorum*, 'the apostle of the apostles'.[116] Yet the problem with her exegesis is that often gender may be merely *one among many* explanations for a text or historical situation.

Ruether published *Sexism and God-Talk* in 1983, and Trible, *Texts of Terror* in 1984. Trible 'recounts tales of terror *in memoriam* to offer sympathetic readings of abused women'.[117] She expounds Hagar's life as being trapped in a circle of bondage (Gen. 16.1–16), though God protects her offspring. She then considers the rape of Tamar, whose dignity stands in contrast to Amnon's brutal violence (2 Sam. 13.1–20), alongside the death of Jephthah's daughter (Judg. 11.29–40). A flood of literature then followed: Adele Yarbro Collins (1985); Letty Russell (1985); Elaine Showalter (1986); Mary Ann Tolbert (1989); Rebecca Chopp (1989); Julia Kristeva (1989); Ursula King (1990); Daphne Hampson (1990); and Alice Laffey (1990). Ann Loades offers a helpful collection of representative essays in *Feminist Theology: A Reader*.[118] The collection challenges examples of stereotypification, injustice, predetermined role-models, and examples of manipulation and control. In the twenty-first century the same themes tend to be repeated, for some believe that they still need to be voiced. The movement was certainly needed in former times; but whether it has become imprisoned now in over-repetitive themes deserves thought. Elizabeth Achtemeier, Susan Heine, and especially Janet Radcliffe Richards, *The Sceptical Feminist*, have voiced serious reservations and criticisms, which also deserve to be heard.[119]

---

113 Schüssler Fiorenza, *In Memory of Her: A Feminist Theological Reconstruction of Christian Origins* (1983).
114 Schüssler Fiorenza, *In Memory*, p. 126.
115 Schüssler Fiorenza, *In Memory*, p. 132.
116 Schüssler Fiorenza, *In Memory*, p. 332.
117 Phyllis Trible, *Texts of Terror* (Philadelphia, Pa.: Fortress Press, 1984), p. 3.
118 Ann Loades, *Feminist Theology: A Reader* (London: SPCK, 1990).
119 Janet Radcliffe Richards, *The Sceptical Feminist* (London: Penguin, 1983).

It is noteworthy that many African women have protested that too many professional middle-class white women have tried to speak on behalf of all women, when they represent only Western academic career women. They prefer the term 'womanism', and concentrate on broader and deeper issues, such as male violence, AIDS and wider cultural questions.

God, theology of

Often the most seemingly abstract or theoretical philosophical character-istics attributed to God constitute qualities of God which are nevertheless of the utmost *practical relevance* to the believer. God's *omnipresence*, for example, means that God is at hand with the believer in any and every situ-ation. His *omniscience* means that the believer does not need to inform him or explain to him every detailed aspect of his or her need or problem, even if prayer is invited. God's *omnipotence* and love means that the believer can trust him in all circumstances. To attribute *personhood* to God means that the believer can constantly talk with him, and that his word, especially through Scripture, is no mere metaphorical notion, but that God commu-nicates with humankind. God's *creation of the world* means that God chose not to remain isolated in lone glory, but positively willed to love created beings who were 'other' than he is: he created us because he loves us.

Yet in the case of unbelievers the problem is different. Karl Rahner (1904–84) and Wolfhart Pannenberg (1928–2014) recognize that, for many, the term *God* has become enigmatic, or even 'a blank face'.[120] Nevertheless, even from the unbeliever's viewpoint, the fact that millions of people listen and pray to God, and talk of God's purposes, presupposes that God is per-sonal. Some describe God as *supra-personal*, because he is not 'personal' in the same way as human beings are personal. God, however, still has pur-poses for the Church and the world.

Biblical writers also portray God as Creator of the world. God is Creator in Isaiah 40.28: 'The LORD is the everlasting God, the Creator of the ends of the earth.' In Isaiah 43.15 Isaiah refers to God's creation of Israel: 'I am the LORD, your Holy One, the Creator of Israel'. God's creation of human-kind is recorded in Genesis 1.27; 5.1–2; 6.7; in Deuteronomy 4.32, and about 20 passages in Isaiah. Christianity firmly rejects the notion that the world constitutes an emanation or outflow of God. Creation remains

---

120 Karl Rahner, *Foundations of Christian Faith: An Introduction to the Idea of Christianity* (New York, N.Y.: Crossroad, 1978 and 2004), p. 46; Wolfhart Pannenberg, *Systematic Theology*, 3 vols (Eng., Edinburgh: T&T Clark, 1991–8), vol. 1, p. 64.

finite, brought into being by God's free, sovereign, will. Jürgen Moltmann (b. 1926) argues that *'creatio ex nihilo'* (from nothing) implies that 'The omnipotent and omnipresent God withdraws his presence and restricts his power', i.e. 'makes room' for what is not-God.[121]

Under 'Systematic theology' we noted that Karl Barth (1886–1968) writes, 'God is known by God and by God alone'.[122] What Barth calls 'the knowability of God' depends entirely on God's readiness to be known.[123] Nevertheless, he points out, the sin of humankind and its fall also express a 'closedness' in our relation to God. We find God 'in Jesus Christ, and in him alone'.[124] Eberhard Jüngel (b. 1934) insists that Christ makes possible the 'knowability', the 'conceivability' and the 'speakability' of God.[125] The need for revelation, Barth urges, arises because 'the hiddenness of God is the inconceivability of the Father, the Son and the Holy Spirit'.[126] Later in that volume, Barth considers the reality of God in terms of his *actions*: 'God is who he is in the act of his revelation. God seeks and creates fellowship between himself and us.'[127] He is also the God who elects and commands; Jesus Christ is the elected man. Barth recognizes that the doctrine of election is not generally recognized today, but considers it self-evident from Scripture. Election is nor arbitrary, but forms part of our election *in Christ*. As a consequence, the believer 'may let go of God, but God does not let go of him'.[128] This demonstrates the faithfulness of God. Pannenberg points out that faithfulness can be demonstrated only through prolonged time.

The love of God is seen not only in his creation of the world, but also in the history of his people, and especially in his gift of Jesus Christ. Jesus said, 'God so loved the world that he gave his only Son, that whoever believes in him should have eternal life' (John 3.16). This includes the humiliation of the Incarnation, and pre-eminently, his crucifixion and resurrection, both for us. This is both the love of Christ and the love of God, for 'in Christ God was reconciling the world to himself' (2 Cor. 5.19). As Donald Baillie entitled his book, *God Was in Christ*.[129] It is important to note that God's

---

121 Jürgen Moltmann, *God in Creation* (Eng., London: SCM Press, 1985), p. 75.

122 Barth, *Church Dogmatics*, II.I, vol. 3, sect. 27, p. 179.

123 Barth, *Church Dogmatics*, II.I, vol. 3, p. 63.

124 Barth, *Church Dogmatics*, II.I, vol. 3, p. 149.

125 Eberhard Jüngel, *God as the Mystery of the World* (Eng., Edinburgh: T&T Clark, 1983), pp. 226–98.

126 Barth, *Church Dogmatics*, II.I, vol. 3, sect. 27, p. 197.

127 Barth, *Church Dogmatics*, II.I, vol. 3, p. 257.

128 Barth, *Church Dogmatics*, II.II, vol. 4, sect. 35, p. 317.

129 Donald M. Baillie, *God Was in Christ* (London: Faber & Faber, 1948), esp. pp. 118–24.

love does not exclude his wrath; although love is his nature (1 John 4.8), his wrath is manifested on specific occasions (see Part 3, Wrath of God). His love is eternal; his wrath is not. This may be part of God's discipline (Heb. 12.7–8).

The holiness of God was originally connected with his majesty or awesomeness. Isaiah's vision of his call in the Temple underlines the unapproachableness of the holy God:

> I saw the Lord sitting on a throne, high and lofty . . . Seraphs were in attendance . . . they covered their faces . . . And one called to another, and said: 'Holy, holy, holy is the LORD of hosts; the whole earth is full of his glory.' The pivots on the thresholds shook at the voices of those who called.
>
> (Isa. 6.1–4)

The focus here is on majesty or *gravitas*, although other passages develop moral and ethical aspects. The Hebrew *qādōsh* (holy) originally meant *separate*, and the holy of holies was the innermost part of the Temple. Edmond Jacob wrote, 'Holiness is not one divine quality among others, for it expresses what is characteristic of God.'[130] O. R. Jones rightly calls it a disposition, which shows itself on specific occasions.[131] Christians are urged to reflect the holiness of God in moral or ethical terms. Many Christians try to reflect this in liturgical practices or worship and prayer, as well as conduct. Jesus taught, 'Hallowed be your name . . . on earth as it is in heaven' (Matt. 6.9–10).

Theologians have long debated how to use language to express God's *transcendence* or otherness from humankind. Paul Tillich (1886–1965) criticized traditional ways. He wrote, 'When applied to God, superlatives become diminutives. They place him on the level of other beings, while elevating him above all of them.'[132] For this reason he rejects the notion of describing God as being even the highest being, but insists on calling him 'Being-itself'. Most thinkers, however, reject Tillich's suggestion, because although they take his point, this unwittingly threatens to reduce the personhood of God in the direction of pantheism. All theists, including Jews, Christians and Muslims, insist on the personhood of God. If any try to reject this on the ground of the huge size of the universe, one significant reply is that the greater the mind, the greater the mind's knowledge of detail. For example, in the teaching of Jesus, 'Not one [sparrow] will fall

---

130 Edmond Jacob, *Theology of the Old Testament* (London: Hodder & Stoughton, 1958), p. 86.
131 O. R. Jones, *The Concept of Holiness* (London: Allen & Unwin, 1961).
132 Paul Tillich, *Systematic Theology*, 3 vols (London: Nisbet, 1953–64), vol. 1, p. 26.

to the ground apart from your Father. And even the hairs of your head are all counted' (Matt. 10.29–30). God's intimate engagement with his people and the world, and his intimate presence through Christ and the Holy Spirit, are often described as his *immanence*. God's immanence is hardly less important than his transcendence. (See Part 2, Trinity, Holy.)

Humankind

(See also Part 2, Sin and alienation.) Many practical themes emerge from the biblical and theological study of humankind. One such feature is the human capacity to relate to one another, and to God. Migliore argues that human beings 'find their true identity in coexistence with each other and with all other creatures'.[133] Karl Barth (1886–1968), similarly, commends 'the differentiation and relationship of man and woman', including 'the relation of sex'.[134] In the same vein, Wolfhart Pannenberg (1928–2014) argues, 'Being with others as others is central to bearing the image of God.'[135]

The image of God is understood and interpreted in a number of ways. Its importance for humanity is affirmed by everyone. Until fairly recently the image of God was associated primarily with particular qualities implanted by God into human beings. One of the most frequently cited was that of dominion, which reflected the words of Genesis 1.26, in which God said, 'Let us make humankind in our image, according to our likeness; and let them have dominion over the fish of the sea, and over the birds of the air . . .' Thomas Aquinas (1225–74) was among the many to stress that dominion or rule reflected God's nature as king. Nevertheless, Jürgen Moltmann (b. 1926) and others have more convincingly interpreted 'dominion' in terms of stewardship or care for the universe. Reinhold Niebuhr (1892–1971), as well as Moltmann, has criticized any notion of 'mastery'. They trace the effects of humankind's mastery of nature and animals to the detriment of nature, and to instances of inflicting pain on animals purely for cosmetics.

From earliest times some, especially Irenaeus (*c.* 130 – *c.* 200), drew a distinction between the image (Heb., *tselem*) and likeness (Heb., *dēmûth*) of God, to argue that whereas at the fall humankind lost its *likeness* to

---

133 Daniel L. Migliore, *Faith Seeking Understanding* (Grand Rapids, Mich.: Eerdmans, 1991), p. 125.
134 Barth, *Church Dogmatics*, III.I, vol. 5, p. 186.
135 Pannenberg, *Systematic Theology*, vol. 2, p. 193.

God, it nevertheless retained the *image* of God. However, the Hebrew terms are almost certainly used in poetic parallelism, to indicate synonyms.

Others have suggested other particular qualities as reflecting God's image. Aquinas and many of the Greek fathers emphasized intelligence and rationality as the quality which distinguished humankind from animals, and which also reflected God. However, it is probable that none of these specific qualities as such refers to the gift of God's image; rather the capacity to live *in a relationship to others.* Perhaps aspects of *all* these particular qualities constitute what it means to bear the image of God. Most of all, the image of God is best seen as a *vocation* through which *God calls his people to show what God is like.* Images of deities in pagan temples were intended in some way to show what the deity was like. The phrase 'in God's image' probably means 'as (Heb., b^e) his image'. The tragic sin of idolatry is that Israel used objects to represent God, when in point of fact God had called *them* to show forth his likeness and image. Although not everyone will agree with him, Vladimir Lossky (1903–58), the Russian Orthodox theologian, has argued persuasively that the image of God is not a natural gift for every person, but a gift of grace for God's people. He argues that God's people should strive to recover and show forth that image in response to God's grace. He regards those who bear the image of God as true '*persons*'; others are merely '*individuals*'.[136]

The Hebrew and Greek terminology for the various human capacities is intriguing. First, the biblical writers offer *no dualism* between mind or spirit and body of the kind envisaged by many Greek philosophers. Biblical traditions presuppose what today we might call an integrated psychosomatic relation of mind and body. Wolfhart Pannenberg (1928–2014) writes positively of the unity of the body and the soul, and of 'the biblical idea of psychosomatic unity'.[137] The Hebrew for *soul, nephesh,* can even denote a dead body, and NT specialists generally agree that the Greek word *psyche* is a theologically colourless word, which is usually translated as *life* or *human life,* even if on rare occasions it is translated as the *soul.*

Every human capacity represented by a Greek or Hebrew term is of great practical relevance to Christians. *Mind* raises questions about the use of the mind for Christians; *heart* shows the relevance of emotions and will, and most of all opens up questions about the *unconscious*; *conscience*

---

136 Vladimir Lossky, *The Mystical Theology of the Eastern Church* (New York, N.Y.: St Vladimir's Seminary Press, 1976; and Cambridge: James Clarke, 1991), p. 117; and Lossky, *The Image and Likeness of God* (London and Oxford: Mowbray, 1974) p. 155.
137 Pannenberg, *Systematic Theology,* vol. 2, pp. 181–202.

conveys meaning not entirely replicated in Western thought; and *flesh* often denotes human weakness, and may also at times be connected to sin and self-reliance. The human body (*sōma*) usually denotes the entire human being, mainly in its public, visible and tangible dimension. Ernst Käsemann offers an accurate definition of Paul's most distinctive concept of body. He describes it as

> that piece of the world, which we ourselves are and for which we bear responsibility, because it was the earliest gift of our Creator to us. Body is not primarily to be regarded from the standpoint of the individual. For the apostle it signifies man in his worldliness (i.e. as part of the world) and therefore, in his ability to communicate . . . In the bodily obedience of the Christian . . . In the world of every day, the Lordship of Christ finds visible expression, and only when this visible expression takes shape in us does the whole thing become credible as gospel message.[138]

Käsemann points out that as God's gift, we should value, never disparage, bodily activities. Bodily conduct also provides the opportunity for the witness of an obedient life, thereby giving credibility to Christ's lordship.

Heart (Heb., *lēbh*; Gk, *kardia*) often expresses deep feeling (Gen. 6.6), such as fear and anxiety (Gen. 45.26), joy or merriment (1 Sam. 2.1). Hearts may be hardened (Exod. 7.13–14), or be pure (Matt. 5.8). The heart may also be the sphere of reflection, reasoning or pondering (Luke 2.19, 51). The term occurs more than 700 times in the LXX and 600 times in the Hebrew Bible. Nevertheless the most significant use of the term for people today is its capacity to denote *the unconscious* operating in *secret*. Paul speaks of 'the secrets of the heart' (1 Cor. 14.20–25). Rudolf Bultmann (1884–1976) suggested that these verses might imply an unconscious striving. Recently, however, Gerd Theissen has made a careful study of the unconscious in Paul, and cites numerous references where, even ahead of Freud, this interpretation is convincing.[139] Thus the Holy Spirit is poured into our hearts, and prompts prayer within our hearts, even with 'inexpressible sighs', because we do not know how to pray as we ought (Rom. 8.26–27).

Conscience translates the Greek *syneidēsis*, but has no Hebrew equivalent. It is not equivalent to conscience today, nor to the normal Stoic usage. In 1 Corinthians 8—10 it is often translated as 'self-awareness'. In 1955 C. A. Peirce published *Conscience in the New Testament*, in which

---

138 Ernst Käsemann, *New Testament Questions of Today* (London: SCM Press, 1969), p. 135.
139 Theissen, *Psychological Aspects of Pauline Theology*, pp. 96–114, 267–341.

he defined conscience in the NT as 'the pain consequent upon the inception of an act believed to be wrong'.[140] More recently Margaret Thrall proposed modifications to Peirce, arguing that conscience could also be used in a positive way. Most recently of all, R. A. Horsley (1978) and P. W. Gooch (1987) argued that 'self-awareness' was the primary meaning in 1 Corinthians 8—10.[141] Those who had a 'weak' conscience were less confident in their convictions than bolder people with a 'strong' conscience.

NT uses of *mind* (Gk, *nous*) present a much more positive picture than tradition has often suggested. Paul saw the positive importance of the use of the mind for Christians, and exhorted the Thessalonians to think rightly (1 Thess. 5.12), and his converts simply to use rational inference and deduction (Gal. 3.1–5). Aquinas (1225–74), Jewett, Bornkamm, Pannenberg, and others, have rightly underlined this point. Christians are urged to reflect positively on ethical conduct and on other matters.

Finally, *flesh* (Gk, *sarx*) is used in numerous ways in the NT. Sometimes, for example, it simply refers to physical substance. At other times it denotes human weakness and fallibility. J. A. T. Robinson rightly distinguishes between flesh and body. He declares, 'While *sarx* stands for man in the solidarity of creation in his distance from God, *sōma* stands for man in the solidarity of creation, as made for God.'[142] 'The mind of the flesh' in Paul (Rom. 8.6) may mean both humankind in its weakness, and humankind in its alienation and sin. When it is used with its *theological* meaning, Bultmann rightly argues that it denotes 'the self-reliant attitude of the man who puts his trust in his own strength'.[143]

Justification

Justification denotes being in a right relationship with God. As Paul stressed especially in Romans, 1 Corinthians and Galatians, and as Martin Luther (1483–1546) also stressed, it constitutes a *free gift* of God, not a purely human aspiration. It is not exclusively a legal or courtroom image, although justice and divine norms feature in the background. A popular evangelist of the last century took as his slogan, 'Get right with God', which reflects justification by grace. Although it is often associated with Paul in

---

140 C. A. Peirce, *Conscience in the New Testament* (London: SCM Press, 1955), p. 22; cf. pp. 13–22, 113–30.
141 P. W. Gooch, 'Conscience in 1 Cor. 8 and 10', *New Testament Studies* 33 (1987), pp. 244–54.
142 Robinson, *The Body*, p. 31.
143 Rudolf Bultmann, *Theology of the New Testament*, vol. 1 (London: SCM Press, 1952), p. 240.

Romans and Galatians, the theme of justification also belongs prominently to the teaching of Jesus, and elsewhere in Paul and the NT.

Suggestions that this theme is not a central one are widely associated with Albert Schweitzer (1875–1965). He argued that this doctrine was 'individualist and uncosmic', and that for those who took it as a starting-point, 'the understanding of the Pauline world of thought was made impossible'.[144] By contrast, he argued, Paul's theology was cosmic and corporate, and 'believing' was not primarily an intellectual matter. Justification, he said, belonged to a different conceptual scheme, where there was controversy about the law. Paul's more prominent theme, he declared, was dying and rising with Christ. More recently Krister Stendahl regarded the doctrine as 'conditioned by the later Western problem of a conscience troubled by the demands of the law'.[145] He repeated Schweitzer's accusation of individualism. J. N. Sanders (b. 1956) regarded justification as 'backward looking' as against a more transformative, holistic and future-orientated understanding of salvation. The charge is that 'justification' interprets Paul through Lutheran eyes, and ignores Paul's setting in first-century Judaism.

Nevertheless Paul derived his characteristic emphasis from the teaching and parables of Jesus of Nazareth. First, the well-known parable of the prodigal son sets in contrast the free forgiveness and welcome granted to the prodigal son with the self-righteous attitude of the elder son (Luke 15.11–32). Second, even more startling is the parable of the good employer and grumbling workers (Matt. 20.1–15). This compares the outlook of the generosity and grace of God with the supposed standards of 'fairness', justice, or law, expected by the grumbling labourers. This parable clearly teaches that *grace eclipses justice*. Those who had worked an 11-hour day received the day's wage that they had agreed upon. Those who worked only for one hour received the same wage, to the consternation of the crowd. The employer responded: 'I am doing you no wrong; did you not agree with me for the usual daily wage?' (v. 13). He asks the pivotal question: 'Or are you envious because I am generous?' (v. 15). It is the 'natural man's' cry of 'it's not fair!' which runs up against the offence of grace over law. Third, the parable of the Pharisee and the tax-collector (Luke 18.9–14) provokes the same attitudes and contrasts. It is addressed to those 'who trusted in themselves that they were righteous' (v. 9). The Pharisee was self-congratulatory about his own supposed achievements (vv. 11–12).

---

144 Albert Schweitzer, *The Mysticism of Paul the Apostle* (Eng., London: Black, 1931), pp. 219–20.
145 Krister Stendahl, *Paul among Jews and Gentiles* (Minneapolis, Minn.: Fortress Press, 1976), p. 81.

The tax-collector simply pleaded with God to be 'merciful to me, a sinner' (v. 13) and 'went down to his home justified rather than the other' (v. 14).

Johannes Weiss (1863–1914), Rudolf Bultmann (1884–1976) and C. K. Barrett (1917–2011) stress that the term is about the non-imputation of sins, and the objective situation of 'peace with God' (Rom. 5.1–2).[146] Weiss asserts: 'It does not say what a man is in himself, but it states what he is considered, in the eyes of God . . . being right with God.'[147] God, he says, declares the ungodly just. Bultmann asserts that this leads to the 'paradox' of God's pronouncing his eschatological verdict in the present.[148] Some older Roman Catholic writers regard this not as paradox, but *self-contradiction*: how can the wicked be righteous?[149] There are two main counter-replies to this. First, John Ziesler argues that we should distinguish carefully between the noun 'righteousness' (Gk, *dikaiosunē*) and the verb 'to declare righteous' (Gk, *dikaioō*). He writes:

> We arrive at an exegesis which satisfies the concerns of both traditional Catholicism and traditional Protestantism. Nothing is lost: justification is entirely by grace through faith, it is declaratory. On the other hand, Paul's ethical seriousness is fully allowed for, within the one section of vocabulary.[150]

Ziesler attempts this task boldly, with careful attention to Hebrew and Greek vocabulary. He declares, 'If God looks on believers only as they are found in Christ, he may properly declare them righteous, for in him . . . they are righteous . . . There is nothing fictional here.'[151] In spite of this clarity and eirenical intention, it is generally agreed that his claims are somewhat exaggerated.

The second reply to older objections takes up the argument of Weiss and Bultmann that justification by faith represents an anticipation of God's eschatological verdict at the Last Judgment. It may further take account of the distinction in Ludwig Wittgenstein and Donald Evans about discerning different interpretations of visual experience and verdicts within a given system.[152] Within the system of eschatological reality, believing Christians are indeed declared righteous. But within the system of

---

146 Johannes Weiss, *Earliest Christianity* (New York, N.Y.: Harper, 1959), p. 498.
147 Weiss, *Earliest Christianity*, p. 499.
148 Bultmann, *Theology of the New Testament*, p. 276.
149 F. Prat, *The Theology of St Paul*, 2 vols (London: Burns & Oates, 1945), vol. 2, p. 247.
150 John Ziesler, *The Meaning of Righteousness in Paul: A Linguistic and Theological Enquiry* (Cambridge: Cambridge University Press, 1972), p. 212.
151 Ziesler, *Meaning of Righteousness*, p. 212.
152 Ludwig Wittgenstein, *Philosophical Investigations* (Oxford: Blackwell, 1967), part 2, pp. 197–214; Donald D. Evans, *The Logic of Self-Involvement* (London: SCM Press, 1963), pp. 124–41.

historical reality, they remain sinners, often bound by their past actions and attitudes. Two *propositions* might seem to contradict each other; but two *verdicts* within *different systems* may be compatible and not contradictory. Verdicts are not propositions, but speech-acts. Luther described Christians as at the same time sinners and righteous (*simul justus et peccator*). I have expanded this point elsewhere, and explained why Paul and James do not contradict each other.[153]

Even if we have reservations about where to place the emphasis, this doctrine or theme is utterly Christ-centred, and shifts the believer's ground of confidence from himself or herself to the free, sovereign, grace of God in Christ. Käsemann emphasizes this. It grants confidence and assurance to the Christian, as nothing else can, and is entirely true to Paul. There are ways to stress correctly the corporate dimension of justification. In liberation theology José Porfirio Miranda underlines this, showing the implications of justification for justice in society.[154] He regards 'the justice or righteousness of God' in Romans 1.18—3.20 as referring to societal institutions and power-structures. Justification is regarded as 'putting things right', and this concerns communities as well as individuals. This seems convincing.

Barrett, Ernst Käsemann (1906–98) and others also regard the 'courtroom' approach as only *part* of the metaphor implied by justification. Käsemann further criticizes Stendahl for allowing the Church to take precedence over Paul's more central concerns about salvation. The importance of justification as judgment with its eschatological connection has been explored by Peter Stuhlmacher and K. Kartelge. They stress the apocalyptic framework of Paul's theme. In recent Catholic theology Hans Küng (b. 1928) has drawn very close to the traditional Protestant tradition. He has investigated Barth's doctrine of justification, and concludes that Barth rightly emphasizes 'the supremacy of God's grace'.[155] This is most helpful in maintaining a clear contrast between justification as a divine verdict and sanctification as a transformative work of the Holy Spirit over time.

Justification is also to be distinguished from forgiveness. Forgiveness is frequently renewed, often each day. Justification is a once-for-all verdict. Paul Tillich (1886–1965) described it as 'accepting that one is accepted';

---

153 Anthony C. Thiselton, *The Two Horizons* (Exeter: Paternoster and Grand Rapids, Mich.: Eerdmans, 1980), pp. 415–22.
154 José Porfirio Miranda, *Marx and the Bible: A Critique of the Philosophy of Oppression* (Eng., New York, N.Y.: Orbis, 1974), pp. 162–3, 178.
155 Hans Küng, *Justification* (London: Burns & Oates, 1964), p. 187.

the believer 'must accept acceptance'.[156] Finally, as Luther and others saw, faith is simply the means by which justification is *appropriated*. It is in no way equivalent to a special kind of work.

Liturgy, liturgical theology

In Greek, *laos*, 'people' + *ergon*, 'work', form *leitourgia*, 'public service'). In the OT, worship often concerned the major festivals of Unleavened Bread, the Feast of Weeks or Harvest, and the Ingathering, and in addition the major festival of Passover. The Passover took place in the home, while the others were public festivals. Exodus 23.4–17 begins, 'Three times in the year you shall hold a festival for me . . .' Exodus 34.18–23 repeats these instructions. Exodus 12.1–51; Deuteronomy 16.1–8; and 2 Kings 23.21–23 enjoin the festival of the Passover, as a reliving of Israel's exodus and redemption from Egypt. 1 Kings 8 recounts worship in Solomon's Temple. The Day of Atonement (Lev. 16) and the celebration of the Passover over time developed a fixed pattern of procedure, in effect, a liturgy.

In Leviticus the Day of Atonement begins with a warning not to approach the holy God unprepared, and much of the theology of Hebrews presupposes this. To approach God is not simply a human 'right'. In the Day of Atonement (Heb., *yōm kippurîm*) Aaron must first prepare a young bull to be sacrificed as a sin-offering for 'himself and for his house' (Lev. 16.6). Then he must prepare a ram to be sacrificed as a burnt offering. He is then to sacrifice two goats, one 'for the LORD and the other . . . for Azazel' (16.8). The former becomes a second sin-offering for the people, while the latter becomes the scapegoat, which will be presented to the Lord, and sent away into the wilderness (16.9–10). The ceremony involves the purification of the sanctuary and the people (16.11–22). The Hebrew word *kipper* (16.11, 16–18) usually means *to expiate* or *to atone*, but in this context denotes *to purify*, involving the purification of the mercy-seat (16.13–14). The aim is to cover all the sins which may not have been cleansed or covered by other sacrifices. Hebrews 9 takes up the theme of the Day of Atonement, insisting that the Aaronic priesthood can never fully and completely atone for sin, whereas Christ's priesthood is finally effective, once for all (Gk, *ephapax*). In Judaism the Mishnah devotes a whole tractate to the Day of Atonement (*m. Yōma*).

The Passover *Haggadah* is detailed in Judaism, and the Lord's Supper or Eucharist is modelled on it. *Haggadah* means narrative or narrative books

---

156 Tillich, *Systematic Theology*, vol. 2, pp. 205–6.

in general, but also denotes specifically the Passover narrative in Exodus and in the contemporary liturgy of the Passover.[157] This contains instructions for the composition of the *Seder* meal: the bitter herbs; the four cups; and the words of blessing, some of which bless God for the herbs and wine, akin to 'saying grace'. It is important that the *Haggadah* and Mishnah state:

> In every single generation it is a man's duty to regard himself as if *he* had gone forth from Egypt, as it is written . . . 'Because of that which the Lord did unto *me*, when *I* came forth from out of Egypt' . . . And he brought *us* out from thence.[158]

Joachim Jeremias (1968–71) and F. J. Leenhardt rightly insist that the Christian institution of the Lord's Supper or Eucharist is closely modelled on the Passover.[159] The words in post-biblical Judaism would have been: 'This is the bread of affliction'; the 'surprise' for the disciples would have been: 'This is my body'. The 'blessing' would have been: 'Blessed art Thou, O Lord, King of the Universe, who redeemed us.'

In 1 Corinthians 11.23–26, or earlier, since Paul is citing a pre-Pauline formula, the Christian recital of the narrative of the Passion became the core of the liturgy of the Eucharist. It has remained the heart of all liturgical canons for the Eucharist in virtually all Christian traditions today. The canon alludes both to the Passover and to the covenant, and occurs in 1 Corinthians 11.25; Matthew 26.28; Mark 14.24; Luke 22.20. In addition to these words, (1) the breaking of the bread (the 'fraction'), (2) the sharing together (1 Cor. 10.16), (3) the eschatological dimension (1 Cor. 11.26; Matt. 26.29; Mark 14.25; Luke 22.16), and (4) 'one bread', 'one cup', 'one body' (1 Cor. 10.17), are all an integral part of the eucharistic canon. 'Remembrance' (Gk, *anamnēsis*) became the focus of much discussion. It cannot denote repetition, for the work of Christ is once-for-all. But it is probably more than a subjective calling to mind. The Passover context suggests 'being there' at the Passion and being involved.

The New Testament also contains non-eucharistic formulae. The Lord's Prayer (Matt. 6.9–13; cf. Luke 11.2–4) and the 'wish-prayers' of Paul became classic examples, especially the 'grace' of 2 Corinthians 13.13.

---

157 Cecil Roth, *The Haggadah* (Heb. and Eng., London: Soncino Press, 1934).
158 Roth, *Haggadah*, p. 36; and *m. Pesahim*, 10.5, in H. Danby, *The Mishnah* (Eng., Oxford: Oxford University Press, 1933), pp. 150–1.
159 Cullmann and Leenhardt, *Essays on the Lord's Supper*, pp. 39–43; Joachim Jeremias, *The Eucharistic Words of Jesus* (Eng., London: SCM Press, 1966), pp. 84–6 and throughout.

The liturgical formulae surrounding baptism and the Eucharist emerge in *Didachē*, 9.1–4 (*c.* 90–120). They allude to scattered bread becoming one. Justin Martyr (*c.* 100 – *c.* 165) recounts regular Eucharist, with the words of institution recited by a 'president' (Gk, *proestōti*) of the brothers, who affirm it with 'Amen'. Only believers can partake, and the deacon distributes bread and wine (Justin, *First Apology*, 65–66). Hippolytus (*c.* 215) sets out a longer service in a manuscript which is now lost. Later the Syrian Church recounts liturgical practice. After the Council of Nicaea (325), further expansions occur.

In the Middle Ages Thomas Aquinas (1225–74) urged transubstantiation, based on Aristotle's philosophy, which the Reformers later rejected as an unbiblical concept (see Part 3, Transubstantiation). The Council of Trent (1551) reaffirmed the doctrine for Catholics, and Vatican II still implies it. The Reformers Luther, Zwingli, Calvin and Cranmer all urged variant interpretations. Today Anglicans represent a spectrum of views, most near to Calvin or Cranmer, but at the extremes ranging from Luther ('High Church' Anglicans) to Zwingli ('Low Church' Anglicans). Richard Hooker (1554–1600) affirmed the 'real presence' of Christ, but with qualifications. The 1971 Agreed Statement on Eucharistic Doctrine suggests a convergence of Catholic and Anglican views, but this is not reflected in official statements in Vatican II.

The Liturgical Movement was a nineteenth-century Catholic movement, influenced by Jean Daniélou, emphasizing the centrality of the Eucharist. It had an effect, in turn, on the Anglican *Alternative Service Book* (1980), but this is generally regarded as superseded by the more recent *Common Worship* (2000). The former went too far using language which is often criticized as 'cheap and cheerful'. *Common Worship* provides also for daily non-eucharistic services and pastoral offices. It is perhaps used more widely than the 1662 Book of Common Prayer, although legally and officially it has not replaced the Prayer Book.

Natural theology

Natural theology denotes knowledge of God that can be obtained by human reason alone, without the aid of revelation. Thomas Aquinas (1225–74) drew a careful distinction between natural and revealed theology. Reason, he believed, can infer the existence of God largely through analogy, but only revelation can give us knowledge of the Incarnation, the Holy Trinity, and understanding of the atonement. Most Roman Catholics endorse this view, and recently Pope John Paul II praised the value of philosophical enquiry. Plato (*c.* 427–347 BC) had first set forth rational arguments for the existence of God, especially from the observance of objects in motion. Among the Reformers, Luther and Calvin argued that everyone has some sense of the deity, and that the natural world contains numerous 'traces' of God's work. Nevertheless, sin and the fall of humankind made the need for divine revelation inescapable.

William Paley (1743–1805), Archdeacon of Carlisle, produced *Evidences of Christianity*, published as *Natural Theology* in 1802. This provided a statement of natural theology used by generations of students. In essence it was a restatement of the teleological argument for the existence of God. He produced the well-known analogy of the watch, found on a heath, the intricate mechanism of which pointed to a designer. He regarded the universe as likewise a machine of notable regularity and design. He therefore inferred the divine 'watch-maker'. Paley drew parallel inferences from the complexity of the human eye. He followed Aquinas' 'fifth way', which had expounded the 'guidedness of nature'.

Paley's arguments, however, had failed to answer the work of David Hume (1711–76), and were also thought to be excluded by the later work of Charles Darwin (1809–82). Hume had argued that 'cause' could not be empirically observed, but only 'constant conjunction'.[160] Hume's *Dialogues Concerning Natural Religion* (1761) took this further, defeating the arguments of the rationalist 'Demea' and the theist 'Cleanthes'. Parts 10 and 11 focus on the problem of evil, where he anticipated some of Paley's arguments. He also considered dysteleology, which suggested only a malign designer. The evolutionary theories of Darwin seemed to raise more objections against natural theology. Both *The Origin of Species* (1859) and *The Descent of Man* (1871) seemed to suggest that all creatures simply evolved by random processes, from natural selection. 'God', it seemed, had been replaced by a mechanism. Darwin's theories held much of nineteenth-century thought in thrall. Unwittingly Georg Hegel (1770–1831) had also encouraged developmental thinking. Herbert Spencer (1820–1903) popularized the slogan, 'the survival of the fittest', in biology and ethics. The theist case was not helped by many literalistic, chronological, accounts of creation in Genesis. Rather than saying with the psalmist, God filled 'all things living with plenteousness' (Ps. 145.16, BCP), many argued that those who were not filled with plenteousness simply died. Nature was 'red in tooth and claw'.

---

160 David Hume, *A Treatise of Human Nature* (3rd edn, Oxford: Oxford University Press, 1978 (1739)), pp. 79–94.

It was left largely to theist philosophers of religion to respond with counter-arguments. In 1930 F. R. Tennant argued, 'The sting of Darwinianism . . . lay in the suggestion that proximate and "mechanical" causes were sufficient to produce the adaptations from which the theology of the 18th century had argued to God.'[161] He continued, 'The survival of the fittest proposes the survival of the fit, and throws no light thereupon . . . Room is left for the possibility that variation is externally predetermined or guided.'[162] During the interwar period, both Tennant and W. R. Matthews insisted that gradualness of development provided no difficulties to theistic belief. In the late twentieth century, Richard Swinburne (b. 1934) similarly moved from an argument for micro-adaptation to a more general notion of order as implying a God of purpose.[163] Objections to a God of purpose, however, have been mounted by the 'new' (i.e. aggressive) atheists, Richard Dawkins and others. Dawkins combines evolutionary theory with genetics, to claim that physics and chemistry, with genetics, provide the basis for life that we need.

A whole regiment of Christian scientists and theologians have offered convincing replies, especially John Polkinghorne (b. 1930), eminent Cambridge professor of mathematical physics and a Christian theologian. Polkinghorne sets out 'levels of explanation' which show that physics cannot 'explain' a great work of art or music in terms of wavelengths or an oscilloscope.[164] He also expounds 'the anthropic principle', whereby, it is argued, life on earth could have emerged only with the exact duration of time and expanding size of the universe which prevails in astrophysics. He concludes, 'The clockwork universe is dead'; the whole is more than the sum of its parts. Stephen Hawking similarly argues: 'If the rate of expansion one second after the big bang had been smaller by even one part in a hundred thousand million million, the universe would have collapsed before it ever reached its present size.'[165] Ian Barbour, Arthur Peacocke and R. J. Berry make similar points. Indeed the outlook of scientists has been radically changing since Heisenberg and Dirac. They no longer view the world as 'objective', as Karl Heim showed in *The Transformation of the Scientific World View*.[166]

---

161 F. R. Tennant, *Philosophical Theology*, 2 vols (Cambridge: Cambridge University Press, 1930), vol. 2, p. 84.
162 Tennant, *Philosophical Theology*, p. 85.
163 Richard Swinburne, *The Existence of God* (Oxford: Clarendon Press, 1979), pp. 134–40.
164 John Polkinghorne, *The Way the World Is* (London: SPCK, 1984 and 1992), pp. 17–19.
165 Stephen Hawking, *A Brief History of Time* (New York, N.Y.: Bantam, 1988), p. 291.
166 John Polkinghorne, *Quarks, Chaos and Christianity* (London: SPCK, 1994); Ian Barbour, *Religion and Science* (London: SCM Press, 1998); Karl Heim, *The Transformation of the Scientific World View* (New York, N.Y.: Harper, 1953).

Among Reformed Christian theologians, Karl Barth (1886–1968) firmly rejected the notion of natural theology. He rejected human religiosity and a self-generated approach to a 'projected' God. God is above all human thought and language, he argued, apart from God's self-revelation through Christ. In 1934 he engaged with his friend and Swiss colleague, Emil Brunner (1889–1966), arguing that Hitler depended on natural theology to tame the Church. Brunner replied to this, but in his famous book, *No!*, Barth rejected any point of contact between God and the 'natural man'. Barth asserted that God can be known through God alone. Brunner had appealed to a modified view of natural theology. He cited the possibility of repentance, the divine ordinances of marriage and the state, and Paul's appeal to knowledge of God in Romans 1.19–20.[167] Because he still had some sympathy with Barth's view, he often avoided the term *natural theology*, preferring instead the term *eristics*. He defined *eristics* as 'the intellectual discussion of the Christian faith in the light of [views] which are opposed to the Christian message'.[168] Natural theology is now valued by almost the whole Christian Church. Wolfhart Pannenberg (1928–2014) insists on its value for providing credibility for the Christian message in public and university circles.

Orthodoxy, Eastern

To define Eastern Orthodoxy is a complex task, especially in view of the history of the subject. Fundamentally, 'Orthodox Church' claims universality in right thought and right worship. This is comparable to the claims of the Roman Catholic Church. Although 'the Orthodox Church' is a convenient label for Western Christians to use, traditionally many in that church have been reluctant to use this term unless it is also called the 'Orthodox Catholic Church'. They recognize, however, that 'Orthodox Catholic' stands in conflict with 'Roman Catholic'. Their full title is 'The Holy, Orthodox, Catholic, Apostolic Church'. Several dates have been suggested for the decisive split between the two churches, but historically it has roots in the distinction between the Greek and Latin fathers. Athanasius (*c.* 296–373) and Augustine (354–430) are often viewed as the respective fountainheads of the two traditions. In the fourth century under Constantine, Rome and Byzantium (later, Constantinople) both came to be regarded as imperial capitals.

---

167 Emil Brunner, *Natural Theology*, with Karl Barth, *No!* (Eng., Eugene, Ore.: Wipf & Stock, 2002).

168 Emil Brunner, *Christian Doctrine of God* (Eng., London: Lutterworth Press, 1949), p. 98.

One symptom of a growing division between East and West was the Latin addition of the 'double procession' (i.e. 'the Holy Spirit, who proceeds from the Father and the Son') into the Ecumenical Creed. Photius (*c.* 810 – *c.* 895), Patriarch of Constantinople, entered into a political struggle with the papacy. He denounced the 'double procession' or *filioque* clause in the creed, and also Rome's sending missionaries to Bulgaria. Mutual moves to actualize excommunication led to the 'Photian schism', with spiralling consequences. Anastasios Kallis traces several key moments of mutual schism to 1054 (when 'Greek Orthodox' came to mean churches in communion with Constantinople), as well as other earlier and later dates.[169] Recently the Church of England has sometimes informally used the Eastern form of the creed, and this form was endorsed by Jürgen Moltmann, among others. *Both* forms offer different advantages.

In terms of theological content, the Eastern Orthodox Church values Scripture, early tradition, the Eucharist and eucharistic theology, the centrality of the teaching office, and the importance and priority of the Holy Spirit. Other churches, however, may also claim these. Liturgical texts and practices are regarded as the surest criteria of faithfulness to apostolic tradition. In place of the Western Church's language about 'sanctification', the Orthodox Church prefers 'deification' (*theiōsis*), an ever-closer relation to God. From the viewpoint of Protestants, both their view of the Eucharist and their deep veneration of Mary would constitute concerns. The Eastern Orthodox Church has no central government of the kind represented by the pope in the Roman Catholic Church. All bishops are regarded as equal by virtue of their ordination. They do not suggest that any bishop can be infallible. In terms of localities, largely through history, this church dominates Russia, Eastern Europe and Greece, parts of the Middle East, and some parts of Africa.

It would be a mistake to assume that Orthodox theology stagnated after the era of the Eastern fathers. Pseudo-Dionysius the Areopagite (*c.* 500) and Maximus the Confessor (*c.* 580–662) constitute very important post-patristic figures. In *The Celestial Hierarchy*, Pseudo-Dionysius expounded orders of angels, the sacraments and mystical theology, which described the ascent of the soul to God through purification, illumination and perfection, i.e. through deification. He also expounded the three orders of bishops, priests and deacons, and allowed for 'apophatic'

---

169 Anastasios Kallis, 'Orthodox Church', in Erwin Fahlbusch *et al.*, *The Encyclopedia of Christianity*, 5 vols (Leiden: Brill and Grand Rapids, Mich.: Eerdmans, 1997), vol. 3, p. 868; cf. pp. 866–72.

theology, in which words are inadequate to speak of God. Maximus the Confessor wrote doctrinal, ascetic, exegetical and liturgical treatises, again stressing 'deification', the Incarnation of Christ, and the restoration of the image of God, damaged by sin.

The most distinctive modern theology, however, emerged initially from the Russian Orthodox Church, originally from those who emigrated from Russia in 1917. The earlier modern period was influenced by Hegel and Schelling, and by the mysticism of Jakob Böhme (1575–1624). The Church rejected the authoritarianism reminiscent of Rome, and the individualism of the Protestant churches in favour of participation or *sobornost*, which may perhaps be translated as catholicity, or togetherness. The modern era saw the rise of several influential Orthodox theologians, including Sergei Bulgakov, Vladimir Lossky, Georgii Florovsky and the Greek Orthodox theologian John Zizioulas.[170]

Bulgakov (1871–1944) was at first a Marxist teacher of economics, but came to Christian belief. He rejected a dualism of spirit and matter, and stressed human participation in God. The Church, he argued, is a participation in the Holy Spirit. He is critical of too Christocentric an emphasis in the Church.

Vladimir Lossky (1903–58) remains among the most influential and important Russian Orthodox theologians of the twentieth century. He studied at the University of St Petersburg, but after expulsion by the Soviet government in 1922, worked first in Prague, and then in the Sorbonne, remaining in France until his death. He opposed the doctrine of Bulgakov, and was especially well known for his work on deification, the image of God and the mysticism of Eckhart. Three of his works are in English translation.[171]

On the image of God, Lossky argued, 'Individual and person mean opposite things'.[172] *Individual* belongs to the empirical realm of biology, to the chain of cause and effect; *person* belongs to God's new creation. As an individual, the self is cut off from the other. The individual is the self-contained narcissistic ego of Descartes. But grace restores the image of God; the self may relate to the other. The 'person' can mirror the nature

---

170 Cf. Rowan Williams, 'Eastern Orthodox Theology', in David Ford with Rachel Muers (ed.), *The Modern Theologians* (3rd edn, Oxford: Blackwell, 2005), pp. 572–88.

171 Vladimir Lossky, *The Mystical Theology of the Eastern Church* (New York, N.Y.: St Vladimir's Seminary Press, 1976; also Cambridge: James Clarke, 1991); Lossky, *Orthodox Theology* (New York, N.Y.: Crestwood, 1959, also New York, N.Y.: St Vladimir's Seminary, 1997); Lossky, *The Image and Likeness of God* (London and Oxford: Mowbray, 1974).

172 Lossky, *Mystical Theology*, p. 121.

of God as self-giving, loving, engagement with others. Second, on *deification*, Lossky regularly quotes a theme from Athanasius, Irenaeus and Gregory of Nazianzus: 'God made himself man, that man might become God.'[173] 'Creation in the . . . likeness of God', Lossky argues, 'implies the idea of participation in the divine being, of communion with God.'[174] The transition to bearing the image of God fully as a person is due entirely to grace, not to some inherent natural quality in humankind.

Georgii Florovsky (1893–1979) graduated at Odessa University, after which he taught philosophy. He lectured in law at Prague, and in 1926 became Professor of Patristics at the Orthodox Seminary in Paris. In 1948 he emigrated to the USA and was professor and dean at St Vladimir's Seminary, New York (1948–55). He then became a professor at Harvard Divinity School (1956–64), after which he was Visiting Professor at Princeton. He published much on the Greek fathers, urging a 'neo-Patristic synthesis', which addressed philosophical questions. He was involved in the World Council of Churches.

Florovsky insisted on the primacy of revelation, and a return to patristic categories of thought. He attacked the bondage of Russian theology to post-Enlightenment thought, in contrast to a needed 're-Hellenizing' of the Christian faith. *Ways of Russian Theology* is a virtually comprehensive view of the history of the Russian Orthodox Church.[175] He gave special importance to the Eucharist and to the related experience of *sobornost* or corporate consciousness. He worked on indeterminacy. The Christian faith, he argued, is historical, and always unfinished. This may have led to his writing also on hermeneutics.

John Zizioulas (b. 1931) has been Metropolitan of Pergamon, chairman of the Academy of Athens, and is a noted and influential theologian of the Greek Orthodox Church. He studied at Thessalonica and Athens, and undertook research on Florovsky. In 1970–3 he was Professor of Patristics and then of Systematic Theology at the University of Edinburgh. He also became a professor at Glasgow (1983–7) and at King's College, London. While he was Metropolitan of Pergamon, he became Professor of Dogmatics at Thessalonica. His main interests are ecclesiology, relationality, the Holy Spirit and ontology. His three best-known works indicate

---

173 Lossky, *Image and Likeness*, p. 97.
174 Lossky, *Mystical Theology*, p. 118.
175 Georgii Florovsky, *Ways of Russian Theology*, <www.holytrinitymission.org/books/english/ way-russian-theology-florosky.htm>; also in *The Collected Works of Georges Florovsky*, 5 vols [of 14] (Belmont, Mass.: Nordland, 1972–9).

this by their titles.[176] The Church, he argues, is founded on a twofold economy, that of Christ and the Holy Spirit. He writes,

> There is, so to say, *no Christ until the Spirit is at work*, not only as forerunner announcing his coming, but also as the one *who constitutes his very identity as Christ*, either at his baptism or at his biological conception.[177]

On relationality, Zizioulas writes, 'God is a relational being: without the concept of communion it would not be possible to speak of the being of God . . . "God" has no ontological content, no true being, apart from communion.'[178] Hence: 'Ecclesial being is bound to the very being of God. From the fact that a human being is a member of the Church, he becomes an "image of God" . . . he takes on God's "way of being".'[179] This mode of being is from the Holy Spirit. He criticized Vatican II for not allowing 'pneumatology' to play a more adequate role. We must relate the institutional in the Church to the pneumatological or charismatic. The Spirit also ensures the place of the *local* church in ecclesiology. Zizioulas' theology is a creative injection into Greek Orthodoxy today, holding much in common with Lossky's Russian Orthodox theology.

Pentecostalism

Pentecostals seek a close, immediate and intimate relation with God, in which this personal relationship is regarded as more important than formal or institutional structures. We hesitate to identify the origins of Pentecostalism simply with Charles F. Parham (1873–1929) and William J. Seymour (1870–1922) alone. Pentecostal churches have become a global phenomenon, and many point to revivals in Korea, Wales and South America as Pentecostal, and do not restrict its origins solely to the United States. A second reason arises from claims to identify 'proto-Pentecostalism' with a series of earlier movements. These range from Montanism in the second century, to the Radical Reformers of the sixteenth, and possibly in

---

176 John D. Zizioulas, *Eucharist, Bishop and Church: The Unity of the Church in the Divine Eucharist and the Bishop during the First Three Centuries* (Brookline, Mass.: Holy Cross, 2001); Zizioulas, *Communion and Otherness: Further Studies in Personhood and the Church* (London: T&T Clark, 2007); and especially Zizioulas, *Being as Communion: Studies in Personhood and the Church* (Eng., New York, N.Y.: St Vladimir's Seminary Press, 1985).

177 Zizioulas, *Being as Communion*, pp. 127–8 (his italics).

178 Zizioulas, *Being as Communion*, p. 17.

179 Zizioulas, *Being as Communion*, p. 15.

a broader sense also to George Fox (1624–91), Edward Irving (1792–1834) and Albert B. Simpson (1843–1919).

1 Origins and development

With these provisos, it remains customary to trace the main origin of the movement to Charles Parham and William Seymour. Some focus on Seymour rather than on Parham, partly because Parham adopted a racist tone in his theology and practice. He founded a Bible School at Topeka (1900), where he taught the 'fivefold' or 'full' gospel of justification, sanctification, Spirit baptism, divine healing and the imminence of the return of Christ. The fifth was combined with a 'premillennial' eschatology, i.e. the belief that a thousand years will follow the return of Christ, or the Parousia. This is usually based on a particular interpretation of Revelation 20.1–10, where Revelation 20.2 speaks of the binding of the devil for a thousand years.

Parham believed that new healings and miracles would follow a period of dryness, because he looked for 'the latter rain' of a new Pentecost in accordance with Joel 2.23 (AV). He further insisted that 'speaking in tongues' was 'an inseparable part of the Baptism of the Holy Spirit'.[180] He viewed sanctification as an 'event' rather than a long process, in common with many in the Holiness Movement. Parham also believed that the narrative of the Acts of the Apostles should be replicated today.

Seymour was pastor of the Apostolic Faith Mission, Azusa Street, Los Angeles. He studied under Parham in 1905. Because of his race, Parham had him study outside his lecture room. He experienced 'baptism in the Spirit', and was called to become pastor of the Azusa Street Holiness mission in 1906. From 1906 to 1909 the Azusa Street Mission became a centre of revival. Seymour used the 'call and response' method of preaching, familiar in many black churches. He often appealed to standard Pentecostal texts such as 'The Spirit of the Lord is upon me' (Luke 4.8–19); the longer ending of Mark, 'They will cast out demons; they will speak in new tongues; they will pick up snakes . . .' (Mark 16.17–18); and, 'All of them were filled with the Holy Spirit and began to speak in other languages' (Acts 2.4).

Splits tragically soon bedevilled the movement. Parham fell out with Seymour, and William Durham set up a rival church. A new phase of

---

180 Charles F. Parham, *A Voice Crying in the Wilderness* (Baxter Springs, Kans.: Apostolic Faith Bible College, 1902), p. 35; Yongnan Jeon Ahn, *Interpretation of Tongues and Prophecy in 1 Corinthians 12—14* (Blandford Forum: Deo, 2013; Journal of Pentecostal Theology Supp., ser. 41), pp. 14–25.

development, however, began with Alfred G. Garr, Frank J. Ewart, Eudorus N. Bell (1866–1923), Aimee Semple McPherson and Ivan Q. Spencer. Garr (1874–1994) received 'baptism in the Holy Spirit' in 1906, and experienced a call to missionary work in India. He had endorsed Parham's principle that the 'initial experience' of baptism in the Spirit was speaking in tongues, which became a standard feature of 'classical' Pentecostalism.[181] When he travelled to Calcutta, to his surprise, Garr discovered that his gift of tongues proved to have no significance for his learning the Bengali language. Henceforth he regarded speaking in tongues solely as an expression of praise, prayer or empowerment.

Ewart (1876–1947) began to anticipate the 'Oneness' movement, and emphasized the centrality of Christ. This movement persisted within the Pentecostal Assemblies of God. Eudorus Bell and the Assemblies of God (founded 1913) originally came out of the Baptist churches. Aimee Semple McPherson (1890–1944) was ordained in the Assemblies of God in 1919 as an evangelist, although she resigned later to join William Durham's community. She married Robert Semple, and they became missionaries in China until Robert's death in 1921. She returned to Los Angeles, and during the early 1920s began to teach and preach the 'Foursquare Gospel'. She formulated the four cardinal principles of Pentecostal thought: (a) Christ as saviour (John 3.16); (b) Christ as baptizer in the Spirit (Acts 2.4); (c) Christ as healer (Jas 5.14–15); and (d) Christ as coming king (1 Thess. 4.16–17).[182] During the 1920s she had an influential ministry, which, especially through the radio, reached several million people. Ivan Quay Spencer (1888–1970) founded the Elim Fellowship of Churches in 1933.[183] He had joined the Assemblies of God in 1919 in New York, and founded the Elim Bible Institute in 1924.

2 The Global South

Meanwhile, Pentecostalism developed and flourished in Latin America, Asia and Africa. Allan Anderson warns us, 'Historians of Pentecostalism have reflected a bias interpreting history from a predominantly white American perspective, neglecting . . . the vital work of Asian, African . . . and Latin Pentecostal pioneers.'[184]

---

181 Gary B. McGee (ed.), *Initial Evidence: Historical and Biblical Perspectives* (Eugene, Ore.: Wipf & Stock, 2007).

182 Aimee Semple McPherson, *The Foursquare Gospel*, ed. Raymond Cox (Los Angeles, Calif.: Foursquare Publications, 1969), p. 9; Yongnan Jeon Ahn, *Interpretation*, pp. 26, 32.

183 E. E. Warner, 'Elim Fellowship', in *NIDPCM*, p. 598.

184 Allan Anderson, *An Introduction to Pentecostalism: Global Charismatic Christianity* (New York, N.Y.: Cambridge University Press, 2004), p. 166.

(a) Latin America: Brazil and Chile

The most spectacular growth occurred in Latin America. Hollenweger calculated the Brazilian Assemblies of God at 13,000 in 1930, and by 1972 it was the largest Protestant Church in Brazil.[185] In 2003 E. A. Wilson argued that nearly three-quarters of the 40 million evangelical Christians in Brazil were Pentecostal, and that Brazil represented the largest number in South America.[186]

Juan Sepúlveda traces the origins of Pentecostalism in Chile only partly to the Azusa Street revival, on the basis of testimony written on behalf of Willis C. Hoover.[187] Hoover mentions 'pre-Pentecostal' meetings in Valparaiso, based on a study of Acts, which resulted in daily prayer meetings. Hoover recounts:

> Laughter, weeping, shouting, singing, foreign tongues, visions and ecstasies, during which the individual fell to the ground and felt himself caught up into another place, to heaven, to Paradise . . . with various kinds of experience: conversations with God, the angels, or the devil. Those who experienced these things were . . . filled with praises, the spirit of prayer and love.[188]

Chilean Pentecostalism differs in several respects from 'classical' Pentecostalism. Speaking in tongues may be *one* gift of the Holy Spirit, but it does not constitute 'initial evidence' of baptism in the Spirit. Indeed the latter may be identified with conversion. Infant baptism is also practised.

(b) Asia: Kerala, India, and Korea

Paulson Pulikottil argues that in the 1920s the southern Indian state of Kerala witnessed the encounter between 'native Pentecostalism' and the Pentecostalism 'introduced by missionaries from the West'.[189] He traces the initial involvement with Pentecostalism to the Syrian church fathers of the early centuries and even to the mission of Thomas to India in the

185 Walter J. Hollenweger, *The Pentecostals* (Peabody, Mass.: Hendrickson, 1972).

186 E. A. Wilson, 'Latin America', in *NIDPCM*, pp. 157–67.

187 Juan Sepúlveda, 'Indigenous Pentecostalism and the Chilean Experience', in Allan H. Anderson and Walter J. Hollenweger (eds), *Pentecostals after a Century: Global Perspectives* (Sheffield: Sheffield Academic Press, 1999; Journal of Pentecostal Theology Suppl., ser. 15), pp. 113, 111–34.

188 Sepúlveda, 'Indigenous Pentecostalism', p. 116 (from Hoover, *Historia* (Valparaiso: Excelsior, 1948), p. 33).

189 Paulson Pulikottil, 'One God, One Spirit, Two Memories: A Pentecostal and Native Pentecostalism in Kerala', in Veli-Matti Kärkkäinen (ed.), *The Spirit in the World: Emerging Pentecostal Theologies in Global Contexts* (Grand Rapids, Mich.: Eerdmans, 2009), p. 69; cf. pp. 19–88.

first century. But references to Thomas in Parthia rest on a reference in Eusebius and to the *Acts of Thomas*, which are perhaps dubious sources. George Berg arrived in Kerala in 1909 representing Parham's teaching on baptism in the Spirit, but by 1923, there were 'three important Pentecostal movements in Kerala'.[190] The first was the South India Pentecostal Church of God, descended from K. E. Abraham; the second was the Assemblies of God; while the third was the South India Full Gospel Church.

The Korean Pentecostal experience is controversial. Lee Hong Jung and Yongnan Jeon Ahn write from different perspectives. Lee Hong Jung argues that after 1960 'Korean Pentecostalism' was materially 'distorted in the process of syncretism with Korean shamanism and North American capitalism', especially in the light of its relations to Korean *minjung* (those 'alienated socially, uneducated in cultural and intellectual matters').[191] Yongnan Jeon Ahn makes no such claims, and focuses on more specific theological issues, including speaking in tongues, spiritual gifts and biblical hermeneutics.[192] Both agree, however, that the outpouring of the Holy Spirit in Pyongyang, now in North Korea, was an indigenous experience for Korea. Over the next three years, 30,000 became Christians. 'The Great Revival' took place in Pyongyang from 1907 to 1910. The Pentecostal concern for the Holy Spirit spread to Seoul. The growth and size of Pentecostal congregations today are huge and impressive. Anderson describes 'the largest Christian congregation in the world, with an estimated 800,000 members in 1995'.[193]

(c) African Pentecostalism

The respected historian Ogbu Kalu writes: 'African Pentecostalism did not originate from Azusa Street; it is not an extension of the American electronic church.'[194] Kalu insists on three fundamental principles: the continuity of African Christianity with African primal religion; the Church as more than an institution with restrictive walls; and an ecumenical perspective which appreciates 'grass-roots' experience and people. The first principle includes the reality of witchcraft, ecstatic prophets and

---

190 Pulikottil, 'One God, One Spirit, Two Memories', in Kärkkäinen (ed.), *The Spirit in the World*, p. 75.
191 Lee Hong Jung, 'Minjung and Pentecostal Movements in Korea', in Anderson and Hollenweger (eds), *Pentecostals After a Century*, p. 138 and n. 1, and pp. 138–63.
192 Yongnan Jeon Ahn, *Interpretation*, throughout.
193 Allan H. Anderson, 'Introduction: World Pentecostalism at the Crossroads', in Anderson and Hollenweger (eds), *Pentecostals After a Century*, p. 27; cf. pp. 19–31.
194 Ogbu Kalu, *African Pentecostalism: An Introduction* (New York, N.Y.: Oxford University Press, 2008), p. viii.

numerous spirits as permeating the everyday world. It also privileges *oral* testimonies over written documents and *narrative* over argumentation. Hence the oral testimony of Pentecostals, together with a key emphasis on healing and often prosperity, makes a ready appeal. Participatory 'call and response' preaching is a phenomenon of most black churches, together with drumming, singing and often dancing, which includes 'a spontaneous verbal and non-verbal interaction between speaker and listener in which statements ("calls") are punctuated by expressions ("responses") from the listener.'[195]

West Africa contains the largest countries of Africa in terms of population. Nigeria claims 130 million people. African cosmology assumes not only the reality of witchcraft and ecstatic prophecy, but also the role of the 'big man', or authoritative, charismatic, leader. Increasingly today what is called the 'prosperity gospel' has made great advances, on the ground that the spiritual and material world are one. Leaders, Olupona suggests, are 'compulsive rather than persuasive'.[196] Ogungbile also maintains that the 'prosperity gospel' spread to Egypt, Ethiopia, Kenya, Sudan, Tanzania and Zambia. Yet Nigeria remains the most prominent. Ogungbile quotes Archbishop Benson Idahosa as declaring, 'My God is not the God of the poor . . . See, by the podium here, my computerized Mercedes Benz. In six months time, I am riding my jet . . . You are having the multiple of ten of what you are offering.'[197]

East Africa is said to have a combined population of around 260 million. Kenya has about two million Pentecostals, including the very large Valley Road Pentecostal Church in Nairobi. The Nairobi Pentecostal Church reaches out to abandoned and abused 'street children', providing guardians, schools and Bible classes for them. The AIDS crisis in Uganda created two million orphans, and the Kampala Pentecostal Church 'initiated an innovative response'.[198]

South Africa has a population of 46 million. Healing through prayer became central. In 1991 South African Pentecostal churches accounted for 30 per cent of the total population. Allan Anderson suggests that some

---

195 G. Smitherman, *Talking and Testifying: Language of Black America* (Detroit, Mich.: Wayne State University Press, 1977), p. 104; Clifton R. Clarke, 'Call and Response', in Clarke (ed.), *Pentecostal Theology in Africa* (Eugene, Ore.: Pickwick Publications, 2014), p. 28.

196 J. K. Olupona, 'African, West', in *NIDPCM*, p. 14.

197 David Ogungbile, 'African Pentecostalism and the Prosperity Gospel', in Clarke (ed.), *Pentecostal Theology in Africa*, p. 141.

198 Donald E. Miller and Tetsunao Yamamiri, *Global Pentecostalism: The New Age of Christian Social Engagement* (Berkeley, Calif: University of California Press, 2007), p. 68; cf. pp. 68–70.

6,000 Pentecostal churches represent some ten million people. Today three streams of Pentecostals continue: Assemblies of God, the Apostolic Faith Mission (each with about a quarter of a million adherents) and the smaller Full Gospel Church of God.

At the same time, worldwide Pentecostalism has undoubtedly reached a new stage of coming-of-age. This is witnessed by such world-class theologians as Amos Yong, Veli-Matti Kärkkäinen, Frank D. Macchia, Donald Miller, Ogbu Kalu, Simon Chan and many more. Pentecostal NT scholars include Gordon Fee, Roger Stronstad and Robert Menzies. What is most impressive is the plethora of contributions to several Pentecostal websites of many ordinary Pentecostals who are raising questions which would have been regarded as settled some 30 years ago. Here assumptions about such vocabulary as 'baptism in the Spirit' and such urgent problems as hermeneutics and the prosperity gospel are addressed.

Is there such commendable self-awareness and self-criticism among leaders of the renewal movement? They seem often to shelter behind the main denominations, while openly changing the style of their worship and practices. Thomas Smail, Mark Bonnington and others are among the rare critics from the Charismatic movement.

Protestantism

Protestantism denotes the Protestant family of churches in the tradition of the Reformation in contrast to Roman Catholicism and Eastern Orthodoxy. The term, however, is not the favoured word among all Protestants. In German Lutheran churches, the German term *evangelisch* denotes 'Protestant' rather than evangelical. The term *Protestant* does *not* denote those making a protest, but is derived from the Latin *pro*, 'for', + *testari*, 'to bear witness'. Initially it can be traced to Luther's 95 theses of 1517, and to the declaration of German princes in support of Luther at the Diet of Speyer in 1529. The original main geographical regions of the Protestant Church are Germany, Scandinavia, the Baltic States, Britain, Bohemia (today's Czech Republic and Slovakia), France (for a time) and Switzerland. The USA represents Catholic and Protestant churches. The Church of England is Protestant, although some argue that it combines reformed and catholic traditions. Its Tudor and nineteenth-century history complicates the issue, but the Thirty-Nine Articles and the Book of Common Prayer are clearly Protestant. William Tyndale (*c.* 1494–1536) was an English and Anglican Reformer, although Henry VIII always held Catholic sympathies. Edward II was firmly Protestant; Mary was Catholic;

Elizabeth I was clearly Protestant, while Richard Hooker (1554–1600) formulated the Elizabethan settlement. Scotland was influenced by John Knox (1513–72).

Protestants, however, embrace differences among themselves. Different traditions follow Luther, Calvin and Zwingli respectively on the theology of the Eucharist, Holy Communion, or the Lord's Supper. All these terms are biblical, but also suggest important differences of practice. Martin Luther (1483–1546) affirmed the real presence of Christ at this service: John Calvin (1509–64) regarded it as comparable to the word, but still centred on the presence of Christ; Ulrich Zwingli (1484–1531) regarded the Lord's Supper as symbolic, or a matter of subjective memory. Anglicans, following Thomas Cranmer (1489–1556), reflect a range of most of these views. Lutherans and Anglicans retain bishops, together with American Methodists. The Reformed Church in Europe and the Presbyterian Church in Scotland, English Baptists, Methodists and Pentecostals do not have bishops formally, and follow Calvin rather than Luther in ecclesiology. On the other hand, all Protestants affirm the importance of justification by grace through faith, the primacy of Scripture over church tradition, and the priesthood of all believers. None accepts the Roman and Thomist doctrine of transubstantiation; none accepts the unqualified primacy of the papacy. All share with Rome and the Eastern Orthodox the creedal view of the Holy Trinity, of the person of Christ and the atonement.

Protestant confessions of faith include the Lutheran Augsburg Confession (1530), the Calvinist Westminster Confession (1647) and the Anglican Thirty-Nine Articles (1566). But these confessions were all regarded as subordinate to Scripture and to the four great ecumenical councils of the church fathers. Attempts to update formulations to match the present propelled a concern for hermeneutics. Germany had led the way in the nineteenth and early twentieth centuries with Schleiermacher, Bultmann, Fuchs and Gadamer, with more recent work in the USA, the UK and France since about 1970. By the end of the twentieth century, Roman Catholic theologians also used every tool of biblical study, including hermeneutics.

In the early twentieth century, some distinguished between 'old' and 'new' Protestantism. 'New' Protestantism hinged on disengagement between church and state. Baptists and independent churches retained no relation to the state, while the Church of England, some Lutheran churches and the Scottish Presbyterian Church constituted established churches. Queen Elizabeth II, like her predecessors, is 'head on earth' of the churches of England.

In terms of the practices of ordinary Christians, three of the most distinctive differences in Sunday worship concern the celebration of the Mass, the veneration of the Virgin Mary and the saints, and the widespread use of images. Protestant worship is plainer. Protestants often argue that an elaborate Mass or Holy Communion can become a distraction, when the purpose of the Lord's Supper was simply to focus on Christ and the cross, and maintain parity with the preached word. Attitudes to visual imagery among Protestants vary. The Reformed tradition adheres closely to the prohibition of images in the Ten Commandments. Lutheranism and Anglicanism came to value the role of visual arts and literature, although with much tighter control than among Roman Catholics. In more recent years, however, ecumenical dialogue has been increasingly held between Protestant churches and Roman Catholics, between Anglicans and Methodists, Anglicans and Pentecostals, and various other combinations. Boundaries are more fluid than they used to be, especially as many academic scholars draw on one another's work.

Resurrection of the dead

The most extensive biblical treatment of the resurrection of the dead is 1 Corinthians 15.1–58, although Paul also refers to the general resurrection in Romans 4.6–25; 8.11; 2 Corinthians 1.9; 5.1–10; and 1 Thessalonians 4.4–17. The emphasis in all of these passages is the *free gift of God's sovereign, creative grace*, in contrast to any inherent capacity for resurrection in humankind. Dead people simply cannot raise themselves. Paul does not teach the view of Plato and that of many Eastern religions; he asserts that God raised Christ, and will raise those who are 'in Christ': 'If the Spirit of him who raised Jesus from the dead dwells in you, he who raised Christ from the dead will give life to your mortal bodies also through his Spirit that dwells in you' (Rom. 8.11).

If the resurrection mode of life is through the Holy Spirit, we should not expect this to be static. The resurrection mode of existence will be as fresh, ongoing and moment-by-moment as renewed life led by the Holy Spirit is now. The Holy Spirit is creative and ongoing; hence no one will find life monotonous when he or she is raised by the Holy Spirit. The raised 'body' will be energized by the living, ongoing God. It will not be like the frozen frame of the end of a film. Normally *body* denotes the *physical* when this is within the conditions of the world. But its *primary* focus is not its physicality, but its *public, observable, communicative* and *recognizable identity*, as Ernst Käsemann has urged (see Part 2, Humankind). As raised people, our identity will be preserved, and we shall be recognizable as individuals, just as God sees us, namely as cleansed, guiltless and reconciled by the work of Christ. Here is a second difference from most other religions. We do not lose our identity by becoming assimilated into some 'all'. God will continue to value us as individuals, just as he demonstrated this by creating and preserving us. On the other hand in Christ we become part of the innumerable multitude of God's raised people in Christ. We are able to offer and to communicate our praise through what Paul calls 'a spiritual body', i.e. a way of existence characterized by the Holy Spirit and public, recognizable identity (1 Cor. 15.44).

In 1 Corinthians 15, first, Paul regards the resurrection of Christ as both the Christian's ground of assurance and the paradigm case of resurrection. In verses 1–5 he points out that belief in Christ's resurrection was transmitted from the testimony of pre-Pauline apostolic witnesses, and handed on as a pre-Pauline creed. The terms for 'received' and 'handed on' (Gk, *parelabon* and *paredōka*) constitute technical terms for the transmission of a tradition. The OT had predicted the vindication of God's Servant. Peter and the other apostles were witnesses. In verse 6 Paul cites 500 further witnesses, and in verse 8 he refers to his own witness as that of an aborted foetus, when the raised Christ appeared to him on the road to Damascus. Admittedly W. Marxsen and Hans Conzelmann insist that 'he appeared' or 'he was seen' (Gk, *ōphthē*) means simply a non-physical notion of 'see', as when a student says 'I see' of a mathematical problem.[199] But W. Künneth, Wolfhart Pannenberg, and many others, argue that the word refers to physical sight. We must also not forget that these appearances concern simply the appearance of Christ *within the conditions of this world*. They do not concern experience of the post-ascension Christ.

From 15.12 and for the rest of the chapter Paul discusses the *credibility and intelligibility* of the resurrection of the dead. Eventually he will expound three principles concerning resurrection: (1) contrast with the earthly body; (2) continuity with it; and (3) transformation from this earthly existence. Meanwhile, Paul first considers the impossible consequences of denying the resurrection: 'your faith has been in vain' (v. 14). But, he argues, in fact Christ's resurrection has occurred, and is the pledge or first fruits (Gk, *aparchē*, v. 20), meaning 'more of the same kind to come'. 1 John agrees with Paul: 'When he [Christ] is revealed, we will be like him, for we will see him

---

199 W. Marxsen, *The Resurrection of Jesus of Nazareth* (Eng., Philadelphia, Pa.: Fortress Press, 1970); Hans Conzelmann, 'On the Analysis of the Confessional Formula in 1 Cor. 15.3–5', *Interpretation* 20 (1966), pp. 15–25.

as he is' (1 John 3.2). Elsewhere Paul speaks of the raised 'body' under the image of a 'house not made with hands' (2 Cor. 5.1), for which Christians long. Elsewhere Paul declares that God will bring 'with him [Christ] those who have died', and 'we will be with the Lord for ever' (1 Thess. 4.14, 17).

Paul now proceeds to address the *intelligibility* of the resurrection. He first suggests the analogy of the planted seed and its transformation into a flower or fruit (15.35–41). If you sow one species of flower, he suggests, another does not come up in its place. What we sow comes out of the earth in a different, even transformed, form. Similarly, each person who dies carries with him or her a unique store of memories, experiences, obligations and grounds for thanks or praise which are not interchangeable with another's. That person is raised, therefore, in a transformed mode, with this stable, recognizable, personhood also intact. Part of the huge contrast will be that weakness, constraints, all that hampers or constrains life, will be left behind. Paul adds, 'God gives it a body as he has chosen' (v. 38). One writer calls the unexpected tense 'an aorist of sovereignty'.

Nevertheless there is also recognizable *continuity* between the 'old' body and the new. Paul's analogies from the natural planting of seeds illustrated this. The third principle is that of *transformation*. Paul explains: 'What is sown is perishable, what is raised is imperishable. It is sown in dishonour, it is raised in glory. It is sown in weakness, it is raised in power. It is sown a physical body (Gk, *sōma psychikon*)' (15.42–44). Paul adds that the first body was characterized by 'Adam', but the second will be characterized by 'the man of heaven', i.e. Christ (v. 49). The NRSV translation of *psychikon sōma* and *sōma pneumatikon* is disappointing. *Psychikos* does not denote 'physical', but whatever stands in contrast to *pneumatikos*. It here means *ordinary body*. By contrast, *pneumatikon* means 'of the Spirit', i.e. animated, sustained and characterized by the Holy Spirit. This reflects the regular meaning in 1 Corinthians and Paul's normal use. The English word 'spiritual' remains too reminiscent of the dualism between material and immaterial, especially with a lower-case 's'. I have argued this for many years, and can so far find only Pannenberg and N. T. Wright adopting the correct translation.[200]

Paul amplifies this with a vision of the end. He explains, 'We will all be changed, in a moment, in the twinkling [i.e. blink] of an eye, at the last trumpet. For the trumpet will sound, and the dead will be raised imperishable, and we will be changed' (15.51–52). He is using the image of a sleeping army. Suddenly the trumpet sounds (a standard signal in the ancient

---

200 Anthony C Thiselton, *The First Epistle to the Corinthians: A Commentary on the Greek Text* (Grand Rapids: Mich.: Eerdmans and Carlisle: Paternoster, 2000), pp. 1, 276–81.

world), and the whole army springs awake, ready for action. Death has been swallowed up in victory. He adds another image or thought: 'Where, O death, is your sting? The sting of death is sin' (vv. 55–56). But if Christ has dealt with the problem of sin, the sting of death has been removed, and transformation into a new form of existence has only to pass through a *stingless* death. As Pannenberg suggests, it will be like the familiar experience of waking from sleep, to new opportunities and life.

The key principles thus remain. First, the resurrection of the dead comes about by *God's creative, transforming, power through Christ and the Spirit.* It is a work in which God as Trinity is involved. Second, it is *not mere resuscitation*, as it was for Lazarus (John 11.17–44). It is no mere parable, as in Ezekiel 37.1–14, or in John 11. It is a *transformed life*, characterized by the ongoing life of the Holy Spirit. The old has been left behind, but ahead will be unimaginable wonders and glory, in progressive, ever-new, experiences. Third, *transformation* constitutes the *bridge between continuity and contrast*.

Revelation

Revelation stands in contrast to human discovery. It denotes the belief that God speaks, and has disclosed himself. He addresses humankind, and has chosen not to remain isolated and silent. In Genesis God's first act after creation is to address humankind in person. Hence it is not surprising that revelation constitutes a central truth in Judaism, Christianity and Islam.

Even in Hinduism different traditions trace their roots to the *Vedas* (*c.* 1500–800 BC), which have the status of sacred scripture (*sruti*). The 108 texts in Sanskrit of the *Upanishads* (*c.* 800–500 BC) also count as Vedic scripture. H. H. Farmer (1892–1981) argued that in the theistic religions revelation underlines 'the essentially personal quality' of our relationship with God, and emphasizes 'the disjunction between *revelation* and *discovery*' (his italics).[201]

Karl Barth (1886–1968) stressed that Christianity stands or falls with God's self-revelation. Humankind does not 'construct God' by aspiring 'upward' from humanity to God. God first addresses humankind, and calls and redeems human beings. Barth declared, 'For me the Word of God is a *happening*, not a thing; [but] an event . . . a living reality' (his italics).[202] He continued, 'God is known through God, and through God alone'.[203] God's

---

201 H. H. Farmer, *The World and God* (London: Nisbet, 1935), p. 77; cf. pp. 77–91.
202 Barth, *Church Dogmatics*, vol. 2, pp. 26, 42.
203 Barth, *Church Dogmatics*, vol. 2, p. 179.

'knowability' is neither a human capacity nor a human right. Bultmann, Fuchs and Ebeling also speak of revelation as an event or a language-event. It may appear that this excludes philosophical reflection. But as a *response* to address, reflection plays an important part in the process of revelation.

In contrast to what is called a theology of the word, Wolfhart Pannenberg (1928–2014) and in part Oscar Cullmann (1902–99) focus on revelation *in history*, but history of two kinds. Pannenberg focuses *on public* history.[204] He writes, 'History is the most comprehensive horizon of Christian theology. All theological questions and answers are meaningful only within the framework of history, which God has with humanity . . . and with the whole creation.'[205] He also stresses, 'The one history . . . binds together the eschatological community of Jesus Christ and ancient Israel.'[206] This theme repeats one of the key contentions of Irenaeus in the second century.

Cullmann and the school of 'Biblical Theology' emphasized the 'sacred history' (*Heilsgeschichte*) of Israel and the Church. He expounds these notions in two books.[207] This division may be more apparent than real. For example, John Webster (1955–2016) stresses the uniqueness of the biblical writings, but in his book *The Domain of the Word* (2012), he argues that the medium of human words does not undermine 'God's providential ordering of all things'.[208]

There is, however, variation between theologians about what revelation amounts to. James Barr (1924–2006) has argued that the term *communication* more accurately reflects biblical thought than the term *revelation*, which is supposedly more limited.[209] F. Gerald Downing argued that the term *revelation* occurs relatively rarely in the biblical writings, although this view has been challenged.[210] We should have to exclude such words as 'spoke', 'promised', and many similar words. Thomas Aquinas (1224–74) distinguished between (1) revelation in the active sense of *God's deed* in imparting his self-communication and (2) the objective sense of a *deposit of truths* which resulted from it. He cites some relevant passages of

---

204 Wolfhart Pannenberg, *Basic Questions in Theology*, vol. 1 (London: SCM Press, 1970), pp. 15–95; *Systematic Theology*, vol. 1, pp. 189–258.

205 Pannenberg, *Basic Questions*, vol. 1, p. 15.

206 Pannenberg, *Basic Questions*, vol. 1, p. 25.

207 Oscar Cullmann, *Salvation in History* (London: SCM Press, 1967); and *Christ and Time* (London: SCM Press, 1951).

208 John Webster, *The Domain of the Word: Scripture and Theological Reason* (London and New York, N.Y.: Bloomsbury, 2012), pp. 14–17.

209 James Barr, *Old and New in Interpretation* (London: SCM Press, 1966), p. 88.

210 F. Gerald Downing, *Has Christianity a Revelation?* (London: SCM Press, 1964), pp. 20–125, 179.

Scripture, for example, Hebrews 1.1–2: 'God spoke . . . in many and various ways by the prophets . . . in these last days he has spoken to us by a Son . . .'

Nicholas Wolterstorff's (b. 1932) *Divine Discourse* shows that it is entirely rational and intelligible to claim that God speaks.[211] His explanation about deputized discourse helps to explain how the divine voice is mediated through human agents. He also speaks of performative language or speech-acts in everyday life, which we take for granted. Other philosophical traditions make similar points. In *Speak That I May See Thee*, Harold Stahmer, with the help of Walter Ong, shows how *irrational* it would be *not* to expect God to address humankind in language.[212] Johann G. Hamann (1730–88) also shows how speech is involved in the ultimate inseparability of human beings from the divine. The Jewish writers Martin Buber (1878–1966) and Franz Rosenzweig (1886–1928) argue, 'Revelation breaks into the world and transforms creation'.[213]

In the Catholic tradition Karl Rahner (1904–84) affirms that the self-communication of God 'reaches the goal and climax in Jesus Christ'.[214] He cites Isaiah 55.8, 'My thoughts are not your thoughts, nor are your ways my ways', to emphasize God's self-disclosure. Similarly Hans Urs von Balthasar (1905–88) addresses the necessity of revelation in *The Glory of the Lord*. He traces God's revelation of grace (Heb., *chesed*) through Amos, Hosea, Isaiah, Jeremiah and other prophets.[215]

On one side, the virtually united testimonies of believers all point to the need for revelation. God is not silent, but addresses humankind. On the other side, differences of interpretation abound. On these issues, philosophical reflection and philosophical clarification of language are required.

Sin and alienation

Sin is one of the few theological terms which people hesitate to use in everyday speech. But it is reductive to substitute the word *wrongdoing*,

---

211 Nicholas Wolterstorff, *Divine Discourse* (Cambridge: Cambridge University Press, 1995), throughout.

212 Harold Stahmer, *Speak That I May See Thee: The Religious Significance of Language* (New York, N.Y.: Macmillan, 1968), esp. pp. 1–63.

213 Franz Rosenzweig in Stahmer, *Speak That I May See Thee*, p. 153; cf. pp. 148–82, and Buber, pp. 183–212.

214 Karl Rahner, *Foundations of Christian Faith* (New York, N.Y.: Seabury Press and London: DLT, 1978), p. 176.

215 Hans Urs von Balthasar, *The Glory of the Lord: A Theological Aesthetics*, 7 vols (Edinburgh: T&T Clark, 1981–91), vol. 6, pp. 161, 254–98, 305–20, 363.

widely used in the media, because it presupposes that sin is an act which is 'done', in contrast to the biblical notion of an *attitude* and *state of being*. It is more accurate to speak of *misdirected desire, alienation* and *self-imposed bondage*. The shallowest of all substitute terms is *failure*, which includes only sins of omission. Among the biblical writers the term has little to do with mere ethics or moralism, but denotes *a turning away from God to self.*

Biblical Hebrew vocabulary conveys three ideas: (1) The verb *chātā'* conveys the notion of straying from the commands of the Lord (Lev. 4—5). If this term stood alone, the notion of sin as disobedience or failure might be said to stand, but it is part of a trio of terms. It occurs in Genesis 4.7; 18.20; Exodus 10.17; 32.32; Leviticus 4.23; Numbers 5.6; 12.11; Deuteronomy 9.18; and so on. (2) The second Hebrew verb is *pesha'*, *to rebel, to revolt* or *to become alienated*. It essentially denotes a *deliberate breach of relationship*. The verb occurs some 41 times in the OT, and the noun 93 times, and often relates to the covenant. It occurs, for example, in Exodus 23.21; 34.7; Leviticus 16.16, 21; Numbers 14.18; Job 7.21; and so on. The term is used not only in relation to God, but also of breaches in political alliances, social relations, and interpersonal friendships. Nationally Israel can become 'a rebellious nation' (Ezek. 2.3) or 'a brood of rebels' (Isa. 57.4, NIV). (3) The *resultant condition* which follows *pesha'* is often conveyed by *'āwen, iniquity*, wickedness, or *deception* or *distortion*. The noun occurs about 74 times in the OT. *'Āwen* has unsettling effects which bring harm, destruction, distortion or deception. God will banish those who commit it from his presence (Ps. 125.5). It is terrifying and deep-seated.

In the NT numerous words denote *sin*, not least because of its many aspects or dimensions. Paul speaks of *anomia*, lawlessness; *akatharsia*, impurity; *asebeia*, impiety; *adikia*, injustice; *planē*, error; *paratōma*, disobedience; *parabasis*, transgression; *hamartia*, sin. Paul is more concerned with the corporate and individual *condition* of sin in these multiple aspects, than with particular individual *acts* of sin. This partly reflects the legacy from apocalyptic, denoting the misery and bondage of humankind apart from grace and new creation. The universality of sin (Rom. 3.23) underlines human corporate solidarity under sin, sometimes referred to as 'this body of death' (Rom. 7.24).

Some have suggested that Paul sets out three versions of 'the fall': Romans 1.18–32; 5.12–21; and 7.11–25. He probably borrowed much in Romans 1.18–32 from the typical synagogue homily on the consequences of idolatry and immorality. The Wisdom of Solomon 14.18–31 provides one of several parallels. The main thrust, in Paul's thought, is that

Jews and Gentiles alike are characterized by fallenness. Romans 5.12–21 demonstrates human corporate liability. On this passage W. D. Davies comments that these verses do 'not aim at explaining the existence of sin'; but assert 'a connexion between the first man Adam's transgression and the sinfulness of the world'.[216]

Humankind, in effect, daily *endorses* Adam's attitude of sin, and shares in his liability. This is not simply Adam's 'fault', because everyone sins on his or her own account. Unlike the *Apocalypse of Ezra* (Esdras), Paul does not 'blame' Adam, but like 2 Baruch sees everyone as the Adam of oneself. In Romans 7.11–25 Paul expounds the seriousness of the human plight as rendering the law powerless as a remedy. The references to 'sin . . . deceived me' (v. 11) and 'I do not do what I want' (v. 15) are *not* biographical or autobiographical accounts, but Paul's reflection on the plight of the Jews and the whole of humanity.

Indeed in a highly influential article Krister Stendahl (1921–2008) has shown that there is much widespread misunderstanding about Paul's personal sense of sin or guilt. He readily admits: 'No one could ever deny that *hamartia*, sin, is a crucial word in Paul's terminology, especially in . . . Romans. Romans 1—3 sets out to show that *all* – both Jews and Gentiles – have sinned.' But he adds, 'It is much harder to gauge how Paul experienced the power of sin in his life.' When we consider his genuinely autobiographical statements, he asserts: 'I know nothing against myself' (1 Cor. 4.4), i.e. he has nothing on his conscience about his ministry; and 'as to righteousness under the law, blameless' (Phil. 3.6). Indeed Stendahl claims that Paul has a 'robust' conscience.[217]

To return to the three 'Pauline versions' of the 'fall', it is well known that C. H. Dodd (1884–1973) described Romans 1.18–22 as a process of cause and effect in a moral universe. Many have rejected this as an unduly impersonal interpretation of Paul's phrase 'the wrath of God'. It is probably more accurate to speak of sin as bringing *internal* consequences, or as bringing its own penalty. Similarly Romans 5.12–20 provides an account of the corporate, trans-individual consequences of sin, in the context of explaining how grace through the cross of Christ can likewise be extended to humankind in a parallel but greater way. But the generosity of solidarity with Christ far outweighs any issue of 'unfairness' by virtue of

---

216 W. D. Davies, *Paul and Rabbinic Judaism* (London: SPCK, 1955), p. 31.

217 Krister Stendahl, 'Paul and the Introspective Conscience of the West', *Harvard Theological Review* 56 (1963), pp. 199–215; and Stendahl, *Paul among Jews and Gentiles* (Philadelphia, Pa.: Fortress Press, 1976), pp. 78–96.

our solidarity with Adam. It also indicates the possibility of *structural* evil, rather than simply corporate or individual guilt. On Romans 7.11–25, a multitude of writers agree that this is *not a personal autobiography*. So-called 'original' sin is better expressed as humankind's being 'under the power of sin' (Rom. 3.9) than any genetic theory. Romans 7.14 speaks of our being 'sold under sin', and Romans 6.6 and 6.20 describe us as 'slaves' of sin. When the Reformers spoke of 'total depravity', they were expressing Paul's theme that 'nothing good dwells within me' (Rom. 7.18), i.e. the bondage of sin taints every aspect of human life, even if we seek to do 'good'.

Oscar Cullmann (1902–99) argued that although Christ has in principle destroyed sin, sin still mars the life of the Christian. He writes: 'The hope of the final victory is so much the more vivid because of the unshakably firm conviction that the battle that decided the victory has already taken place.'[218] But meanwhile, Christians still sin, just as they still die: 'The time tension is manifest in the Church through the continuances of sin, which nevertheless has already been defeated by the Spirit.'[219]

The Gospels and Johannine writings confirm this. The prologue of John affirms that light shines in the darkness, and 'the darkness did not overcome it' (John 1.5). The light illumines everyone, or (better) sheds light upon them (*phōtizō*) in judgment, as well as grace (1.19). Before the discovery of Qumran in 1948, Bultmann and others claimed that the dualisms of light and darkness, truth and falsehood, and Spirit and flesh, reflected Greek or Gnostic sources of a relatively late date. But with the discovery of the same dualisms in the Dead Sea Scrolls, this view is no longer tenable. In John, humankind stood in need of new birth (or birth from above; John 3.3–6); it stood in need of salvation (3.16); it needed living water, which was ever-fresh and ongoing (4.14); needed to be transformed from death to life (5.24); and it needed the living bread (6.35). Sin is a quality of life which leads to death, slavery and blindness (John 8.24, 34; 9.25). Above all, sin in John is distinctively lack of trust or faith in the person of Christ (John 16.9; cf. 15.21–22). 1 John asserts, 'If we say that we have no sin, we deceive ourselves, and the truth is not in us' (1.8). Christians still sin, but do not habitually sin as an expression of their new life.

In the Synoptic Gospels, Jesus' proclamation of the kingdom of God involves repentance or 'turning' (Mark 1.15). Parables often depict the rescue of sinners through everyday imagery (e.g. Luke 15.7–10). In Acts, early Christian preaching calls for repentance (Acts 2.38; 3.19). It also proclaims

---

218 Cullmann, *Christ and Time*, p. 87.
219 Cullmann, *Christ and Time*, p. 155.

the need for 'universal restoration' (3.21). The 'Lord's Prayer', enjoined by Jesus, includes 'forgive us our debts' (Matt. 6.12), and 'may your kingdom come'. In the Epistle to the Hebrews, Jesus is the high priest who 'made purification for our sins' (Heb. 1.3); makes 'a sacrifice of atonement for . . . sins' (2.17); and offers 'gifts and sacrifices for sins' (5.1; cf. 7.27).

Over the centuries *historical interpretations* show how basic concepts of sin have varied. Irenaeus (*c.* 130 – *c.* 200) viewed sin as *inadequate growth and maturity*. On Adam, he writes: 'Humankind was little, being but a child. It had to grow and reach full maturity . . . Its mind was not yet fully mature, and thus humanity was easily led astray by the deceiver.'[220] This view may invite the critical question of whether he does justice to the term 'image of God'. The fall, in effect, supposedly achieves an *educational* purpose; it was not an unmixed evil. Clement of Alexandria (*c.* 150 – *c.* 215) also regarded sin primarily as *ignorance and irrationality*: 'The sources of all sin are but two, ignorance and inability.'[221]

Tertullian (*c.* 150 – *c.* 225) was the classic advocate of traducianism, the notion that each human being inherits his or her 'soul' from Adam. Allegedly this derived from such passages as Romans 5.12–20 and 1 Corinthians 15.22: 'As all die in Adam'. But it may owe as much to the Stoic view of the soul (Lat., *anima*) as a quasi-material substance. He contradicts himself, however, for while he insists on following only the Bible and the apostolic rule of faith, in practice he borrows extensively from Stoic thought. Each generation, he claims, is an offshoot (*tradux*) of the previous one. Sin is hereditary, transmitting the qualities of fallen Adam to all of his descendants.

Origen (*c.* l85 – *c.* 254), like his teacher Clement, stressed freedom of the will, and interpreted the account of Adam's sin and Eden as purely allegorical.[222] The 'fall' occurred before the creation of the world. Athanasius (*c.* 296–373) showed caution about how much we can infer from biblical texts, which primarily concern Christ and the gospel. He explicitly *rejected* the view of Irenaeus that Adam before the fall was immature, like a child. After all, before the fall, he had intercourse with God and bore his image. Hence he almost reaches a doctrine of 'original righteousness'. Sin brings *corruption* (Gk, *phthora*). Ambrose (*c.* 338–97) provided a stepping-stone in the Western Church to Augustine. It is crucial, as we saw in the biblical section, that sin is viewed *as a state or condition, not simply*

---

220 Irenaeus, *Demonstration of the Apostolic Teaching*, 12.
221 Clement of Alexandria, *Stromata*, 7.16.101 (Eng., *ANF*, vol. 2, p. 553).
222 Origen, *De Principiis*, 4.1.16 (Eng., *ANF*, vol. 4, p. 365).

as an act. For Ambrose, sin is a *state of human nature.* On Romans 5.12 he stressed, as Paul did, the solidarity and unity of humankind. He also states: 'Death is alike to all . . . although through the sin of one alone, yet it passed upon all.'[223]

Augustine (354–430) speculated about the state of humankind before the fall, ascribing to 'Adam' the possibility of sin. This *equipoise of choice* between good and evil was *lost* at the fall. He states, 'The enemy held me and thence made a chain for me, and bound me.'[224] Sin and the sinful state have *become universal.* On Romans 7.7–25, Augustine argued that sin became ingrained in human nature. N. P. Williams commented, 'For the first time in the history of Christian thought we meet the epoch-making phrase *originale peccatum,* meaning sinful quality, which is born with us and is inherent in our constitution.'[225] Humankind as such constitutes a single corporate *massa peccati,* or 'lump of sin'. Williams calls this 'the fully rounded . . . "African" or "twice born" type of the Fall-doctrine.'[226] He is hostile to Augustine's teaching.

One notorious problem concerns Augustine's reading of Romans 5.12, 'because all have sinned' (Gk, *eph' hō pantes hēmarton*), where he depends on the Latin Vulgate *in quo,* 'in whom', i.e. Adam.[227] In the view of Pelagius (354–420), freedom brings responsibility only when it brings an equal opportunity to choose good or evil. For Augustine it denotes freedom to express the *desire of the will,* without external compulsion. Hence if the heart is corrupted, sin may become an unconscious expression of the will.

The dominant thinker of the Middle Ages was Thomas Aquinas (1225–74). Much of his work constitutes a reinterpretation of Augustine. He explicitly appeals to Augustine that sin brings its own punishments.[228] Death, he concludes, is the punishment for sin. Sin is 'committed by habit', and 'this corrupt disposition is either a habit acquired by custom, or a sickly condition . . . The will, of its own accord, may tend toward evil.'[229]

Luther (1483–1546) and Calvin (1509–64) underlined Augustine's doctrine. Writing on the consequences of the fall, Calvin says: 'This is

---

223 Athanasius, *On the Belief in the Resurrection,* 2.6 (Eng., *NPNF,* ser. 2, vol. 10, p. 175).

224 Augustine, *Confessions,* 8.10.11.

225 N. P. Williams, *The Ideas of the Fall and Original Sin* (London: Longmans, Green, 1929), p. 237.

226 Williams, *Ideas of the Fall,* p. 323.

227 Augustine, *On the Merits and Remission of Sin,* 1.10 (Eng., *NPNF,* ser. 2, vol. 5, p. 9).

228 Aquinas, *Summa Theologiae,* I.II, qu. 71–80, qu. 81–5 (on original sin), and qu. 86–9 (on the effects of sin); cf. also Augustine, *On Nature and Grace,* 67.

229 Aquinas, *Summa Theologiae,* I.II, qu. 80, art. 3.

the hereditary corruption to which early Christian writers gave the name "Original Sin", meaning by the term the depravation of a nature formerly good and pure.'[230] Calvin continues, 'The orthodox . . . laboured to show that we . . . bring an innate corruption from every womb . . . "I was shapen in iniquity . . ." (Ps. 51.5) . . . All of us . . . come into the world tainted with the contagion of sin . . . in God's sight defiled' (*Institutes*, 2.1.5).[231] His reference then to 'all the parts of the soul' explains what the Reformers meant by *total depravity*. It means not the impossibility of ever aiming at good, but that *every* part of humanity as a totality was tainted by sin. By contrast Friedrich Schleiermacher (1768–1834) regarded sin primarily as an inadequacy of God-consciousness. The deepest problem is his typically nineteenth-century concern with 'development'. Albrecht Ritschl (1822–89), however, sought to reinstate the corporate and communal character of sin. Sin is whatever is contrary to the kingdom of God. In Frederick R. Tennant (1866–1957) we find yet another contrast. He provided a philosophical, empirical and individualist account of sin. 'Adam' becomes a wholly mythological or symbolic figure. In essence sin is described in exclusively *moralistic* or *ethical* terms, which wholly falls short of the biblical concepts.

Karl Barth (1886–1968) regarded human sin as alienation from God and pride, in the sense of trust in the self, rather than finding one's security in God. Further, what sin amounts to must be assessed in the light of Jesus Christ: 'Jesus is man as God willed and created him.'[232] Sin is revealed, he continued, as a human's

> personal act and guilt . . . his arrogant attempt to be his own master, provider and comforter, his unhallowed lust for what is not his own, the falsehood, hatred and pride in which he is enmeshed in relation to his neighbour, the stupidity to which he is self-condemned . . .[233]

Similarly Emil Brunner (1889–1966) writes: 'Through sin man has lost . . . his God-given nature.'[234] Like Barth, he perceived sin as the assertion of human independence over against God. Reinhold Niebuhr (1892–1971) in his powerful *Moral Man and Immoral Society* showed that human sin is more pernicious in groups than as individuals. He wrote, for example, 'the family may become a means of self-aggrandisement'.[235]

---

230 Calvin, *Institutes*, 2.1.5, vol. 1, p. 214.
231 Calvin, 2.1.5, vol. 1, p. 214; cf. also sect. 9.
232 Barth, *Church Dogmatics*, III/2, sect. 43, p. 50.
233 Barth, *Church Dogmatics*, III/3, sect. 50.3, p. 305.
234 Emil Brunner, *Man in Revolt* (London: Lutterworth Press, 1939), p. 94.
235 Reinhold Niebuhr, *Moral Man and Immoral Society* (London: SCM Press, 1932–63), p. 47.

Karl Rahner (1904–84) perceived the essence of sin as 'rejection of God'. He did not reject the *term* 'original sin', but sought to retain the basic *idea* without its unfortunate baggage. Wolfhart Pannenberg (1928–2014) realistically uses the term '*misery*' rather than 'lostness' or other terms, to denote humankind's sinful condition. He writes: 'The term "misery" sums up our detachment from God . . . The term "alienation" has a similar breadth.'[236] Emphatically, he states: 'The decay of the doctrine of original sin led to the anchoring of the concept of sin in acts of sin, and finally the concept was reduced to the individual act.'[237] The Bible and Augustine, he says, remind us of sin's structural, corporate and destructive effects.

Theodicy

Few pastoral problems are as acute as the problem of evil and suffering. If God is both sovereign and loving, why does he permit evil and suffering to occur in the world? It appears to be part of human nature to cry out, 'Why has this happened to me?' when tragedy or suffering hits life, but hardly ever to ask, 'Why?' or 'What have we done to deserve this?', when life is blessed with health or prosperity. Some suggest that the problem of evil can be addressed only when we ask about the problem of *good*. Why not ask, 'Why has this good happened to me?' Some insist that evil is a personal punishment, and also that good is a personal reward. But this would undermine what we have noted about God's love and sheer grace. This answer also contradicts the reply of Jesus about those who were killed when the tower of Siloam fell on them (Luke 13.2–5).

The biblical material gives us several examples of deep experiences of suffering, ranging from Job, Ecclesiastes and the Psalms to the suffering and death of Jesus. Job reflects ironically on the gift of life 'to one in misery . . . to the bitter in soul, who longs for death' (Job 3.20–21). Job 3.3 declares, 'Let the day perish on which I was born.' The writer of Ecclesiastes concedes, 'I hated life' (2.17); Psalm 73.21, I was 'embittered'; Jesus cried, 'My God, my God, why have you forsaken me?' (Mark 15.34). *Evil is real*, as biblical writers recognize.

The Greek philosopher Epicurus (341–271 BC) was probably the first to formulate the dilemma, although it is usually expressed in the form quoted by David Hume (1711–76). Hume asks, 'Is [God] willing to prevent evil, but not able? Then he is impotent. Is he able, but not willing? Then he is

---

236 Pannenberg, *Systematic Theology*, vol. 2, p. 179.
237 Pannenberg, *Systematic Theology*, vol. 2, p. 234.

malevolent. Is he both able and willing? Whence, then, is evil?'[238] We may have radically to qualify what we mean by the omnipotence and love of God, or else qualify the nature of evil. The Christian religion, like Islam and Judaism, cannot relegate the problem to a dualistic world-view, as if all evil came from a rival power, equivalent to the Gnostic demiurge. It does not solve the problem to ascribe evil to Satan, or 'monotheism' would not genuinely mean monotheism.

Key issues include, first, what do we mean by God's being *sovereign*? As Richard Swinburne (b. 1934) insists, God's sovereignty cannot facilitate acts which are *logically* self-contradictory. God 'cannot' (*logically*) create a square circle, cannot tell lies and cannot change the past.[239] Second, What do we mean by divine 'goodness'? If God were constantly to intervene, would it manifest his goodness, or would it make free will impossible? Would humans then become robots? In Job, Satan says, 'Does Job fear (serve) you for nothing?' He implies that Job is good simply for the sake of reward. The third key issue is whether human happiness constitutes the ultimate goal in life. Is our ultimate goal happiness or holiness? Is all 'evil' only evil *if it serves some 'higher' goal*?

First, we enquire into what God's sovereignty really means. Some have attended prayers in which a devout believer prays that an event 'may have happened'. Does sovereignty mean ability to *change the past*? There must also be *moral* limits. God 'cannot' lie, because this would contradict the constraints imposed by his own character as faithful and true. There is a difference between *logical* and *empirical impossibility*. A schoolboy question was allegedly: 'Can God make a stone so big and heavy that he can't lift it?' Can he make a square circle? In terms of *logic*, this would be impossible. From a Deist viewpoint, God cannot intervene in 'laws' or regularities which relate to medical conditions in the natural world. On the other hand, there are events, such as the resurrection of Christ, which appear on special occasions to modify generally predicted laws. The Bible generally recounts miracles in special redemptive eras: those of Moses, Elijah and Christ. So the majority of informed Christians suggest not that God *cannot* modify such regularities of nature, but that he chooses *normally* not to do so. The debate about miracles is a separate topic, but is largely related to the fulfilment or non-fulfilment of the kingdom of God, i.e. in what sense it is present or future. If, in the message of Jesus, the kingdom of God is still

---

238 David Hume, *Dialogue Concerning Natural Religion* (New York, N.Y.: Harper, 1948 (1779)), part 10, p. 66.
239 Richard Swinburne, *The Coherence of Theism* (Oxford: Clarendon Press, 1977), pp. 149–58.

in *process* of being fulfilled, then at present, as Oscar Cullmann (1902–99) argued, 'Christians still sin and still die'.[240]

Medical or therapeutic examples remind us of the major distinction between natural and moral evil. Natural evils arise from the natural processes of the world; moral evils arise from a decision to embark on a course of action by an act of human will. J. S. Mill (1806–73) writes, 'Nearly all the things for which men are hanged or imprisoned for doing to one another are Nature's everyday performances.'[241] Whether or not this is an exaggeration, it is noticeable that whereas 50 years ago the 'Fact and Faith' films were regularly shown with a message of divine purpose in nature, today such films as those by David Attenborough equally show birds, beasts and insects preying on one another. Alfred, Lord Tennyson wrote that while man trusted God as love, 'Nature, red in tooth and claw . . . shriek'd against his creed'.

Several 'replies' have been made to this. The Catholic mystic Simone Weil (1908–43) gloried in the wild and dark beauty of a storm at sea, but acknowledged that this may bring shipwrecks. In a more classic philosophical mode, Augustine (354–430) and Aquinas (1225–74) appeal to what Arthur Lovejoy called 'the Principle of Plenitude'.[242] Lovejoy argued that the created universe contains the fullest variety of creatures from the highest to the lowest, and that this is a richer and better universe than one consisting only of the higher creatures. Thus Augustine asked, 'What is more beautiful than a fire? What is more useful than the heat and comfort? . . . Yet nothing can cause more distress than the burns inflicted by fire.'[243] In this sense 'difference' can potentially become a root of evil. Similarly Aquinas declared, 'The wisdom of God is the cause of the distinction of things . . . the cause of their inequality . . . Species seem to be arranged by degrees.'[244]

This is sometimes related to an argument which may seem needlessly to inhibit God's almightyness. Edgar S. Brightman (1883–1952) spoke of a 'finite God'.[245] William H. Vanstone (1923–99) compared God with an artist who must 'go with the grain and limitations' of his materials.[246] Augustine and Calvin (1509–64) did not hold this view of the sovereignty of God.

---

240 Cullmann, *Christ and Time*, pp. 69–93.

241 John Stuart Mill, *Three Essays on Religion* (London: Longmans, Green, 1875), p. 28.

242 Arthur Lovejoy, *The Great Chain of Being* (Cambridge, Mass.: Harvard University Press, 1936).

243 Augustine, *City of God*, 12.4.

244 Aquinas, *Summa Theologiae*, I, qu. 47, art. 2, reply.

245 Edgar Brightman, *A Philosophy of Religion* (New York, N.Y.: Skeffington and Prentice Hall, 1940), pp. 157–8.

246 W. H. Vanstone, *Love's Endeavor, Love's Expense* (1st edn, 1977; London: DLT, 2007).

Nevertheless this approach has helped many to cope with the problem of evil and suffering, not least because of its insights into the 'costly' nature of the love of God.

Augustine and Aquinas also deploy what philosophers call the free-will defence argument, in which the *possibility* of evil is bound up with the capacity of the human will to choose freely. Evil, Augustine believed, arises from a wilful turning of the self from desire of the highest good. Granted that God's gifts are good, evil comes when we misuse them. Certainly evil is not, as the Manichaeans claimed, a positive entity in its own right. The whole creation is good, but humankind can abuse it, and misunderstand its function and purpose. Augustine wrote, 'An evil will is the cause of all evils'.[247] In the *Confessions* he declared, 'Free will is the cause of our doing evil, and . . . [God's] just judgment is the cause of having to suffer from its consequences'.[248] He also recalled, 'I had gone astray of [my] own free will and fallen into error'.[249] Humankind substitutes its own private good for the highest good of God's will.

Clearly this does not imply that human freedom is the cause of evil, but the cause of only *potential* evil, its *possibility*. If humankind is free to sin, moral evil is *potentially inevitable*. Otherwise God would (in theory) need to programme robot-like humans who would *always* choose *only* the right or good. Thomas Aquinas endorsed this argument. Evil has no causal efficacy of its own. Aquinas writes, 'God allows evils to happen in order to bring a greater good therefrom; hence it is written (Rom. 5.20): "Where sin abounded, grace did much more abound"'.[250]

In modern philosophy, some have questioned this 'free-will defence' argument. J. L. Mackie (1917–81) insists, 'All forms of the free-will defence fail'.[251] He claims that God *could* supposedly have created human beings who *always freely choose* to do the right. Much of this argument depends on analogies with freedom and predictability. We may construct the following hypothetical situation: Tom lives in a fairly dreary town, where most young people of his age have left school at the first opportunity, and speak of nothing but TV soaps, sport, holidays and clothes. However, next door lives Mary. Like Tom, she enjoys higher education,

---

247 Augustine, *On Free Will*, 3.17.48.

248 Augustine, *Confessions*, 7.3.5 (Eng., Augustine, *Confessions and Echiridion*, ed. A. C. Outler, LCC, vol. 7 (Philadelphia, Pa.: Westminster Press, 1965, p. 137).

249 Augustine, *Confessions*, 4.15.26, p. 91.

250 Aquinas, *Summa Theologiae*, III, qu. 1, art. 3, reply to obj. 3.

251 J. L. Mackie, *The Miracle of Theism* (Oxford: Clarendon Press, 1982), p. 176.

classical music and politics. Gradually their common interests bring them together. One day Tom freely chooses to propose marriage, and Mary freely chooses to accept. Everyone, including both sets of parents, says: 'We knew it would happen.' Mackie and others argue that what was inevitable was freely chosen.

Alvin Plantinga (b. 1932) has provided the most successful 'reply' to Mackie. Plantinga formulates an argument which at first is negative, and concerns *logical*, not empirical (or actual), *necessity*. He argues, 'It is possible that God, even being omnipotent, *could* not [*logical* 'could not'] create a world with free creatures, who never choose evil.'[252] It is *logically possible*, however, for an 'omnibenevolent' God to create a world which contains evil, 'if moral goodness requires free moral creatures'. Plantinga is not so much concerned with what is true, as with what is *logically possible* or *logically impossible*. Freedom, he argues, is *a presupposition* of people's capacity to perform moral good. To create moral good without the *possibility* of moral evil is *not logically possible* even for an omnipotent God. Robert Adams is quoted as saying that 'Plantinga has solved the problem'.[253] Mackie himself and Antony Flew argue that he succeeds only if we hold an 'incompatibilist' view of freedom, i.e. the doctrine that freedom and determinism cannot both be true. Yet Plantinga cannnot be called 'a hard determinist', nor 'a libertarian'. He spends considerable time in elucidating the ideas of freedom and the sovereignty of God.

Of the three supposedly incompatible realities, namely the sovereignty of God, the love of God and the presence of evil in the world, each has been qualified logically in such a way as to minimize a stark paradox. Evil is still real, but is seen as part of a bigger picture. Divine goodness and love are real, but have undergone *logical* constraints. Finally, Plantinga argues that just because we do not *know* of a *ready* 'answer' to the problem of evil, this does not imply that there is none, *in the inscrutable counsel of God*. Why should we assume that God's self-revelation tells us *everything* about God and the universe?

As we have noted above, Simone Weil's witness was primarily one of sheer acceptance of God's ways, even if she also spoke out against

---

252 Chad Meister, *Introducing Philosophy of Religion* (New York, N.Y. and London: Routledge, 2009), p. 133; cf. Alvin Plantinga, *God, Freedom and Evil* (Grand Rapids, Mich.: Eerdmans, 1977), pp. 29–55; and Plantinga, 'Free Will Defense', in Max Black (ed.), *Philosophy in America* (Ithaca, N.Y.: Cornell University and London: Allen & Unwin, 1965); and Plantinga, *The Nature of Necessity* (Oxford: Clarendon Press, 1974), pp. 165–90.

253 Daniel Howard-Snyder and John O'Leary-Hawthorne, 'Transworld Sanctity and Plantinga's Free Will Defense', *International Journal of Philosophy of Religion* 44 (1998), pp. 1–28.

'humiliation' by human oppression.[254] Other writers who adopt this more existential approach include Terrence Tilley, F. Dostoevsky and Elie Wiesel in his autobiographical experiences of the Holocaust in *Night* (1969). Jürgen Moltmann (b. 1946) recounts part of Wiesel's experience, citing the question of a youth in his death-throes: 'Where is God?' Moltmann regards his answer, 'He is hanging on the gallows', as a rabbinic equivalent to the Christian response, 'God is hanging on the cross'.[255]

We must also cite John Hick's (1922–2012) book *Evil and the God of Love*. He describes his approach as the 'minority report' in Christian theology, to which Irenaeus and Schleiermacher belong. Rather than looking *back* to the fall with Augustine and Aquinas, Hick looks *forwards* to the end, with its goal of maturity and holiness. He declares, 'The *telos* [goal] of man's nature consists in a relationship to God.'[256] Evil has a part to play in achieving *maturity of character*. Hick borrows the term 'soul-making' theodicy from Keats.

For ordinary Christians, this means that evil and suffering may be endured as *an opportunity for growth and holiness*. Austin Farrer, especially in his *Love Almighty and Ills Unlimited*, stresses the redemptive and eschatological nature of God's providence and grace.[257]

Whether we should drive a sharp wedge between the so-called Augustinian and Irenaean approaches may be doubted. Pastorally each approach discussed above offers something constructive to say to those who pass, or have passed, through suffering or conflict with evil.

Trinity, Holy

The doctrine of the Holy Trinity is much more practical and simple than popular opinion often seems to suggest. Three factors help to make this clear. First, Gregory of Nyssa and Gregory of Nazianzus argued convincingly that the Trinity has *nothing whatever to do with mathematical numerals*. Numerals apply only to created, finite, objects or people. Second, Jürgen Moltmann, Wolfhart Pannenberg, and especially Eugene Rogers, have urged that the biblical foundations of the doctrine expound it in terms of a *narrative* of God's activity as Father, Son and Holy Spirit. This has been

---

254 Simone Weil, *Waiting for God* (London: Routledge, 1974 (1939)).

255 Jürgen Moltman, *The Crucified God* (London: SCM Press, 1974) pp. 273–4; cf. Elie Wiesel, *Night* (New York, N. Y.: Hill & Wang, 1960 and 1969), pp. 75–6.

256 John Hick, *Evil and the God of Love* (London: Macmillan, 1966), p. 16.

257 Austin Farrer, *Love Almighty and Ills Unlimited* (New York, N.Y. Doubleday and London: Collins, 1962), esp. ch. 7.

called the *narrative approach* to the Trinity. Third, Wesley Hill builds on the approaches of Pannenberg, Francis Watson, Richard Bauckham and John Zizioulas, to show that neither God the Father, nor God the Son, nor God the Holy Spirit can be understood, even in Paul, without presupposing an *implied relation to the other Persons*. The second and third approaches appeal to a *relational* concept of God, Jesus and the Holy Spirit.

A further, fourth factor is the recognition since the Cappadocian Fathers that each person of the Holy Trinity is fully involved in our creation, redemption and destiny. Further, in particular, prayer can be understood as a divine dialogue, which is *prompted by the Holy Spirit*, normally addressed *to God the Father*, and mediated *through Jesus Christ*. In Romans 8.26–27 Paul declares.

> The Spirit helps us in our weakness; for we do not know how to pray as we ought, but that very Spirit intercedes with sighs too deep for words. And God, who searches the heart, knows what is the mind of the Spirit, because the Spirit intercedes for the saints according to the will of God.

On the first of these four factors, it would not help to explain the Trinity in terms of the numerals 'three' and 'one'. Gregory of Nyssa (*c.* 330–95) stressed this in a treatise called 'On "Not Three Gods"'. He argued that the use of numerals may well denote the different identities of three finite people, such as Peter, James and John, but this is quite different from the use of 'three persons of the Holy Trinity'.[258] He further wrote,

> The Father does not do anything by himself in which the Son does not work co-jointly, or again the Son has no special operation apart from the Holy Spirit . . . Every operation . . . has its origin from the Father, and proceeds through the Son, and is perfected in the Holy Spirit.[259]

Similarly Gregory of Nazianzus (*c.* 330–90) declared both that numbers are irrelevant, and that each person of the Holy Trinity was fully involved in the activity of the other two persons. Even 'God is one' may well refer to exclusive allegiance, exclusive worship and absolute sovereignty, not to the numeral 'one'.

Our second key factor, the *narrative* approach to the Trinity, enables us to be freed from the mistaken notion that this doctrine is a fourth-century complicated concoction unknown in the NT. The simplest accounts of Trinitarian narrative occur in the life of Jesus. All four Gospels recount

---

258 Gregory of Nyssa, 'On "Not Three Gods"', 3 (Eng., *NPNF*, ser. 2, vol. 5, p. 331).
259 Gregory of Nyssa, 'On "Not Three Gods"', 3 (Eng., *NPNF*, ser. 2, vol. 5, p. 334).

how the Holy Spirit descended upon Jesus in visible form, as if in the likeness of a dove. So the narrative is already about both Jesus and the Holy Spirit. All four Gospels record that God spoke as Father, saying, 'This is my Son, the Beloved, with whom I am well pleased'. It is therefore a narrative about the joint acting together of God the Father, God the Son and God the Holy Spirit. The account of the baptism of Jesus would not make sense if any of the three persons of the Trinity were omitted (Matt. 3.3–17; Mark 1.9–11; Luke 3.21–22; John 1.32–34).

Probably the most detailed account of the three persons of the Trinity acting together in the baptism of Jesus comes from Eugene F. Rogers.[260] He writes,

> The baptism of Jesus is primarily to be understood as an entrance Trinitarian event . . . It is an event in which the Spirit bears witness to the love between the Father and the Son. In the baptismal interaction, the Father expresses his love . . . The Spirit hovers over the waters of the Jordan . . . And Jesus receives the love and witness in a way that other human beings can participate in . . . to accomplish its potential for initiating human beings into the tri-union life.[261]

Moltmann (b. 1926) makes exactly the same point. He declares (his italics): '*The New Testament talks about God by proclaiming in narrative the relationships of the Father, the Son and the Spirit, which are relationships of fellowship and open to the world.*'[262] He exemplifies this first with reference to the baptism and call of Jesus.[263] Under the same heading he considers the sending of the Son and the surrender of the Son at the cross. Rogers also illustrates the sending of the Son with reference to the annunciation and birth of Jesus. God the Father shows his favour to the Virgin Mary, and the Holy Spirit rests upon her to initiate the birth of Jesus.[264] Like most other writers, he shows the Trinitarian work of the resurrection of Jesus. In Romans 8.11 Paul declares, 'If the Spirit of him who raised Jesus from the dead dwells in you, he who raised Christ from the dead will give life to your mortal bodies also through his Spirit that dwells in you.' Rogers quotes Robert Jenson as calling this 'the most remarkable Trinitarian passage in the New Testament', and part of the Trinitarian logic of

---

260 Eugene F. Rogers, *After the Spirit* (London: SCM Press, 2006), pp. 135–74.
261 Rogers, *After the Spirit*, pp. 136–7.
262 Jürgen Moltmann, *The Trinity and the Kingdom of God* (London: SCM Press, 1981), p. 54 (his italics).
263 Moltmann, *The Trinity and the Kingdom of God*, pp. 65–71.
264 Rogers, *After the Spirit*, pp. 98–134.

Romans 8.[265] David Yeago and Sarah Coakley (b. 1951) have also made expanded comments about this verse.

Perhaps more speculatively, Rogers includes the Transfiguration among the narrative examples of Trinitarian activity. The Holy Spirit has a constant role in glorifying Jesus; and Jesus explicitly obeys the Father's will.[266] The Spirit, he suggests, transfigures Jesus, just as he will transfigure Christians. Pannenberg (1928–2014) also makes much of the narrative portrayal of the Holy Trinity in the earthly life of Jesus, as well as in his resurrection. Indeed he also argues that the very identity of Jesus depends on his relation to God the Father and to the Holy Spirit. He introduces the subject by declaring: 'The words "God" and "Father" are not just time-bound concepts from which we can detach the true content of the message.'[267] He adds, 'The Spirit of God is either presupposed or expressly mentioned as the medium of the communion of Jesus with the Father.'[268] We cannot fully understand the identity of Jesus without understanding something of God the Father and the Holy Spirit.

We are already beginning to introduce our third and fourth key factors. Wesley Hill has expounded them most fully in *Paul and the Trinity* (2015).[269] Hill cites Francis Watson, who declared, 'God [is] defined in relation to Jesus'; or more fully, 'Jesus is integral to God's own identity, and this is a statement both about who God is, and about who Jesus is. Paul's understanding of deity is ... relational in form'.[270] In effect echoing Pannenberg, Hill comments, 'It was obvious that "Father" implies a corresponding "Son", and vice-versa.'[271]

Hill's most distinctive work concerned his careful exegesis and linguistic examination of relational texts concerning the Trinity in Paul. He carefully examines Romans 4.24 and 4.5, which he regards as identity markers of God and Christ in their mutual interrelation.[272] He then carefully examines Romans 8.11, which he defines as 'Christ-shaped divine *telos*'.[273] In his careful examination of grammatical and syntactical forms he concludes

265 Rogers, *After the Spirit*, p. 97.
266 Rogers, *After the Spirit*, p. 175; cf. pp. 172–99.
267 Pannenberg, *Systematic Theology*, vol. 1, p. 263.
268 Pannenberg, *Systematic Theology*, vol. 1, p. 266.
269 Wesley Hill, *Paul and the Trinity: Persons, Relations, and the Pauline Letters* (Grand Rapids, Mich.: Eerdmans, 2015).
270 Hill, *Paul and the Trinity*, p. 29; Francis Watson, 'The Triune Identity', *Journal for the Study of the New Testament* 80 (2000), pp. 111–12; cf. pp. 99–124.
271 Hill, *Paul and the Trinity*, p. 33.
272 Hill, *Paul and the Trinity*, pp. 54–60.
273 Hill, *Paul and the Trinity*, p. 61.

that this passage is closely parallel with Romans 4.17 and 4.24. He then considers Galatians 1.1, which he considers to be 'a personal mark of God's identity' as one who raised Jesus from the dead and is called 'Father'.[274] Hill also undertakes a careful exegetical rereading of Philippians 2.6–11, and 1 Corinthians 8.6 and 15.24–28.[275] His discussion also interacts with Gunton, Zizioulas and Lossky on relationality. Perhaps the one surprise is his lack of interaction with Pannenberg.

Hill acknowledges that the 'intricate fourth-century debates' similarly turned on relationality, but it is not his aim to pursue them.[276] Much debate on the Trinity was given new life and attention by Athanasius and the Cappadocian Fathers when they heard from Serapion about the 'Tropici', or *pneumatomachi*. These claimed that the Holy Spirit was not *created* by God, i.e. he was not a mere 'creature' (Gk, *ktisma*). Michael Haykin has well surveyed this debate.[277] Athanasius (297–373) expounded the subject in his *Letters to Serapion*. He made much of central passages in 1 Corinthians to show that the Holy Spirit is intimately related to God, and 'proceeds from' God, and not as a finite creation. Like the Son, he is 'begotten, not made'.[278] Basil of Caesarea (*c.* 330–79) stressed the co-equality of God the Father, the Son and the Holy Spirit. He insisted on the threefold Gloria: 'Glory be to the Father, and to the Son and to the Holy Spirit'. This is prominent today in our worship. The phrase 'proceeding from the Father' is today also recited in our creeds.

We shall not trace the 'intricacies' of the fourth-century debate. Briefly, however, theologians often use the terms 'economic Trinity' and 'social Trinity', and we may offer a brief definition of these. The term *economic Trinity* generally denotes the Trinity considered in *relation to the world*, in contrast to the *immanent* Trinity, which concerns only internal or immanent relations between the persons. The *social* Trinity is important for understanding intratrinitarian relations between the persons, and usually denotes their mutuality. Moltmann is probably the best-known exponent of this, although Hill, Stanley Grenz and Paul Fiddes also explore it, not least for pastoral reasons. All stress *relatedness* as part

---

274 Hill, *Paul and the Trinity*, pp. 64–7.

275 Hill, *Paul and the Trinity*, pp. 70–174.

276 Hill, *Paul and the Trinity*, p. 50.

277 Michael Haykin, *The Spirit of God: The Exegesis of 1 and 2 Corinthians in the Pneumatomachian Controversy of the Fourth Century* (Leiden: Brill, 1994).

278 Athanasius, *Letters to Serapion*, 1.31, 3.2, and so on (Eng., C. R. B. Shapland (ed.), *The Letters of Athanasius Concerning the Holy Spirit* (London: Epworth, 1951)).

of the nature of God.[279] Some today express concerns that this approach has become a fashion which too easily reflects Western democracy. The Catholic theologian, Karen Kilby, recently suggested the danger of falling into Feuerbach's trap of projecting current human values on to our concept of God.

---

279 Paul S. Fiddes, *Participating in God: A Pastoral Doctrine of the Trinity* (Louisville, Minn.: Westminster/John Knox Press, 2000).

Part 3

KEY TERMS

Agnosticism (Gk, *a-gnōsis,* no knowledge) is different from *atheism.* Agnosticism is the denial of *knowledge* of God; not of the *existence* of God. It may appear to be more humble and more open than atheism but it is no less dogmatic. It asserts that knowledge of God is impossible, when Christians, Jews and Muslims believe that knowledge of God comes not primarily from human discovery, but from God's self-revelation. It tries to shortcut the paradox of scepticism: how can I know that I cannot know?

Allegory, allegorical interpretation (Gk, *allos,* other) signifies a meaning 'other' than the normal historical and grammatical meaning of a word or a text. A Stoic defined it as saying one thing and meaning something other than what it says. But Andrew Louth argues that to view allegory as dishonest is mistaken. He regards it as a way of plumbing the depth of an idea's signification. The origins of allegorical interpretation go back to sixth-century BC Greeks. Philo and Origen used it extensively to expound meanings of the OT. However, the Reformers broadly opposed it.

Analogy provides a way of speaking of God, which does not attribute to him an exact match with human beings or things. Thomas Aquinas (1225–74) writes, 'Words are used neither univocally nor purely equivocally of God and creatures, but analogically, for we cannot speak of God at all [otherwise]' (*Summa Theologiae,* I, qu. 13). The analogy of being constitutes a major concept in medieval thought. However, Karl Barth (1886–1968) rejects this approach, to speak only of the analogy of *faith.* Most Protestant theologians do not share Barth's position so strongly. Emil Brunner (1889–1966) finds its justification in the image of God and the Incarnation.

Angels (Heb., *mal'kh*; Gk, *angelos*) normally denote messengers. About half of 200 uses of the term in the OT denote humans, while half denote heavenly beings or the armies of God. Heavenly angels are called *seraphim* (Isa. 6.2–7) or *cherubim* (Exod. 25.20), awesome winged creatures. Angels are more than human in Revelation, Luke and Acts. In Matthew 18.10 angels appear as guardians of children. It is *forbidden to worship* angels. Twelve legions of angels could be readied for Jesus' defence at his arrest (Matt. 26.53). Personal names are given mainly in the apocryphal writings.

Anglicanism denotes the belief and practice of churches formally in communion with the archbishop and province of Canterbury, although the 'being in communion' still remains under discussion. It is conventional to describe Anglicanism as 'reformed' and catholic. The 1552 Book of

Common Prayer represents the 'reformed' aspect; the 1549 Prayer Book and the Tractarian Movement represent the 'catholic' aspect. The Thirty-Nine Articles of the 1662 Prayer Book provide the basis of Anglican doctrine, although some Anglicans would not assent to all 39 articles. The Anglican view of the Bible still adheres to Richard Hooker's (1554–1600) settlement under Elizabeth I. Worldwide Anglicanism includes some 30 provinces and 300 dioceses.

Antinomianism devalues the law of God. It exaggerates salvation by grace, as if the law were not relevant to Christians. It removes from its context, 'all who rely on the works of the law are under a curse' (Gal. 3.10), and 'for freedom Christ has set us free' (Gal. 5.1), Paul insists that we cannot rely on the law *for salvation*; but he insists that it guides us, like the Ten Commandments, as a standard for practical behaviour. In this sense, it is 'just and good' (Rom. 7.12). Jesus preaches both freedom from the law as a means of salvation, and observance of the law as a rule of life (Matt. 5.17–48).

Apocalyptic. The literature of apocalyptic contains certain themes, whether it is Jewish or Christian. It emphasizes God's new creation, rather than human aspirations, the place of judgment and resurrection, and God's dealings with the whole world, not just Israel and the Church. H. H. Rowley (1890–1969) suggests that it implies that the world is too bad to be reformed; hence God's intervention and new creation become necessary for salvation. It also majors on symbolism and epochs within world-history. Klaus Koch (b. 1926), Wolfhart Pannenberg (1928–2014) and Alexandra Brown are among those who stress its value for Christian theology.

Apologetics (Gk, *apologia*, a defence) denotes attempts to provide rational defence of the Christian faith against pagan or atheist objections. The second-century Christian apologists provide classic examples from Aristides to Irenaeus. The minimum aim is to demonstrate that Christian belief is not irrational. Origen, Augustine (354–430) and Aquinas (1225–74) also constitute classic cases. Barth (1886–1968) rejected apologetics as natural theology. Brunner (1889–1966) preferred the term *eristics*; but Tillich (1886–1965) regarded himself as a thoroughgoing apologist. Roman Catholic theologians, especially Rahner (1904–84) and Küng (b. 1928), strongly advocate apologetics.

Apostle (Gk, *apostolos*, one who is sent) in the Gospels denotes especially the Twelve, chosen by Jesus. In Paul and the epistles the meaning is wider, including Paul and many others. It appears that one has to have witnessed the resurrection to be an apostle (1 Cor. 9.1–2). In Romans 16.7, Paul includes Junia (feminine) as 'prominent among the apostles'. In Ephesians 2.20 the Church is built 'upon the foundation of the apostles and prophets', which suggests that apostles constitute a once-for-all foundation. Irenaeus stressed the 'rule of faith' as following the witness of the Scriptures and apostles. Crafton spoke of them as 'windows' through which we see Christ.

Apostolic fathers denote the successors to the Apostles, who mainly belong to the second century. The earliest was Clement of Rome (*c.* AD 96), followed by the *Didachē* (*c.* 900), Ignatius (*c.* 112) and Polycarp of Smyrna (d. 155). They generally include the *Shepherd of Hermas*, Papias and the *Epistle of Barnabas*. Justin Martyr (*c.* 100 – *c.* 165) is more usually classed as an early apologist, and Irenaeus (*c.* 130 – *c.* 200) as the first of the church fathers. Clement writes to Rome about the unity of the Church; Ignatius writes on his way to martyrdom in Rome, and stresses church order under the bishop.

Ascension of Christ. All biblical accounts of the ascension of Christ occur in the Lucan writings. Acts 1.6–11 is the most extended, especially verse 9: 'As they were watching, he was lifted up (Gk, *epērthē*), and a cloud took him out of their sight.' Luke 24.51 says, 'he withdrew from them and was carried up (Gk, *anephereto*) into heaven'. Hebrews and the longer ending of Mark presuppose the event. Paul uses the term 'exalted'. No one seriously questions Christ's exaltation, but some debate its mode. It may probably constitute an *acted-out metaphor* for those who experienced *earthly* time and space. We do not have to assume a constant journey through interstellar space in the same mode.

Asceticism denotes extreme self-discipline from property, luxury, wine, marriage, wealth, or any form of self-indulgence. Positively it entails poverty. Paul commends self-control (Gk, *enkrateuomai*) as among athletes (1 Cor. 9.25). He even speaks of punishing (Gk, *hupōpiazō*) his body (9.26), putting 'to death the deeds of the body' (Rom. 8.13). Some church fathers, the desert fathers and all monastic orders placed a high value on world-denying self-discipline, and the practice of renunciation. However, Luther and the Reformers thought of this as 'works', which also devalued the body. All Christian living entails struggle and conflict.

Assurance denotes a state of certainty or confidence, usually about one's personal salvation. Luther (1483–1546) believed that an accurate understanding of justification by grace through faith constituted the foundation of such assurance. In the biblical writings, *trust* and *reliance* (Heb., *bātach*, Ps. 31.14–15), and *full assurance* (Gk, *plērophoreō*, 1 Thess. 1.5), express this concept. Assurance is also based on the covenant, in which people know where they stand with God. It is commended, but it does not mean complacency or arrogance. God pledges himself to act in stated ways in promises; hence unbelief would doubt the faithfulness of God.

Athanasian Creed, the, must be dated later than Athanasius (*c.* 296–373). It was composed in Latin, not Greek. It is found in the Catholic Daily Office, the Lutheran Book of Concord, the Synod of Dort, and the Anglican 1662 Book of Common Prayer, to be said on 13 holy days. These include Christmas, Easter, Ascension Day and Whitsun. It is headed 'At Morning Prayer' in the Prayer Book. Its theme is that of holding the catholic faith, and it greatly expands the Nicene and Apostles' creeds. However, it has considerably less authority than they have.

Atheism affirms that God does not exist. It is distinguished from agnosticism, which asserts that we cannot know whether God exists. Practical atheism (i.e. the belief that the existence of God makes no difference) occurred mainly before the seventeenth century. But after the Enlightenment, many affirmed a mechanistic world-view, and held explicit and avowed atheism. Feuerbach, Nietzsche and Paul von Holbach held such avowed atheism, while Feuerbach, Nietzsche and Freud attributed belief in God to human projection. Karl Marx (1818–83) viewed God as a human construct to serve power-interests. Richard Dawkins' book *The God Delusion* (2006) constitutes the more polemical 'new atheism'.

Baptism in Romans 6.1–11 concerns participation or sharing in the death and resurrection of Christ. It entails dying to the unbelieving world, and being raised to new life in Christ. It has also become a mark of belonging to the visible Church. Like the Lord's Supper, it involves a pledge of loyalty to Christ, and the promise of God to own and save the baptized. It is also a corporate or communal rite, inviting both the prayers and faith of the Church, and prayers and commitment on behalf of the candidate.

Baptists reserve baptism to believers alone, and hold a more individualist confession of faith by the candidate. The primacy of the individual and the local congregation shapes their view not only of baptism, but also of their ecclesiology. Historically they may have come from a 'separatist' tradition, but claim today that worldwide they may be the largest Protestant denomination. Their first church in London was founded between 1612 and 1616. British Baptists divided into General and Particular Baptists, in which Particular Baptists represented a Calvinist (Reformed) tradition and belief in 'limited' atonement for believers only.

Calvinism denotes doctrines broadly modelled on *The Institutes of the Christian Religion* written by John Calvin (1509–64), the second-generation systematizer of Reformation theology. More strictly the term refers to Reformed theology, in contrast to Lutheran theology. In popular thought it is sometimes used disparagingly to allude to a preoccupation with predestination, in contrast to Arminianism (or the theology of James Arminius, 1559–1609). But Calvin's theology is far more comprehensive, and his emphasis on predestination and election serves to promote the sovereignty of God, and undeserved character of grace. He seeks to follow Scripture and Augustine.

Cappadocian Fathers, the, denote Basil of Caesarea (*c.* 330–79), Gregory of Nyssa (*c.* 330–95), Basil's brother, and his friend, Gregory of Nazianzus (*c.* 330–90). Basil wrote *On the Holy Spirit*, in which he defended the deity, holiness and personhood of the Spirit, and attacked the 'Pneumatomachi'. He pressed for the threefold Trinitarian Gloria. Similarly Gregory of Nyssa passionately defended the Nicene concept of the Holy Trinity, arguing that the numeral 'three' could be applied only to created, finite, things or people. Gregory of Nazianzus largely repeated these views, and contributed to the Council of Constantinople.

Cataphatic theology uses positive language to speak of God, largely on the basis of Aquinas' defence of using analogical language to speak of what cannot readily be described by human beings. It is derived from the Greek *kata*, down, and *phemi*, I speak, i.e. to bring God down to human language. It stands in contrast to apophatic theology, which is a theology of negation, often associated with Pseudo-Dionysius (*c.* 500). He would have regarded cataphatic language as presumptuous when applied to the transcendent God. Most theologians follow the cataphatic way, except perhaps some mystics.

Celtic Christianity denotes a twentieth-century reconstruction of an 'ideal' type of early Christianity, in contrast to the more hierarchical and authoritarian structures of the Roman Church or Latin world. Although it may have a historical core, many twenty-first-century historians regard it as owing more to popular myth than to historical and archaeological research. Its main truth lies in dissociation from the view of sin in the Augustinian tradition. Much Irish and Northumbrian Christianity was independent of Rome, but 'Celtic' cannot denote any unified tradition of faith and practice.

Chalcedon, Council of, was the fourth ecumenical council held in 451. It followed Nicaea (325), Constantinople (381) and Ephesus (431). It was largely based on the *Tome* of Leo I of Rome. It excluded the Christology of Eutiches, and confirmed the earlier three councils, including the Nicene Creed. It set the standard of Christological orthodoxy, at least perhaps until the Enlightenment and the modern era, when fresh reformulations began.

Charismatic describes those Christians who are committed to the practice of what Paul describes as gifts of the Holy Spirit (Gk, *charismata*), especially those of the more 'supernatural' or spectacular kind. Critics lament that they often tend to hold a dualist contrast between natural and supernatural gifts, as if to imply that the Holy Spirit does not equally work through 'natural' processes, e.g. through rational reflection, medicine or science. Unlike Pentecostals, the Charismatic renewal movement can be found in all major denominations or traditions, and seeks the renewal of a more intimate and spontaneous relation with God. They rely less on institutional structures.

Communion of saints. Belief in the communion of saints is affirmed as the ninth article of the Apostles' Creed. It has at least three or four senses. Luther (1483–1546) defined it as the bond of communion (Gk, *koinōnia*) between Christians in a congregation or church, as against only isolated, individual, believers. Pannenberg (1928–2014) understood the term to denote the universal unity of the Church across the ages, in fellowship with saints and martyrs. Among Catholics and others it has been understood as fellowship between living Christians and those who have died. J. Pearson understood it to denote fellowship with God the Holy Trinity and the angels.

Covenant denotes an agreement or contract whereby two people or two institutions pledge to adhere to terms formally agreed. Colloquial English might suggest the term 'deal'. Covenant rests on a binding *promise*. A promise limits options, so that alternative actions must be excluded, if they countermand the promise. Walther Eichrodt (1890–1978) rightly comments that through the covenant, 'With this God men *know exactly where they stand*; an *atmosphere of trust and security is created*' (*Theology of the Old Testament*, vol. l, (London: SCM Press, 1961), p. 38, his italics). God's covenant with Israel and the Church permeates Scripture, and forms the basis of the sacraments.

Creation, *Creatio ex nihilo*, focuses not on a moment in time, but on the dependence of all created beings on God. It is also an expression of his love, and desire for a relationship with others. Creation differs from emanation; the world is not just an outflow of God, but remains finite and creaturely. It means that matter constitutes a gift of God, and is not evil. Creation 'out of nothing' stresses that *God alone* is the only source of all being. No pre-existent matter was used. Creation is also the work of the whole Trinity: Father, Son and Holy Spirit.

Creationism has two different meanings: one in contrast to evolutionary natural selection; the other in contrast to traducianism (see pp. 13 and 153). The first is more widespread, and denotes the view that God directly created each species. It arose in immediate reaction to Darwin, but nowadays most theologians regard 'evolution' (broadly) as such as entirely compatible with the biblical account of creation. Tennant (1866–1957), Swinburne (b. 1934), Polkinghorne (b. 1930), and many others insist that *order and purpose*, rather than chronology, define the heart of divine creation. In contrast to traducianism, a second meaning of creationism holds that each person is created directly by God.

Creed (Lat., *credo*, I believe). The Nicene Creed is recited at every Anglican service of Holy Communion, and in many other churches. It is older than the so-called Apostles' Creed, and much older than the Athanasian Creed. In effect it is based on the Council of Constantinople (381), and draws on the earlier Old Roman Creed. It affirms the four ecumenical councils (see Chalcedon, Council of). Adolf von Harnack (1851–1930) claimed that the Nicene Creed was later, originally without reference to the Virgin Birth. But H. B. Swete (1835–1917) defended its early date, and more recently O. Cullmann (1902–99) and V. H. Neufeld have detected embryonic creeds and confessions in the NT.

Cross, the, stands at the heart of the gospel. Paul calls it 'the power of God' for believers, although a scandal for others (1 Cor. 1.18). The Gospel of Mark regards the cross as the goal of Jesus' life. Matin Hengel has shown the offensiveness of the cross in Graeco-Roman society, and its being exceptionally humiliating and painful. Moltmann (b. 1926) laments: 'We have surrounded the cross with roses', regarding it as decorative, rather than painful. Paul described it as a curse on our behalf (Gal. 3.13). Luther (1483–1546) saw the theology of the cross as opposing a theology of glory, which says 'bad is good, and good is bad'. The crucifixion and resurrection are the work of God as Trinity.

Death and mortality. The Hebrew *chayyîm* and *chayyah* mean 'span of life' or 'allotted life'. It implies the finite life-span of human beings. God alone remains the source of life; he gives life or death (2 Kings 5.7). Death has today become a taboo subject, whereas the Bible openly grieves over death. To repress thoughts of death or grief is unhealthy. The Book of Common Prayer quotes Psalm 90.12, 'Teach us to number our days that we may apply our hearts to wisdom' (BCP). Jesus wept at the death of his friend Lazarus (John 11.35). 'Flesh' also denotes humankind in its weakness and mortality.

Death of God theology, the, flourished in the 1960s, mainly in the USA. Its origins lie with Nietzsche (1844–1900) and Feuerbach (1804–72). T. J. Altizer (b. 1927) borrowed from Nietzsche and superficially from Hegel (1770–1831), alluding with the latter to the death of God at the cross. His aim, however, unlike Nietzsche, was to stress the transcendence of God. Like Bonhoeffer (1906–45), he repudiated a God who merely served human wishes and needs. Paul van Buren (1924–98) and William Hamilton (1924–2012) also demanded a radical interpretation of God. But few were convinced, and the movement appears to have fizzled out today.

Deification (Gk, *theōsis*) has often been regarded as the Eastern Orthodox equivalent of sanctification in the Western Church. It has often been rendered as *divinization*, but this term can seem ambiguous. On the other hand, many cite Athanasius (*c.* 296–373) as saying, 'God made himself man that man might become God'. Gregory of Nyssa (*c.* 330–95) uses similar words. But this does not denote assimilation into the being of God. In its proper context it entails transformation into God's image and likeness through Christ's redemption and the work of the Holy Spirit.

Deism flourished in the seventeenth and eighteenth centuries. Deists worshipped God as Creator, but believed that divine intervention in the world would imply that God's creation was imperfect and needed regular repair. They viewed creation as a kind of mechanism, which God left to run as a self-regulating machine. Lord Edward Herbert Cherbury (1583–1643) upheld 'common notions' of reason and natural religion. Matthew Tindal (1657–1733) promoted natural theology. John Toland (1670–1722) characterized deism in his title *Christianity Not Mysterious*. Anthony Collins (1676–1729) rejected any authority. Thomas Carlyle (1795–1881) attacked deism as promoting 'an absentee God, sitting idle . . . watching the universe go'.

Demons. The Greek words *daimōn* and *daimonion* occur over 1,200 times each, and the verb *daimonizomai* over 1,200 times, in the Synoptic Gospels. Matthew 8.31 recounts demons speaking to Jesus. By contrast, Paul uses the term only five times, although he speaks of 'the god of this age' (2 Cor. 4.4). The Hebrew term for demon is *shed*; Leviticus 16.8 names one as Azazel. *1 Enoch* and Philo regard demons as fallen angels. They cause illness and mental disturbance, and sometimes invite exorcisms (Mark 1.23–27, etc.). This view flourished in the Middle Ages, and with Aquinas (1225–74) and Luther (1483–1546). Bultmann (1884–1976) and others regarded them as expressing a 'pre-scientific' world-view. Yet while many biblical episodes may reflect accommodation to current beliefs, it is doubtful whether all such references can be so understood.

Desert fathers describes the monks, ascetics and hermits who lived in the desert of Egypt for solitude and devotion to God in the third and fourth centuries. Anthony of Egypt (*c.* 251–356) was the most widely known, along with Paul of Thebes. They anticipated, in effect, the monastic movement. They gave away property in accordance with the Sermon on the Mount. From about 310 Anthony supported the Nicene party. They also prefigured the term 'abbot', and initiated a mystical tradition of piety.

Devil. Matthew records that Christ was tempted by 'the devil' in Matthew 4.1; and Jesus tells 'Satan' to go away (Matt. 4.10), thereby suggesting that the two terms are synonymous. Matthew and Luke use 'the devil' a dozen times. Jesus says that Satan cannot cast out Satan (Matt. 12.26); and Luke says that Satan entered Judas (Luke 22.3). Paul says that Satan may be disguised as an angel of light (2 Cor. 11.14).

Dialectical theology denotes the earlier theology of the theologians Karl Barth (1886–1968), Friedrich Gogarten (1887–1967) and Eduard Thurneysen (1888–1974). In the 1920s Rudolf Bultmann (1884–1976) also joined their number. Language about God, they believed, could never take the form of direct assertion, because God transcends human language. But a 'yes' and 'no' of assertion and counter-assertion could grasp the address of the transcendent God to humankind, and express his word. Barth's *Commentary on Romans* communicated a 'yes' of divine grace, and a 'no' of divine judgment. The journal of the movement was *Between the Times* (1920–30), after which it declined.

Dispensationalism is the belief that God's dealings with the world are divided into different 'dispensations' or periods of time. Christians will accept the distinction between the Mosaic and Christian eras. But Dispensationalists go further. John Nelson Darby (1800–82), founder of the movement, was followed by the Scofield Reference Bible (1909). It regards 'the rapture', based on 1 Thessalonians 4.16–17, as an event that involves the bodily ascent of the faithful to heaven. One era extends from the fall of the Temple (AD 70) to the founding of the state of Israel (1948). Darby believed that the return of Christ would occur twice, first at the rapture. Today the movement is associated with Hal Lindsey, J. F. Walvoord and, often, Dallas Theological Seminary.

Dogmatics differs only marginally from systematic theology. 'Dogma' is technically what the Church has received or recognized as doctrine. Hence most universities prefer the term *systematic theology* for Christian doctrine. Notably Barth (1886–1968) and Brunner (1889–1966) retain the term dogmatics, since it denotes what serves the Church. Pannenberg (1928–2014) uses the term systematic theology to highlight his concern for the university and the public credibility of theology. The term is more open, whereas 'dogmatics' might suggest a norm or rule of faith.

Dualism denotes the belief that reality or humankind is divided into two. Its application to reality may take the form of belief in two powers, perhaps of equal strength, sometimes God and Satan; sometimes light and darkness. Or it may sharply divide natural from supernatural, as if to imply that one is more closely associated than the other with divine action. The second type of dualism separates mind or spirit from body. Both philosophers (e.g. Gilbert Ryle) and modern theologians reject this dualism. Biblical writers do not hold it.

Ecumenical theology usually refers to conversations between different Christian traditions or denominations in an attempt to promote unity, or at the very least mutual understanding. The term may also be used to refer to increased understanding between the major world religions. These constitute very different tasks and agenda. One clear example is the ongoing conversation by the Anglican–Roman Catholic International Commission (ARCIC). This produced ARCIC I in 1970–1, on eucharistic doctrine. ARCIC II followed (1983–2011), mainly on teaching authority, but this engendered more controversy than ARCIC I. ARCIC III began in 2011 and is continuing. Other inter-denominational conversations also continue.

Election is based on the biblical words for *choose* and *chosen* (Heb., *bāchîr*; Gk, *eklegomai, eklektos*). One classic verse is: 'It was not because you were more numerous than any other people that the LORD loved you' (Deut. 7.7–8). God chose Israel (Deut. 4.37), as 'my servant' (Isa. 41.7–8). 1 Peter declares: 'You are a chosen race, a royal priesthood' (2.9). As Barth stressed, this applies especially to 'my Son, my Chosen' (Luke 9.35). The sole ground of election is the sovereign will of God. Ephesians 1.4–6 asserts, 'He [God] chose us in Christ before the foundation of the world to be holy'.

Enthusiasm denotes in theology the beliefs of the Radical Reformers (Müntzer and Karlstadt) whom Luther called 'the fanatics', often the Montanists (see p. 19), and often also many Pentecostals and Charismatics (see Part 2, Pentecostalism; Part 3, Charismatic). Knox hesitates to include John Wesley (1703–91) in the fullest sense, but the earliest Quakers, Edward Irving (1792–1834) and John Fletcher are often so described. John Locke (1632–1704) wrote against their disparagement of reason and reasonableness. Today the name may include many in worldwide Pentecostalism. But the term is elusive, with blurred edges.

Epiphany (Gk, *epiphaneia*, appearance, manifestation) originally meant the appearance or manifestation of God, especially in Christ. In the Eastern Church it denoted the birth of Christ on 6 January, but in the West it came to denote the manifestation of Christ to the Gentiles in the persons of the Magi. The chronological date of Christmas is unknown. Some Western liturgies have built into Epiphany the celebration of the baptism of Jesus in accordance with early Eastern usage. However, the Greek word in the NT is also associated with appearance of the Christ at the Parousia or end time.

Erastianism denotes the control of the civil state over the Church or churches. Thomas Erastus (1524–83) gave his name to this movement when the Swiss civil authorities claimed jurisdiction over the Church. The Oxford Movement began as a protest against the British government's appointment of Irish bishops. The Westminster Confession and the Barmen Declaration rejected it. Richard Hooker (1554–1600) is occasionally criticized for Erastian tendencies, but most Church of England theologians dissociate the establishment of the church from Erastianism.

Eucharist, the, is also known as Holy Communion and the Lord's Supper. Each of these terms has biblical basis. Paul speaks of the *Lord's Supper* (*kuriakon deipnon*; 1 Cor. 11.20). He also calls it 'a *sharing* (*koinōnia, communion*) in the blood of Christ . . . [in which] we all partake' (10.16–17). The central 'handing on' of pre-Pauline apostolic tradition begins, 'Jesus . . . *having given thanks*' (*eucharistēsas*). It pledges in visible and tangible form God's promises to believers, and pledges their allegiance to God. The Eucharist, as F. J. Leenhardt and Joachim Jeremias (1900–79) insist, is based on the covenantal meal of the Passover, except that it makes us dramatically present at the *cross of Christ*.

Evangelicalism. The term is widely misunderstood today, especially since its meaning differs in the UK, the USA, Germany and elsewhere. In popular thought it is often confused with *evangelistic*, which means a concern to propagate the gospel, and can apply to many traditions. It is also popularly confused with *Charismatic*. It does not denote 'happy, clappy worship'. The term stresses the *primacy of Scripture*. Anglican Evangelicals follow Richard Hooker (1554–1600) in stressing, first, Scripture, then reason and tradition. Second, it emphasizes *the all-sufficiency of the work of Christ* for salvation, and justification by grace through faith. In practice, an Evangelical church gives priority to biblical preaching and to the 'reformed' tradition of worship. Within this definition there are broader and narrower concerns.

Faith, faithfulness. Faith varies in meaning according to its context, and to whom it is directed. The Hebrew root *'-m-n* means in adjectival form *firm, reliable, trustworthy*, while the verb means *to trust in*. The Greek *pistis* (noun) and *pisteuō* (verb) begin with these meanings in the NT. A classic example is: '[Abraham] believed the LORD, and the LORD reckoned it to him as righteousness' (Gen. 15.6). In other contexts *'emeth* denotes *fidelity* or *faithfulness*. In the NT in some contexts faith denotes 'the conviction of things not seen' (Heb. 11.1), where things are not seen because they are yet to occur, and rely on God's *promise*. In Paul, faith in Christ often denotes appropriation of his work, almost amounting to 'being in Christ'. *Faithfulness* takes time to prove itself in different situations. Martin Luther (1483–1546) defined *faith* as a 'living, daring, confidence in God's grace', which is utterly certain. It is impossible to indicate the varied scope of the terms in a short article.

Fall, the, is recounted in Genesis 3.1–24, Romans 5.12–44, and arguably in Romans 1.18–32 and 7.7–23. Genesis 3 recounts the entry of sin into the world, and the consequences of alienation from God. In Romans 5.12–21 Paul expounds the universal significance of Christ's work, but to do this he needs also to expound the universality of human sin and alienation (see Part 2). In verses 12–14 he paints the picture of 'the many in one', and uses Adam as his example. Although Adam seems to have acted as an individual, his act had universal consequences. This does not simply imply that humankind suffered because of his disobedience. For everyone, Paul says, endorses his act of alienation, and the fall extends to all humanity. The purpose of the passage is less to describe the fall, than the universal effects of both sin and grace. Augustine (353–430), unfortunately, rendered the Greek *eph' hō* by the Latin *in quo*, which suggested that humans sin *in* Adam. Today many debate whether 'Adam' is a historical individual. The Hebrew *ādām* simply means *man*, but elsewhere he seems to be a particular person, and this issue is hotly debated.

Fideism includes a spectrum of meanings. At the moderate end it insists on the priority of faith over reason. At the more extreme end, it regards faith as in effect blind belief or trust, which reason cannot support or discredit. Kierkegaard (1813–55) believed that trying to prove the existence of God was 'a shameless affront'. Aquinas (1225–74) and Pannenberg (1928–2014) insist that faith is not contrary to reason, not least to demonstrate its public credibility. Both, however, acknowledge that some revealed truths are beyond reason. John Locke (1632–1704) argued for the reasonableness of belief.

Filioque (Eng., 'and the Son') denotes the double procession of the Holy Spirit 'from the Father and the Son', interposed into the creeds by the Western Church. Photius (819–90) denounced the clause, insisting that the Eastern Church retain only 'from the Father'. Each side may appeal to good reasons for its belief. In John 14—16, Romans 8.9 and elsewhere, the Holy Spirit is mediated through Christ. But the Eastern view is older, and seems to do better justice to the co-equality of the Holy Trinity. There are signs of softening in the Western Church: Jürgen Moltmann (b. 1926) advocates the Eastern formula, and recently (2013) Justin Welby, Archbishop of Canterbury, used it at his installation.

Forgiveness reflects three Hebrew words, *kipper* (to cover, atone), *nāsā'* (forgive, pardon), and *shākach* (to let go, forget). The normal Greek words are *aphiēmi* (to forgive) and *apoluō* (to loose away). One classic verse is Jeremiah 31.34: 'I will forgive their iniquity, and remember their sin no more.' The Greek *aphiēmi* occurs 100 times in the first three Gospels. Whereas justification is a permanent status, forgiveness is regularly renewed. It is a petition in the Lord's Prayer, and is part of the earliest apostolic preaching (Acts 2.38).

Foundationalism denotes a set of beliefs which are considered to be *self-evident* either from reason (with many rationalists) or from experience (with many empiricists). The key point is that this stands in contrast to beliefs which depend on a *chain of inferences* from other beliefs. In Reformed epistemology these are called 'basic' or 'immediate' beliefs, in contrast to inferred beliefs. Classical foundationalism occurred in René Descartes (1596–1650) on the rationalist side. He attempted to build upon a foundation beyond doubt, and to demolish inferred ideas. Arguably John Locke (1632–1704) appealed to 'sense-experience' in a parallel way.

Fundamental theology denotes, first, the branch of theology mainly within Catholicism which establishes the fact that God has made a supernatural revelation and established the Church, founded by Christ. It came into prominence in the nineteenth century when J. H. Newman (1801–90) used the term, and followed Aquinas (1225–74) in regarding it as a science dealing with God. It is fundamental because its role is to set forth the rational foundations of the Catholic faith. It denotes the science of the fundamental doctrines of the Christian faith.

Fundamentalism derives its name from a 12-volume paperback series entitled *The Fundamentals* (1910–15). About three million copies were distributed to pastors, evangelists and missionaries. The content reflected the doctrines of the older Princeton theologians Charles Hodge (1797–1878) and Benjamin Warfield (1851–1921). Specifically it was hostile to Darwin and his theories of evolution by natural selection. W. B. Greene and H. Beach were said to be 'pugnaciously anti-Darwin'. The writings addressed the infallibility of the Bible, the Virgin Birth and the deity of Christ. Its influence reached a peak in the 1920s. James Orr (1844–1913), P. T. Forsyth (1848–1921), and other evangelicals adopted a 'softer' approach.

Gnosticism (Gk, *gnōsis*, knowledge) emphasized secret knowledge by secret revelation, and a sharp dualism between God and evil powers.

Gnostics flourished from the second to the fifth century. Some trace 'proto-Gnosticism' in Paul's opponents. Like later Gnostics, they claimed to be 'spiritual' in contrast to 'fleshly' (Gk, *sarkikos*) or ordinary (Gk, *psychikos*) Christians. Paul shows that 'spiritual' means 'of the Holy Spirit', who is given to all Christians (1 Cor. 12.3). Irenaeus (*c.* 130 – *c.* 200) insisted on the *public* nature of apostolic tradition; Tertullian (*c.* 150 – *c.* 225) and Origen (*c.* 185 – *c.* 254) opposed Gnosticism equally. The church fathers regarded God as Creator and sovereign, and revealed in the OT and NT. The *Gospel of Truth* and the *Gospel of Thomas* are largely Gnostic gospels.

Gospel. The Greek word for gospel (*euaggelion*) means simply good news. Mark calls his Gospel 'the good news of Jesus Christ' (1.1), and recounts Jesus as declaring, 'Repent and believe in the good news' (1.15). Paul asserts, 'I am not ashamed of the gospel; it is the power of God for salvation' (Rom. 1.16). The cognate verb, *euaggelizō*, means to bring good news or specifically to announce God's message of salvation. It soon became the technical term for providing details about the life and teaching of Jesus, and referred mainly to our four canonical Gospels.

Grace translates the Hebrew *chēn* and *chesed*, and the Greek *charis*. Exodus 33.19 tells us that the basis of grace lies solely in God's will and choice: 'I will be gracious to whom I will be gracious'. Isaiah 55.7–9 tells us how differently God is motivated from humankind. *Chēn* originally meant *favour*, as in *finding favour*. In the NT the supreme manifestation of grace comes in Jesus Christ. Jesus, the Word of God, was 'full of grace and truth' (John 6.14). The parable of the grumbling labourers (Matt. 20.1–16) shows that grace eclipses human notions of justice. Paul exclaimed, 'By the grace of God I am what I am' (1 Cor. 15.10). For Christians grace is everything.

Hamartology (Gk, *hamartia*, sin) is the theological study of the doctrine of sin, and concerns the origin, nature and consequences of sin. It studies the way in which sin is transmitted across the human race. Sin is not just an individual *act*, but a corporate *stance or attitude*, hostile to God. *Alienation* from God is its major consequence. It consists of misdirected desire and results in bondage. The Hebrew terms *chattā'th*, *pasha*' and *'āwōn* must be given full weight, as well as numerous Greek terms. They suggest not simply failure, but rebellion, distortion and lack of communion with God. Paul says that humankind is 'under the power of sin' (Rom. 3.9), and that 'the wages of sin is death' (Rom. 6.23).

Healing. The Gospels regard healing (Gk, *iaō, therapeuō*) as bound up with the coming of the kingdom of God. Otherwise healing is not usually universal, because God often works through natural laws. Isaiah 35.5 also associates healing with the fulfilment of God's purposes. Sickness was sometimes regarded as a sign of God's disfavour. Hence the Gospels also associate healing with the messianic work of Jesus (Mark 1.27; Luke 5.17–26). The apostolic age was also a special opportunity for healing (Acts 3.2–10). Paul speaks of 'gifts of healing' (1 Cor. 12.9). But the notion that God *always* enacts supernatural healing implies too sharp a dualism, as if God did not also work through medicine or natural processes.

Heart (Heb., *lēbh*; Gk, *kardia*) denotes depth of feeling, resolve of will, rational reflection, subconscious depth, or the core of one's human being. God regards emotion, will, intellect and even our subconscious as all proper functions of being human. Paul declares that God poured his love into our hearts 'through the Holy Spirit . . .' (Rom. 5.5). Calvin (1509–64) stressed the heart and its deceptions as needing God's work. Bultmann (1884–1976) and especially Gerd Theissen (b. 1943) draw particular attention to the subconscious in Paul's writings. In 1 Corinthians 4.5 the secrets of the heart are revealed to God. In 1 Corinthians 14.20–25 preaching discloses such secrets. In 1 Corinthians 4.1–5 ministers are capable of self-deception.

Heaven (Heb., *shāmayîm*; Gk, *ouranos*) may sometimes mean sky, but more often denotes the abode of God and angels. The dead in the OT more often depart for She'ol. God *created* heaven (Ps. 33.6), so heaven cannot be simply his dwelling-place. God is exalted 'above' the heavens (Ps. 57.11), Yet Jesus taught us to pray, 'Our Father in heaven' (Matt. 6.9). Heaven is a holy sphere for God to dwell in. Jesus uses the language of accommodation by speaking of 'up' in the ascension, as in Revelation. But much of Revelation is metaphorical and symbolic. Heaven reveals the ceaseless worship of God (Rev. 4.8–11), but is never static or timeless.

Heilsgeschichte is the German word for salvation-history. J. K. Hoffmann used it first, but it was most widely associated with Oscar Cullmann (1902–99). In *Christ and Time*, he traced a line of God's purposes until they reached fulfilment in Christ, although the end was still awaited. Since 1970 it is contrasted with universal history in contrast to what Pannenberg (1928–2014) called the ghetto of redemptive history.

Hell. We should not view 'everlasting punishment' as the sole orthodox view of hell, since throughout the centuries three views have been held. (1) Augustine (354–430) held to everlasting punishment (*City of God*, 13.2). He also cites Revelation 2.11 and 20.6, 14. He is joined by Aquinas (1225–74) and Calvin (1509–64). (2) Irenaeus (*c.* 130 – *c.* 200) argued that humankind can he deprived of life (*Against Heresies*, 3.19.1 and 4.39.2). God alone is the source of life. (3) Origen (*c.* 185 – *c.* 254) believed in the restoration of all things (*Catechism*, 24), and quoted Acts 3.21 to this effect. Moltmann (b. 1926) claims that all things will be united in Christ. In 1997 a report was commissioned for the Evangelical Alliance, which sets out these three views.

Heresy and orthodoxy. Irenaeus (*c.* 130 – *c.* 200) defined orthodoxy as life and thought in accordance with 'the rule of faith', i.e. biblical and apostolic public tradition. The term is derived from Greek *orthos*, right, and *doxa*, opinion. It stands in contrast to Greek *hairesis*, choice. Tertullian (*c.* 150 – *c.* 225) and Origen (*c.* 185 – *c.* 254) followed Irenaeus closely, exposing Gnostic writings as heresies. Walter Bauer (1877–1960) formulated his different thesis in *Orthodoxy and Heresy in Earliest Christianity* (Ger., 1934). He argued against the fathers that orthodoxy and heresy varied from such local regions as Edessa, Egypt and Antioch, and that therefore these concepts could not be applied. Nevertheless, creeds and confessions date from the NT, and Bauer's theory depends on a *purely historical* account of tradition.

Historical Jesus. The phrase 'the quest of the historical Jesus' was invented by the publisher of the English translation of Schweitzer's (1875–1965) book *From Reimarus to Wrede* (1960). This book became outdated, and became known as the 'first quest'. The so-called 'new quest' (Bornkamm, Käsemann) was still inadequate. The 'third quest' from 1985 onwards took account of Jesus' Jewish context, but reached wildly differing conclusions. The 'Jesus Seminar' in the USA (Funk and Robinson) interpreted Jesus as a rustic peasant uttering wise aphorisms. A largely British group (James Dunn (b. 1939), N. T. Wright (b. 1948), Richard Bauckham (b. 1946) and others) made more realistic assessments, in Bauckham's case, the value of eyewitness testimony to Jesus. Their work was sober, meticulous and positive about what we can know about the historical Jesus.

Holiness (Heb., *qādesh, qādōsh*; Gk, *hagios*) denotes what is separate or belongs to God, in contrast to what is common or in ordinary use. In the OT *holy* is often cultic, e.g. the Sabbath as a holy day (Isa. 58.13). But most characteristically it refers to God as 'majestic in holiness' (Exod. 15.11), or as 'the Holy One in your midst' (Hos. 11.9). In Isaiah 6.3 'Holy, holy, holy' signals that God cannot be approached. 1 Peter 1.15 is classic in the NT: 'As he who has called you is holy, be holy yourselves . . .' O. R. Jones has shown that holiness may be a disposition: what it consists in depends on what situations require its manifestation.

Holy Communion. See Eucharist.

Homiletics denotes the study and practice of preaching, including its composition, rhetoric and reception. Jesus, Peter and Paul provide different examples (Luke 4.16–21; Acts 2.14–36; 1 Thess. 2.1–12). Paul comments, 'You accepted it not as a human word, but . . . God's word' (1 Thess. 2.13). Accurate exegesis is the starting point. This is why many learn Hebrew and Greek. Augustine (350–430) asserts this, together with the need for prayer. Hundreds of books have been written on this, urging identification with the congregation's needs, emotions and imagination, together with a clear aim, and the disciplined use of words.

Homoousios (Gk, *homos*, the same, and *ousia*, being or substance) represents the Greek behind '*being of the same substance* as the Father' in the Nicene Creed. The phrase confesses belief in the co-equality of God the Father and God the Son. The Latin term *substance* is synonymous with *being* in the NT. The Council of Constantinople (381) used the formula to exclude the Arians, who had insisted that the Son was subordinate to the Father. It also excludes the compromise formula that the Son is merely 'like' (Gk. *homoios*) the Father.

Hope. Hebrew uses four words for *hope*: *betach, chāsāh, yāchal* and *qāwāh*, while Greek tends to use simply *elpizō*. It denotes confidently looking forward to some future good. In Psalm 16.9 (AV), 'My flesh shall rest in hope' (*betach*) denotes *confidence*. Paul says, 'We hope for what we do not see' (Rom. 8.25). Hebrews also declares that 'faith is the assurance of things hoped for' (11.1). Its multiform contexts impose a variety of meanings on to the word. But its OT background suggest that it is rooted in God's promise, which may take years to reach final fulfilment.

Hypostasis is Greek for *essential nature, reality* or *underlying structure*, although it has other meanings also. Even some Greek-speaking theologians found the term confusing, while it was more difficult for Latin speakers. Yet it played an important role in debates about the Holy Trinity. In this context it could be translated as *persona* or *substantia*. Latin and Greek theologians agreed on the formula 'three *hypostases* (persons) in one *ousia* (being or substance)'. Details of writers are in G. W. H. Lampe, *Patristic Greek Lexicon* (Oxford, 1961), pp. 1454–61.

Icons (Gk, *eikōn*, image) are flat pictures, usually crafted in mosaic or special paint, which are venerated by the Russian and Greek Orthodox churches. They often commemorate a biblical character or event. Leo I ordered a restraint on excessive uses of icons in the eighth century, which is usually called the iconoclastic controversy.

Image of God means to represent God, as images in pagan temples often did. The English 'Let us make humankind *in* our image' (Gen. 1.26) may arguably be translated '*as* our image' (Heb., *beᵗtsalmēnû*, understanding; Heb. *beth*, of essence, signifying representative). It was the task of Adam, and then of God's people, to show forth God's nature. They failed in this task. Hence Jesus Christ, as the *true image of God*, fulfilled this vocation: 'Christ . . . is the image of God' (2 Cor. 4.4; Col. 1.15). Vladimir Lossky (1903–58) argues that to bear the image of God is attained *by grace* (*The Mystical Theology of the Eastern Church*, 1991, p. 118). As image-bearer he or she becomes a 'person'; no longer a mere individual. This approach is more fruitful than cataloguing qualities of God's image, such as intelligence, dominion and relationality. Dominion, in any case, means stewardship, not mastery.

Immaculate conception. This dogma was first promulgated by a papal bull of Pope Pius IX for Roman Catholics in 1854. It asserted, 'From the first moment of her conception the Blessed Virgin Mary was . . . in view of the merits of Jesus Christ . . . kept free from all stain of original sin.' The Council of Trent had exempted Mary from statements about original sin. But most Protestants reject it. The translation 'Hail, Mary, full of grace' is based only on the Vulgate's rendering of Luke 1.28; the Greek renders the phrase 'favoured one' (as NRSV).

Immanence. The immanence of God denotes God's being or acting *within* humankind, or *within* the world, in contrast to the transcendence of God, which denotes his being above and beyond humankind and the world. In Christian theology these are not alternatives, for God is both immanent and transcendent. Indeed as immanent, God sustains the world, and acts providentially within it. An unqualified immanental view of God would be pantheistic.

Immortality denotes continuing human existence after death. Materialists dismiss it on the grounds that life depends on a body or brain. Many Eastern religions regard it as release of life from a cycle of bodily existence. Plato (d. 348 BC) argued for immortality on the ground that the soul belonged to the realm of eternal ideas. Christianity, however, distinguished the resurrection of the *whole person* (in biblical language, the 'body') from the immortality of an unknown entity called the *soul*. It will be a fresh divine act of new creation. This is partly on the basis of biblical witness to the sovereign, living God, partly on the basis of the resurrection of Christ.

Incarnation can be understood only against the background of the OT and Jewish expectations of the end. Prophetic witness looked forward to a figure who would be anointed by the Holy Spirit in an unprecedented way. Apocalyptists expected God himself to intervene in human history, since human leaders had so often disappointed their hopes. Jesus fulfilled both streams of hope, in being born as a man anointed for service by the Holy Spirit, and as the intervention of God himself. Pannenberg (1928–2014) is one of many who stress that the Incarnation can be understood only in the light of OT and Jewish expectations. *Incarnation* means the becoming flesh of the divine Word in Jesus Christ.

Incommensurability properly denotes a term in philosophy of science, not originally theology. Thomas Kuhn (1922–96) applied the term to two conceptual systems that do not strictly contradict each other, but can find no common arbiter to decide between their competing claims (1962 and 1970). The conventional example is the physics of Newton and Einstein. The postmodernist Lyotard found numerous examples of such 'undecideability', arguing that only rhetoric pronounced the winner. But in theology too much is ascribed to 'incommensurability', which became a fashion. Often patient logic will find an answer.

Intermediate state, the, supposedly refers to the state between the death of Christians, and the final judgment and resurrection of the dead, which they still await. On the one hand Paul uses the language 'to depart and to be with Christ' (Phil. 1.23). Jesus says, 'Today you will be with me in Paradise'

(Luke 23.43). On the other hand, Paul speaks of the Lord descending from heaven, 'and the dead in Christ will rise first' (1 Thess. 4.16–17). But is the intermediate state something of which we are conscious? A solution may depend on a difference of logic between an observer and a participant, as Gilbert Ryle stated it. On Christmas Eve I may tell a child, 'The sooner you fall asleep, the sooner Christmas will come.' But as observers, adults often have much to do in preparing for the next day. There is no outright contradiction between the two, depending on the logic used in each case. The term is partly valid, but also problematic.

Irresistible grace is the doctrine that God's grace cannot finally be resisted or rejected. It finds a place in Augustine (354–430) and is strongly affirmed in the sixteenth and seventeenth centuries by Calvin, the Jansenists, Reformed theology and the Synod of Dort. It is related to views on predestination and election. It does not necessarily contradict free will, as 'compatabilist' philosophers imply, and Moltmann (b. 1926) regards the grace of God as inevitably triumphant at the last day.

Kairos is the Greek word for *point in time* or favourable opportunity, in contrast to Greek *chronos*, which denotes time as duration. Characteristically *kairos* denotes 'an acceptable time' (2 Cor. 6.2). In 1985 a group of South African theologians published *The Kairos Document*, arguing for the right time to end apartheid. Oscar Cullmann (1902–99) first suggested favourable moments in the execution of God's plan of salvation.

Kenotic theology refers to Christ's 'emptying himself' (Gk, *ekenōsen*) in Philippians 2.7. The self-emptying of Jesus led to his anguish, suffering, constraints, God-forsakenness and death on the cross. Jesus did not rely on himself, but looked to God and to the power of the Holy Spirit. The late nineteenth century saw a flourishing of 'kenotic theology'. Charles Gore wrote *The Incarnation of the Son of God* (1891), to provide a popular exposition of kenotic theology. It became a fashionable way of accepting the deity of Christ, while avoiding the so-called dualism of Chalcedon. The central truth is that love accepts constraints. Barth stressed the humility of God in this sense.

Kingdom of God, the (Heb., *malkhuth*; Gk, *basileia*) denotes *the royal reign of God as king*. Mark and Luke regularly use the term 'kingdom of God'; Matthew prefers the reverential 'kingdom of heaven'. It does not denote kingdom in the sense of a territory. Jesus proclaimed, 'The time is fulfilled, and the kingdom of God has come near (Gk, *ēggiken*)' (Mark 1.15). The kingdom of God is certainly not the Church, which is fallible and sinful. The Gospels declare that the kingdom of God is *in process of arriving*. Jeremias (1900–79) called it 'in process of realization'. Hence such signs of the kingdom as healing occur, but are not for all.

Last Judgment. Biblical writers, far from being fearful about the Last Judgment, anticipate it with joy and enthusiasm: 'Sing for joy before the LORD, for . . . he is coming to judge the earth' (Ps. 96.10–13); and 'Let the nations be glad . . . for you [God] judge . . . with equity' (Ps. 67.4). God will remove all deceit, and *put everything to rights*. Hence, 'We must all appear before the judgment seat of Christ' (2 Cor. 5.10) is not like hearing exam results from a head teacher, but hearing the *public and definitive verdict* on how God sees everything. Evil will not be ignored. Even when they have faults exposed, believers will also receive the verdict of justification through Christ alone. The theme is vindication of the oppressed.

Law, the (Heb., *Torah*; Gk, *nomos*) has at least three meanings in Scripture. (1) It may mean the use of the law as a mirror, to show us ourselves in relation to God's standards: 'If it had not been for the law, I would not have known sin' (Rom. 7.7). (2) The law may also have a *civil* function, to restrain evil. Jesus came 'not to abolish but to fulfil' the law (Matt. 5.17). Paul says, 'The law is . . . holy, just and good' (Rom. 7.1). (3) The law may stand in contrast to gospel (2 Cor. 3.1–18). Sometimes it may lead to self-achievement or religious 'works'. Thus the plural *tōrōth*, laws, may mean the rules and regulations of OT sacrifices and worship. For Christians the law has a *moral* function, to indicate the goal of sanctification. Luther (1483–1546) and Calvin (1509–64) urge the three senses of the law.

Liberal Protestantism flourished mainly in the 1920s, following Harnack (1851–1930). He had reduced the teaching of Jesus to the fatherhood of God, the brotherhood of man and the infinite value of the human soul, and regarded 'doctrine' as deriving from Paul and the church fathers. Liberal Protestantism today varies enormously, from those who champion impartiality and scientific research against dogmatic and ecclesial claims, to those who deny many biblical traditions and miracles in the name of 'modern man', and what he 'could believe'. Both Evangelicals and Tractarians fiercely oppose the movement.

Liberation theology emerged in the late 1960s and 1970s in Latin America. It then spread to virtually every part of the world, and often developed into post-colonial theology. In 1968 the Conference of Latin American bishops at Medellín, Colombia, marked a decisive point, together with Vatican II in 1963–5. Gustavo Gutiérrez (b. 1928) of Peru devised the agenda for the conference, publishing it as *The Theology of Liberation* (1971; Eng., 1973). He called for solidarity with the poor and oppressed. He referred to the biblical exodus from bondage. Other early liberation theologians included José Porfirio Miranda and Juan Luis Segundo. The 'second generation' of liberation theologians included Leonardo and Clodovis Boff and numerous others. Critics claim that they use biblical texts selectively, and constantly repeat the same themes.

Logos. This Greek word simply means *word, statement, communication* or *rational principle.* In John 1.1 it describes Jesus Christ as God's eternal self-communication. Because *logos* was used in a variety of ways in the first-century Graeco-Roman world, including its meaning as rational principle in philosophy, many of the early church fathers used the term in Christology to reach a non-Jewish audience.

Love (Heb., *'āhēb, 'ahabāh*; Gk, *agapaō, agapē*) is part of the command to love God 'with all your heart' (Deut. 6.5). The fact that love can be commanded shows that it is *not an emotion*, but an act of *will* and habit. Thus God set his love upon Israel (Deut. 7.7), not because they were more numerous than any other people, but because God loves them. Jesus also urges, 'You shall love the Lord your God' (Mark 12.28–34), and 'Love your enemies' (Matt. 5.44). Paul declares, 'Nothing in all creation will be able to separate us from the love of God in Christ Jesus' (Rom. 8.39). Anders Nygren (1890–1978) showed that in NT *uses* of the word, *love* is spontaneous and creative of value. It does not depend on merit.

Lutheranism denotes the theology of those who follow Martin Luther (1483–1546), founder of the Reformation. It often stands in contrast to Calvinism or Reformed theology, as well as to Catholicism. It also excludes the charismatic theology of the Radical Reformers, and Zwingli's notion of the Eucharist. Justification by faith alone is central. Lutheran theology is enshrined in the Augsburg Confession (1530) and the Book of Concord (1580), and Lutheranism has become the state church in some Scandinavian countries and the main Protestant church in much of Germany. It has also spread to North America.

Mediation, Mediator (Heb., *mēlits*; Gk, *mesitēs*) denotes one who stands between two parties, a go-between, one who represents one party to the other. Priests represent the prayers of their people to God, and are therefore called 'ascending' mediators; prophets represent the commands of God to the people, and are therefore called 'descending' mediators. In the OT Moses represents a classic mediator, and in the NT Jesus Christ is our mediator (Heb. 8.6). Paul is a mediator; he and Moses are willing to be blotted out of God's book if he will hear them (Exod. 32.32; Rom. 9.3). Such a mediator is 'a man torn in two'.

Mennonites originally derived their name from Menno Simons (1496–1561), who became an Anabaptist. The group insists on believers' baptism and congregational government, but in particular on non-violence and withdrawal from magistrates. In the twentieth century there were 226,000 in the USA at one time, and 18,000 in Germany. Stanley Hauerwas (b. 1940) has firm Mennonite roots.

Mercy, divine (Heb., *r-ch-m*; Gk, *hilaskomai, eleos*) occurs respectively in 'O God, have mercy on me, a sinner' (Luke 18.13), and 'God, who is rich in mercy' (Eph. 2.4). The Hebrew noun denotes *pity, compassion* and *love* (Ps. 103.1). The Greek *eleos* denotes compassion, but is not exclusive to God. Blind men cry for sight, based on mercy (Matt. 9.27). As the mercy of God, it overlaps with *chēn, grace*. Paul also speaks of 'the mercies of God' (Rom. 12.1; Gk, *oiktirmos*). This denotes God's collective compassion.

Messiah (Heb., *māshiakh*; Gk, *christos*) means *Anointed One*. Kings and high priests were anointed in Israel, but three things characterized the Messiah: (1) the anointing would be an unprecedented anointing by the Holy Spirit of God; (2) this would be for the end time; (3) the Messiah would be anointed to bring in the kingdom of God. The figure of the Messiah has royal roots, as exemplified in the title 'Son of David'. He would exceed David in every way. Peter in Acts 2.34–35, and Hebrews 1.5, 8, cite the royal Psalms 2.7 and 110.1 as applying to Jesus as Messiah. In the prophetic tradition Isaiah 11.1–9 looks forward to a kingly, Anointed One. The resurrection of Christ depends, as Pannenberg (1928–2014) asserts, on its being a cosmic event of the end. Further, the entire preaching of Jesus Christ concerns the imminence of the kingdom of God, or the reign of God (Mark 1.15).

Methodism's origins lie with John Wesley (1703–91). The term 'Methodist' derived from his student days at Oxford, when John and his brother

Charles, together with George Whitefield and their friends, were nick-named 'the Holy Club' or 'Methodists', because of their strict rules for holiness. Wesley sought to preach the gospel in America, where he was influenced by the Moravians. Both Wesley brothers were ordained as Anglicans. John dated his conversion to 1738. The break came when he ordained Francis Asbury and Thomas Coke, even though Anglican authorities recognized only episcopal ordination. Wesley founded chapels in London, Bristol and Newcastle. The first Methodist Conference was held in 1744, and a system of 'circuits' set up. Charles had urged that in spite of blemishes, the Church of England remained nearer to Scripture than other churches.

Millennium, millenarianism signifies belief in a thousand-year period in which saints will rule, while the devil is bound. This depends on a debatable reading of Revelation 20.1–10. Some claim that 1 Corinthians 15.22–28 and 1 Thessalonians 4.15–17 also support the idea, but Paul, John, the Synoptic Gospels and Hebrews seem silent about the notion, and exegesis of these passages remains doubtful. 'Premillennialists' believe that the millennium will follow the Parousia (or future return of Christ); 'postmillennialists' believe that it will occur *before* the return of Christ. A premillennial view was defended by J. N. Darby, the Scofield Reference Bible (1909), J. F. Walvoord and the popular writer Hal Lindsey. The respected NT scholar G. B. Caird calls the theory 'demonstrably false'.

Missiology denotes the study of the theology and practice of mission. As a specific sub-discipline of practical theology, it developed only in the nineteenth century, with Alexander Duff in Edinburgh. Gustav Warneck founded a journal for the subject in 1874, and became Professor of Mission at Halle. In the 1960s a debate about the nature and goal of mission began. Many still stress the Great Commission of Matthew 28.18–20. Others urge the broadening scope of mission beyond evangelism. Some stressed its social aspect, or related it to Christ's 'sending' by the Father. Often the broader and narrower concepts became polarized. Religious pluralism seemed to question the evangelistic concept, although some tended to forget that first-century preaching took place in a pluralistic environment.

Modernism arose from the desire to free theological studies from its commitment to supposedly outworn ecclesial dogmas which were perceived to place obstacles in the way of what 'modern man' could find credible. In practice this impinged mainly on biblical criticism and scientific research. Much biblical criticism emerged to offer a *purely historical* approach to the biblical writings without the supposed 'distraction' of theology. Similarly in the wake of Darwin, modernists sought to show that they took account of scientific discoveries. The modernist Protestant movement owed much to Harnack (1851–1930). Catholic modernism had similar motivations, and owed much to Alfred F. Loisy (1857–1940), and George Tyrrell (1861–1908).

Monism sought in origin to reduce a dualism of mind and body radically into *one*. The term was coined by Christian Wolff (1679–1754). Spinoza (1632–77) represents substantival monism, i.e. whatever exists is part of a single substance. It rejects both dualism and pluralism, and primarily constitutes a philosophical world-view.

Monotheism (Gk, *monos*, one or alone, and *theos*, God) denotes belief in one God. Judaism, Christianity and Islam are monotheistic religions. But it would be mistaken to assume that 'one' is solely or primarily *numerical*. Numerals, Gregory of Nyssa argued, apply only to finite, created, people or objects. The Ten Commandments rightly prohibit 'other gods' because the God of Israel demands total loyalty and obedience (Exod. 20.1–4; Deut. 5.6–8) to the sole Creator and Redeemer. Hence to worship Jesus as Lord does not infringe monotheism.

Mysticism denotes a sense of the immediacy of God which transcends cognitive thought. Some appeal to Paul's experience of being 'caught up to the third heaven' (2 Cor. 12.2). Positively, many medieval monks and nuns have been inspired to express their experience in beautiful prayers. Negatively, Luther questioned the notion of 'ascent' and 'ladders' *upwards* to God, in contrast to the downward direction of grace *from above*. Some mystics have suggested a needed measure of 'control'. Walter Hilton (*c.* 1343–96) and Bernard of Clairvaux (1090–1153) offer examples. But the lack of critical awareness may sometimes be deceptive, e.g. in the frequent use of 'pictures', which Wittgenstein rightly says can be 'variously interpreted'.

Narrative theology follows from the very positive research into the *many functions* of narrative which literary theory has exposed. Narratives do not merely report, as Paul Ricoeur stresses. Such concepts as 'narrative time' and 'narrative world' have released theology and biblical studies from remaining imprisoned in an unduly *chronological* understanding of *all* biblical narratives. Mark, for example, clearly varies narrative time to show that events proceed to the cross. In narrative theory a flood of light is shed on narrative by Genette, Ricoeur, Chatman, Frei, Crites, Kort and others. Yet on the negative side, narrative theology has become almost an uncritical fashion. 'Story' has come to be used in a loose, undisciplined, way. At its best, however, it remains of great value to theology.

Neo-orthodoxy is perhaps a dated label for the early twentieth-century theologies of Barth, Brunner, Niebuhr, Bonhoeffer and Aulén, who reacted against the liberal theology of the previous generation. It is unclear whom this label includes. Many would include the earlier Bultmann. Perhaps it has now served its purpose, especially since its scope is debated.

Nicaea, Council of, known as the First Ecumenical Council, was held in 325. It was convened by the Emperor Constantine to address the Arian controversy and to promote church unity. Eusebius, in effect court theologian, probably presided. Athanasius and the Alexandrians persuaded the council to accept that the Son was 'of the same being (Gk, *homoousios*)' as God the Father, and the Trinitarian formula was introduced. Arius was sentenced to be exiled. The 'Nicene' Creed, as it is known, was a revision approved by the Council of Constantinople (381).

Numinous, as a term, is drawn from Rudolf Otto's *The Idea of the Holy* (1917; Eng., 1923). Otto used it to describe the experience of reverence, 'creature-feeling', awe, wonder and overpoweringness, in the presence of the holy, transcendent, God. God, who is regarded as 'wholly other', inspires the experience of '*mysterium tremendum et fascinans*'. This experience stands in contrast to what is rational or intellectual.

Ontological argument, the, is one of the three (or four) classic arguments for the existence of God. It was first formulated by Anselm (*c.* 1033–1109) as a statement of faith. In its basic form Anselm declared, 'We believe that You [God] are that than which nothing greater can be conceived.' It represents an *a priori* argument which demonstrates the impossibility of the non-existence of God. Descartes (1596–1650) formulated it as a philosophical argument. Kant (1724–1804) and Russell (1872–1970) proposed devastating criticisms of it, mainly insisting that 'existence' could not count as an attribute. Malcolm (1911–90) and Plantinga (b. 1932) defended it through modal logic, and it is the subject of vigorous philosophical debate today.

Open theism suggests that God is 'open' in two ways. First, God may choose to limit his absolute sovereignty in response to human actions. Arguably, as Swinburne (b. 1934) suggests, the biblical God may 'repent' of a proposed act when humankind repents. Second, God is also open to the future; every single event is *not pre-ordained*, even if the ultimate goal is. Moltmann (b. 1926) and Polkinghorne (b. 1930) tend towards this view, but Thomist theologians oppose it.

Original righteousness denotes the view that God imparted perfect righteousness to humankind before the fall. Ambrose and Augustine imply it, and Roman Catholicism officially holds it. Today most theologians decline to speculate about the period before the fall.

Orthopraxis denotes right behaviour and action, in contrast to orthodoxy which denotes right opinion, belief or doctrine. It concerns a practical way of life.

Panentheism is compatible with theism, whereas pantheism is not. Panentheism simply emphasizes the immanence of God, as the One who sustains all life and everything, alongside his being holy and transcendent.

Pantheism (Gk., *pan*, all, and *theism*, belief in God) denotes the belief that God is everything, in contrast both to *theism* and *deism*. Either God is identified with the world (as in Spinoza) or the world is regarded as an emanation or outflow of God (as in neoplatonism). Many Eastern religions are pantheistic. Christianity, Judaism and Islam carefully differentiate God the Creator and his world, which is finite and creaturely.

Paraclete (Gk, *paraklētos*) is the term used for the Holy Spirit in John 14—16. It means *mediator, helper* or *one who intercedes on another's behalf.* The Paraclete is given as a witness to Jesus Christ. Many argue that the term means *advocate* or *defending counsel,* although recently the legal use has been questioned. Barrett has suggested that it may also mean *prosecuting counsel,* for he 'convicts the world of sin' (John 16.8). The Spirit continues the presence of Jesus (14.16–17). Jesus also declares, 'I will not leave you orphaned; I am coming to you' (14.18). The Paraclete effaces himself and advertises Jesus: 'He will not speak on his own (Gk, *aph' heautou*, of himself) . . . He will glorify me' (16.13–14).

Parousia. In academic circles the term Parousia is usually preferred to the more popular 'Second Coming' of Christ. The Greek term *parousia* includes both the royal arrival in pomp of an emperor, and the final, public, coming of Christ at the end. Some scholars prefer the ambiguity of this term to include both Christ's coming in the present and his future coming as a vindication of his promises and public glory.

Pietism is an influential post-Reformation movement, which included P. J. Spener (1635–1705), F. C. Oetinger (1703–82) and Nikolaus, Count von Zinzendorf (1700–60). It was concerned to promote personal holiness and renewal, and Zinzendorf influenced John Wesley. It reacted both against the shallow rationalism of the eighteenth-century Enlightenment, and the rigid formalism of much Protestant orthodoxy. It emphasized the work of the Holy Spirit, new birth, justification, sanctification and vocation. The movement reflected a spectrum of opinions, and Johann Bengel (1687–1752) was one of its most scholarly advocates.

Pluralism, religious, is not a new phenomenon. From its beginnings until the reign of the Emperor Constantine (*c.* 313) the Christian faith had always been no more than one among many religious voices, and had learned not only to cope with this, but to use it as an opportunity, even in times of persecution. The monopoly of 'Christendom' in the West lasted only from Constantine (or perhaps Gregory of Rome) until Muslim expansion into Europe, and otherwise until the mid-twentieth century. Then Hick (1922–2012) on the Protestant side (with 'mutual acceptance'), and Rahner (1904–84) on the Catholic side (with 'anonymous Christianity'), began attempts to make overtures to other religions.

Pneumatology (Gk, *pneuma*, spirit) denotes the Christian doctrine of the Holy Spirit. In practice Pentecostals and Charismatics often favour this term. Traditionally this doctrine has been largely neglected. It developed far more slowly than Christology. But from the 1980s there has been an explosion of works on this subject, not least from Moltmann (b. 1926) and Zizioulas (b. 1931), among others. Moltmann stresses that the Spirit makes, preserves and perfects the world, 'indwelling, sympathizing . . . delighting and glorifying' it, as well as urging the importance of practical experiences and gifts. He argues for his personhood and co-equality in the

Trinity. Zizioulas urges, 'There is . . . no Christ until the Spirit is at work' (*Being as Communion*, p. 127). Some stress his holiness and transcendence. There are today growing conversations of mutual respect between Pentecostals and others.

Polytheism (Gk, *polus*, many, and *theos*, god) denotes the view that many gods exist. It stands in contrast to monotheism, the view that only one God exists or is sovereign. Monotheistic faith may also mean the pledge of total loyalty to the one God. Some hold to a purely subjective polytheism, namely that in practice people believe in many gods, irrespective of their objective existence. Some call this 'paganism'.

Postcolonial theology is regarded by many as a development of liberation theology. It aims to liberate theology from an imperialist mindset and conceptual framework. R. S. Sugirthararajah, a major exponent of it, argues that it is often connected to neo-Marxism. Gerald West regards it as a movement of indigenous peoples against specific forms of oppression. Edward Said seeks to unmask 'Eurocentric' assumptions. In more extreme forms, it seeks to remove such terms as 'king' from biblical traditions.

Post-liberal theology has been defined in two ways. More recently it reflects the aim of George Lindbeck (b. 1923) to avoid 'polarization between tradition and innovation' by drawing on Clifford Geertz's 'thick description' of intertextual worlds. On the positive side, it seeks to be ecumenical and to give primacy to the text of 'a scriptural world'. Negatively, some argue that it reduces truth in favour of the Church. An older meaning of post-liberal theology concerns the protest of Barth and others against the liberalism of Harnack (1851–1930) and his era. Kelsey, Frei and the 'Yale' School are broadly associated with the more recent view.

Postmodern theology. As David Griffin and Graham Ward insist, there is no single postmodern theology, but only varieties of postmodern theologies. Their status is vigorously debated. As is the case with postmodernism in general, some themes are hugely valuable, while others are disastrous. At best, it follows Foucault in investigating the relation between knowledge and power. It also investigates concepts which lie beyond standard questions, for example, indeterminacy, uncertainty, scepticism, and issues more familiar in the philosophy of religion. At worst, it goes too far in accepting these concepts too uncritically. In the USA, Rorty and Fish are over-ready to accept pragmatic criteria of truth. Kevin Vanhoozer (b. 1957) is one warning voice.

Prayer includes many different ways of communicating with God. It may include: worship, adoration, praise, thanksgiving, confession, petition, intercession, lament and much else. Paul urges that the *Holy Spirit* initiates prayer in accordance with the mind of God (Rom. 8.15, 27). Jesus taught that prayer is normally addressed to God as Father. The Lord's Prayer concerns God's holiness, kingdom and will, daily food, forgiveness and deliverance from evil. It is part of *a Trinitarian dialogue: to* the Father, *through* the Son and *by* the Holy Spirit. Kant thought that prayer meant *only subjective* adjustment to God's will. If God knows our needs, many ask, why pray? We pray for the 'best possible', because the best possible when people pray is 'better than' the 'best possible' when they do not.

Predestination is the doctrine that God has determined the goal and purpose of humankind in advance. Usually this is to salvation; in harsher forms, this is also to damnation. Paul speaks of being 'predestined to be conformed to the image of his Son' (Rom. 8.29), and of God's calling 'those whom he predestined . . . [to be] justified . . . glorified' (v. 30). Mainly to stress God's sovereignty, Augustine (354–430) and Calvin (1509–64) in effect taught double predestination. This needs to be understood in context, and in the light of concepts of dualism and hell (see above). In Paul it assures us that nothing can stop God's plan.

Pre-existence in theology usually refers to the pre-existence of Christ. But it may also refer to the pre-existence of the human soul, as in Origen (*c.* 185 – *c.* 254) and Plato. Origen, however, needed to presuppose a dualist view of the 'soul' for his argument, and it rests more on Plato than Scripture. On the pre-existence of Christ, traditionalists cite Philippians 2.5–11 as decisive, usually together with the birth narratives, John 1.1–4 and 1 Corinthians 8.6. Dunn (b. 1939), among others, considers that 'born of a woman' does not imply the pre-existence of Jesus. But Pannenberg (1928–2014) and many others argue that 'The eternal relation of the Father to the Son may not be detached from the Incarnation of the Son . . . We can thus speak of the pre-existence of the Son of God'. Jesus is the 'eternal' Son. Paul and Hebrews regard the Son as co-Creator of the world (1 Cor. 8.6; Col. 1.16; Heb. 1.2).

Prevenient grace denotes grace that goes before, i.e. grace also gives us the will to receive it. Augustine (354–430) is said to have coined the term: 'Grace anticipates us . . . that we may be called.' Similarly Thomas Aquinas (1225–74) spoke of prevenient and subsequent grace. It reflects the belief that we owe everything to grace alone.

Key terms

Promise, promissory language (Gk., *epaggelia*; Heb., simply *dābār*, word) occurs 50 or 60 times in the NT. It is used in God's promise to Abraham (Rom. 4.13–20), and God's promise to Israel (Rom. 9.4–9). God makes promises primarily in the context of the covenant. A promise is a pledge or commitment, which ties one's options to perform what one has promised. Few things indicate the grace and faithfulness of God more strikingly. It is not surprising that Luther, Tyndale, Barth, Rahner, Moltmann and Pannenberg regard promise as a primary mode of God's word. The philosopher J. L. Austin has shown how promise is a speech-act, which can change situations.

Providence (Gk, *pronoia*) occurs in the LXX of apocryphal books, but not in the NT. Jesus taught that God the Father cares for birds (Matt. 10.29; Luke 12.24), 'clothes the grass of the field' and cares for disciples (Matt. 6.30). The overarching purpose of Acts reflects God's oversight of the expansion of the Church, in spite of setbacks (Acts 8.4). God's purpose in the crucifixion of Jesus provides a pre-eminent example. God has control of history, as 'the fullness of time' (Gal. 4.4) implies. Ephesians 1.10 speaks of God's plan. H. P. Owen argues that several factors combine to form the concept of providence: God's foresight, control of history, care of the world and purpose.

Purgatory. Pope Benedict XII declared in the fourteenth century, 'There is a purgatory that is a state of punishment and purification, in which . . . souls . . . are purified.' Earlier, Aquinas (1225–74) had declared that purgatory supplements Christ's satisfaction. Most Protestants, however, reject the idea, on the ground that the work of Christ is wholly complete and perfect, and once-for-all. If the resurrection body is characterized by the Holy Spirit, this doubly obviates any need for other means of purification. The passage about fire in 1 Corinthians 3.11–15 is irrelevant.

Puritanism emerged during the reign of Elizabeth I. It was originally a protest against the Elizabethan settlement of 1559, and the inclusion of more 'Romish' elements in the Book of Common Prayer, compared with the 1552 Prayer Book of Edward VI. Most Puritans belonged to the Reformed tradition, but some, like Richard Baxter (1615–91), remained loyal clergy of the Church of England. The movement continued until the seventeenth century and afterwards.

Queer theology is a very recent development. It concerns human sexuality in marginalized groups. Thus it considers 'heteronormativity' among gays, lesbians and transgendered people. It tends to regard 'given' categories as mere conventions. It owes much to the postmodernism of Foucault.

Rapture, the. This concept owes much to John N. Darby (1800–82) and the Scofield Reference Bible (1909). Supposedly Paul predicts the rapture in 1 Thessalonians 4.16–17. Bernard McGinn describes it as 'Christ's bodily rescue of the faithful by way of a collective, physical ascent to heaven'. Christ will 'snatch' true believers to heaven. In 'premillennial dispensationalism' (see Dispensationalism; Millennium) this rescue will occur from the dire tribulation that comes before the end. Such an interpretation is often tied to a particular hermeneutic of the book of Revelation. It is influential in the USA, but is not favoured by biblical specialist scholars.

Recapitulation (Lat., *recapitulatio*; Gk, *anakephalaiōsis*), often based on Ephesians 1.10, is generally associated with Irenaeus (*c.* 130 – *c.* 200). The NRSV translates God's purpose as 'to gather up all things in him [Christ]'. Irenaeus writes, 'The only-begotten Son came to us . . . summing up His [God's] own handiwork in Himself' (*Against Heresies*, 4.6.2). He means by this restoring humankind's defects by reliving every stage of life on our behalf.

Reception theory enquires into the effects which texts generate on subsequent readers. It shows how successive generations of interpreters, communities, artists and literary figures have read the texts in question. It resists the notion of a 'closed past'. In the modem era its founder was Hans Robert Jauss (1921–97). Texts, he argued, perform a socially formative function. A central feature is a horizon of expectation, which radically affects understanding. He was influenced by Gadamer's (1900–2002) notion of an unfinished meaning, questioning the text, and *Wirkungsgeschichte* (effective history). In biblical studies Ulrich Luz pioneered this approach, and it has now become a major field of study.

Reconciliation (Gk, *katallagē*) is distinctive to Paul as his way of explaining God's overcoming the alienation or estrangement brought about by sin. He describes the gospel as the word of reconciliation (Rom. 11.15). In 2 Corinthians 5.19 he writes, 'In Christ God was reconciling the world to himself'; in Romans 5.10, 'If while we were enemies (Gk, *echthroi*), we were reconciled to God . . . much more . . . will we be saved by his life.' The logic of reconciliation depends on change of status (cf. Gk, *allos*, other) from enemy to friend (cf. Rom. 8.7). The brilliance of Paul's concept can be seen when we recall how frequently reconciliation is used in modern life: e.g. in marriage and divorce, in industrial disputes, in relations between nations, and so on. Its meaning is transparent.

Redemption (Heb., *pādāh, gā'al*; Gk, *agorazō*) denotes purchase or rescue *from* a state of jeopardy or oppression *to* a new status of safety or new ownership *by* a costly or redemptive act. The classic example or paradigm-case is Israel's redemption *from* oppression in Egypt *to* a new secure status as God's people *by* the redemptive act of the exodus. In Greek *agorazō* regularly means *buying* in everyday life. But the metaphor should not be pressed. To ask, 'To whom is a price paid?' is not part of the theological metaphor. The word simply indicates *cost*. We must not be distracted by Deissmann's alleged parallels with Graeco-Roman freedom from slavery. Dale B. Martin has shown that redemption was not to 'freedom' as such, but to Christ as our new gracious master.

Reformation. In spite of more obscure uses of the term, the Reformation widely denotes the theology instigated by Martin Luther (1483–1546). In 1517 he nailed up his famous Ninety-five Theses, which were primarily directed against papal indulgences. These supposedly exempted those who paid for indulgences from a number of years in purgatory (see Purgatory). Luther regarded them not only as instruments of papal control, but as implying salvation by works. In 1519 the Leipzig Disputation was decisive in urging the authority of Scripture, and justification by grace through faith alone followed. Luther was excommunicated at the Diet of Worms in 1521. In England William Tyndale (*c.* 1494–1536) owed much to Luther's thought, and like Luther translated the Bible into the common tongue. Ulrich Zwingli (1484–1531) and Philipp Melanchthon (1497–1560) were also first-generation Reformers. John Calvin (1509–64) was a second-generation Reformer, who brilliantly systematized Reformation theology. In advance of the Reformation John Wycliffe (*c.* 1330–84) heralded the authority of the Bible and misgivings about the papacy.

Repentance (Heb., *nācham, shûbh*; Gk, *metanoeō*) does not mean simply remorse or regret; indeed its meaning is closer to the Hebrew, *to turn round*, than to the Greek component terms, *to have an after-mind*. 2 Kings 17.13 can be translated: 'Turn from your evil ways.' In Mark 1.15 Jesus begins his ministry with, 'The kingdom of God has come near; repent, and believe in the good news.' Peter's sermon after Pentecost includes the words: 'Repent and be baptized . . . in the name of Jesus Christ so that your sins may be forgiven' (Acts 2.38). Paul declares, 'Godly grief produces a repentance that leads to salvation' (2 Cor. 7.10).

Sacrament. This term (Lat., *sacramentum*; Gk, *mustērion*) does not appear in the biblical writings, but emerged in the second century. In Protestant theology the two sacraments are baptism and the Eucharist or Lord's Supper. Whether we conceive of seven sacraments or two depends largely on how we define *sacrament*. (1) At its broadest almost any object can represent a spiritual reality. (2) Roman Catholic and Eastern Orthodox traditions include ordination, marriage, confirmation, penance and often extreme unction. These all include visible, tangible signs, e.g. a wedding ring, the laying on of hands, and so on. (3) Biblical writers validate baptism and the Lord's Supper as dominical and pre-Pauline visible means of grace. Both sacraments associate grace with the death of Christ (Rom. 6.3–11; 1 Cor. 11.23–26). Paul says that in the Lord's Supper 'you proclaim the Lord's death' (1 Cor. 11.26). Controversy about repetition in the Mass may be partly solved by understanding sacraments as dramatic re-presentations of the one unrepeatable event.

Sacrifice could be of four types in the OT, also broadly divided between gift sacrifices and expiatory sacrifices. (1) The *minchah*, meal-offering or gift, was often enacted in response to some favour or blessing. (2) The burnt offering (Heb., *'olā*) expressed devotion, and formed part of the regular morning and evening sacrifices. (3) The *sheˡāmîm*, or peace offerings, expressed communion with God. (4) The guilt offering or sin offering (*'āshām*) expressed expiation for sin. In the NT, Hebrews regards Christ as the perfect fulfilment of all types of sacrifice. He is the full, perfect and sufficient sacrifice for sin, as well as that with which God is well pleased. His sacrifice is therefore once-for-all (Gk, *ephapax*; Heb. 7.27; 9.12; cf. Rom. 6.10). Hebrews shows that sacrifice is not merely a culture-relative ordinance of the OT, as does Paul.

Sanctification (Gk, *hagiōsunē* from *hagios*) means either *made holy* or *being made holy*. The difference may seem trivial, but it explains deep controversy about the subject. Most Christians regard sanctification as a *long process enacted by the Holy Spirit*, which may at times involve temptation and struggle, and which has being like Christ as its goal. Some, especially many Pentecostals, regard 'baptism in the Spirit' (at times almost a synonym) as an event, not a process. 'Holy' means set apart for God. Hence it may apply to objects (holy city, holy ground) and people (Holy Father, holy apostles). In the history of thought, sanctification is a major work of the Holy Spirit.

Sinless perfection is often based on those biblical passages which speak of being perfect: 'Be perfect, therefore, as your heavenly Father is perfect' (Matt. 5.48). But the Greek word translated *perfect* (*teleios*) may be translated *mature, being full-grown*. A further difficulty is whether this constitutes an immediate goal or an ultimate one. Some claim that John Wesley believed in sinless perfection, but this remains controversial. Others regard John Fletcher, his deputy, as holding this view. 1 John is clear: 'If we say that we have no sin, we deceive ourselves' (1.8).

Sobernost is a virtually untranslatable Russian term that characterizes much in Russian Orthodox theology. Some have suggested catholicity, solidarity or *koinōnia* (fellowship, mutual participation) as its meaning.

Soteriology (Gk, *sōtēria*, salvation) denotes the doctrine of salvation, which in practice relates closely to the saving work of Christ. It also means attention to the three tenses of salvation as past deliverance and justification, the present process of growth and sanctification, and the future destiny of resurrection and hope. In practice it involves the purpose of God the Father, the redemptive work of Christ, and the constant agency of the Holy Spirit. Many terms indicate it, including grace, election, covenant, reconciliation, redemption, perseverance, assurance and beatific vision.

Soul (Heb., *nephesh*; Gk, *psychē*). The Hebrew and Greek terms seldom mean *soul* rather than *life*. The Hebrew *nephesh* can even mean *dead body*. Admittedly the term may *sometimes* mean *soul* in contrast to *body*, but this is not the characteristic NT meaning. It frequently means *life, self, person* or *living being*. Thus Jesus asks, 'What will it profit them if they gain the whole world but forfeit their life' (Gk, *tēn psychēn*)? Or what will they give in return for their life?' (Gk, *tēs psychēs autou*; NRSV rendering of Matt. 6.26). In Paul the adjective *psychikos* usually means *ordinary* in contrast to *spiritual* (1 Cor. 2.14; 15.44). In Romans 2.9 *psychē* means simply *person*. It is a very different matter in the post-biblical period. 'Soul' remains important in Thomas Aquinas (1225–74) and probably Augustine. Following Aquinas, the Roman Catholic *Catechism of Christian Doctrine* (1971) declares, 'My soul is like God because it is a spirit and is immortal.' This is a popular view, but not a biblical one. Edmund Hill laments that it commits Catholics to the dualist view satirized by Gilbert Ryle of 'the ghost in the machine'.

Spirit (Lat., *spiritus*; Heb., *rûach*; Gk, *pneuma*) often has meanings in philosophy and popular thought which would be alien to characteristic biblical uses of the term. Plato popularized the notion that *spirit* usually means *mind* in contrast to the physical body. In philosophy the German *Geist* may mean both, and nineteenth-century idealism reflects this, with Fichte, Hegel and others. Sometimes biblical writers also use the word in this way. The Hebrew *rûach* may mean *wind* (perhaps Gen. 1.2) or attitude of mind (Gen. 43.27; Prov. 11.13). But overwhelmingly the term alludes to the Spirit of God (Isa. 42.1). Similarly *pneuma* in the NT may refer to evil spirits (Matt. 10.1; Mark 5.8) or to what stands in contrast to body (1 Cor. 5.3), but the overwhelming majority of uses denote the Holy Spirit of God (Rom. 8.9–11; 1 Cor. 2.12). In the history of theology, Greek philosophy and Plato influenced many, and then *spirit* often means 'immaterial'. But the biblical use has today become more prominent among theologians.

Spirituality may be defined in two radically different ways, which correspond with the two uses of *spirit*. In popular terms, it has come into vogue in the last 50 years to denote virtually any concern for what lies beyond this world. In the nineteenth century people spoke of humankind's 'higher' aspirations. It is sometimes used as a softer alternative to 'religious' faith, or to a specific faith. The second sense of *spirituality* is what earlier Christians called *godliness*. More specifically it denotes that for which Paul used *pneumatikos*, namely what is prompted and characterized by the Holy Spirit (1 Cor. 2.13; 12.1; 14.1; 15.44). The first use may be convenient in avoiding giving offence, but the two uses must not be confused.

Subordinationism broadly regards God the Son (or the Son and the Holy Spirit) as subordinate to God the Father. Arius was one of those who supported this view. Some have quoted Paul: 'God is the head of Christ' (1 Cor. 11.3) as implying such a view. But there is a special context in Corinth that accounts for this. The church fathers emphatically argued for the co-equality of the persons of the Trinity. They pointed to their mutual participation in salvation and to the uniqueness of their status as uncreated beings.

Syncretism (Gk, *sunkretizō*, to combine) denotes the blending of different philosophical or religious schools of thought to gain a unified viewpoint.

It began with philosophical viewpoints in Plutarch, but nowadays refers especially to the blending of religions, and is often viewed by critics as compromise between them.

Teleological argument, the, (Gk, *telos*, goal, purpose) is also known as the argument (for the existence of God) from design. It is one of the classic three (or four) arguments, and is said to depend on the cosmological argument, on causality. Kant rejected the formal validity of the argument, but respected humankind's sense of design. Plato and Aristotle used it, and it was the fifth of Aquinas' 'five ways'. William Paley's (1743–1805) formulation is classic. The discovery of a watch, he argued, would be different from drawing inferences from a stone. Its delicate mechanism would suggest a watchmaker. Earlier, however, David Hume (1711–76) had doubted whether 'cause and effect' could be observed, rather than constant conjunction. Darwin's theory of evolution constituted a more serious challenge. This, appeared to substitute the random 'survival of the fittest' for divine design. Nevertheless, F. R. Tennant (1866–1957) argued that order and purpose could be gradual, and today Richard Swinburne (b. 1934) has expanded his arguments. Richard Dawkins has recently combined evolutionary difficulties with genetic ones to attack the argument. However, John Polkinghorne (b. 1930) has deployed a number of convincing arguments in defence of it.

Temptation (Heb., *massah*; Gk, *peirasmos*) may denote either *testing* or *temptation*. The Greek may refer to the eschatological trial or to daily testing. Linguistically, *temptation* is just as likely. James 1.2 regards it as an occasion for joy, and assures us that it 'produces endurance' (1.3). 1 Peter 1.6–7 suggests that it shows whether faith is genuine. The Holy Spirit 'drove' (*ekballei*) Jesus toward his messianic temptations (Mark 1.2). Yet Jesus urges us to pray, 'Lead us not into temptation' (AV) or 'Do not bring us to the time of trial' (NRSV; Matt. 6.13; Luke 11.4). But Jesus does not advocate withdrawal from the world. Struggle is essential for growth in the world, as Luther and more recently Käsemann (1906–98) insist. Hebrews also regards Jesus in his struggles, as 'in every respect . . . as we are, yet without sin' (4.15).

Theism denotes belief in God who engages with the world in communication and action. It affirms both his transcendence and his immanence. Hence it differs from both deism and pantheism, as well as from atheism and agnosticism. Moltmann (b. 1926) has questioned whether the term is too static, in comparison with the living God of the Bible.

Thomism denotes the philosophical theology which emerged from Thomas Aquinas (1225–74). Thomas utilized the rediscovery of Aristotle, and drew deeply on Augustine. His system became the standard theology for official Roman Catholicism. Pope Leo XII renewed the call to return to his philosophy in 1879. More recently Étienne Gilson (1884–1978) and Jacques Maritain (1882–1973) provide examples of Thomist philosophers. Both faith and reason are defended.

Time has become increasingly important today. Clock-time is but one manifestation of time. Heidegger has explored subjective time, i.e. how humankind perceives it. Literary theorists (e.g. Genette) show how narrators use temporal speed, flashbacks, and so on, as tools which transcend chronological time. Physicists since Einstein and Dirac show how time takes a different form and speed in space travel. In theology it is generally agreed that, as Augustine expressed it, God created the universe *with* time, not *in* time. Eternity is not, most argue, timelessness. Nor is it everlasting duration. It may involve what Boethius called simultaneity, which holds together past, present and future. Or (plausibly in view of scientific and literary advances) it may be an aspect of time, not as we know time, but in a new, unprecedented dimension.

Transcendence is *not* to be confused with *transcendental*, which concerns Kant's philosophy. *Transcendence* applies to God, to indicate that he is infinitely *beyond* and *above* the universe. 'Above' and 'beyond' can only hint at God's otherness, majesty and holiness. Isaiah's throne vision conveys the idea: 'Holy, holy, holy' declare the angels, and cover their faces in reverence (Isa. 6.1–6). Kierkegaard (1813–55), Otto (1869–1937) and Barth (1886–1968) are three of those who urge that God is transcendent; humankind is creaturely.

Transubstantiation denotes the theory of Aquinas (1225–74) through categories drawn from Aristotle, that accounts for how bread and wine can become the body and blood of Christ in the Mass. The elements *appear* to remain bread and wine, while their substance changes. Aristotle had distinguished *substance* from *accidents*. Aquinas urged that in the underlying *reality* of *substance* the bread and wine became the body and blood of Christ. But the *accidents*, which are what we see and touch, remain to all *appearances* simply bread and wine. Luther did not dissent from the transformation, but resisted Aquinas' use of a pagan philosopher to explain it. This is still the official doctrine of the Catholic Church.

Unitarianism is a form of religious belief that rejects the doctrine of the Holy Trinity. The Racovian Catechism (1605) was the first formal statement of Unitarianism. The movement began in Poland, and spread to parts of Europe. In the eighteenth century some Baptists became Unitarians. Unitarians stress the unity of God.

Universalism. Many today defend 'hoped-for universalism', while rejecting 'dogmatic universalism'. The latter states, 'We *know* that all humankind will be saved'; the former states, 'We *hope* that all humankind will be saved'. F. D. Maurice (1805–72) was ejected from his university chair on the ground of holding universalism. But he had merely expressed it as a *possibility*, not a certainty. Today Hans Urs von Balthasar (1905–88) and Karl Rahner (1904–84) hold it as a hope, and Moltmann (b. 1926) sees anything less than this as a defeat for grace. In the patristic era Origen and Gregory of Nyssa held to the restoration of all things. Irenaeus regarded separation from God, the source of life, as leading to loss of life or extinction. This avoids the difficulty of eternal dualism.

Vatican II was convened by Pope John XXIII (1958–63), and was held from 1963 to 1965. It proved to be a watershed in Roman Catholicism. It aimed to renew the Church and its vision, and to initiate dialogue with other churches. About 2,600 bishops participated, with over 200 theologians as advisors. These included Karl Rahner, Yves Congar and Hans Küng. About a third of the bishops came from Europe, a third from the Americas, and a third from Asia, Africa and Australia. The most memorable conclusions included the following: parts of worship need no longer be in Latin, but in the vernacular; the priesthood of all believers was emphasized; bishops were to observe a collegial relationship, and were to teach and preach; the word of God was to be heard with reverence; and the social order, peace and dignity of humankind was to be observed. Yet transubstantiation and the reserved sacrament were retained.

Wrath of God, the, is often misunderstood. It is not the opposite of the *love* of God, but the opposite of *indifference*. Further, love and holiness are *eternal* characteristics of God, whereas his wrath may be temporary and manifested *at particular times*. Nygren (1890–1978) declared that God cannot be indifferent if or when his creation is destroyed. Even a human analogy illustrates this. Would parents or grandparents remain indifferent if a child is bent on self-destruction? Oppressors provoke the wrath of God when they harm God's people. Although C. H. Dodd (1824–1973) notoriously described wrath in impersonal terms as cause and effect in a moral universe, what is true is that often evil acts bring ill effects *internally*. God does not always need to intervene. Yet a God who never shows wrath would be bland and unfeeling, and frequently the wrath of God has a redemptive purpose.

Bibliography

Recommended as textbooks ***
Recommended as seminal works **
Also of special value for this subject *

Abelard, Peter, *Exposition of the Epistle to the Romans*, in Fairweather (ed.), *A Scholastic Miscellany*, pp. 276–87.

Achtemeier, Paul, *The Inspiration of Scripture* (Philadelphia, Pa.: Fortress Press, 1980).

Ahn, Yongnan Jeon, *Interpretation of Tongues and Prophecy in 1 Corinthians 12—14* (Blandford Forum: Deo, 2013; Journal of Pentecostal Theology Supp., ser. 41).

Albright, William F., *From Stone Age to Christianity: Monotheism and the Historical Process* (Baltimore, Md.: Johns Hopkins University Press, 1940).

Anderson, Allan, 'Introduction: World Pentecostalism at the Crossroads', in Anderson and Hollenweger (eds), *Pentecostals after a Century*, pp. 19–31.

**Anderson, Allan, *An Introduction to Pentecostalism: Global Charismatic Christianity* (New York, N.Y.: Cambridge University Press, 2004).

Anderson, Allan H., and Walter J. Hollenweger (eds), *Pentecostals after a Century: Global Perspectives* (Sheffield: Sheffield Academic Press, 1999); Journal of Pentecostal Theology Suppl., ser. 15).

Anselm, *Why God Became Man*, Eng. in Fairweather (ed.), *A Scholastic Miscellany*, pp. 101–46.

Aquinas, Thomas, *Summa Theologiae*, 60 vols (Eng. and Lat., Blackfriars edn, London: Eyre and Spottiswoode, 1963).

Athanasius, *Letters to Serapion*, in C. R. B. Shapland (ed.), *The Letters of Athanasius Concerning the Holy Spirit* (London: Epworth, 1951).

Athanasius, *On the Incarnation* (London: Mowbray, 1963).

Atkinson, James, *The Great Light* (Grand Rapids, Mich.: Eerdmans, 1968).

Atkinson, James (ed.), *Luther: Early Theological Works*, Library of Christian Classics, vol. 16 (London: SCM Press, 1962).

Augustine, *City of God* (Eng., *NPNF*, ser. 1, vol. 2, pp. 1–165).

Augustine, *Confessions and Enchiridion*, in Albert C. Outler (ed.), *Confessions and Enchiridion*, Library of Christian Classics, vol. 7 (Philadelphia, Pa.: Westminster Press, 1965).

Augustine, *On Free Will*, in J. H. Burleigh (ed.), *Augustine: Earlier Writings*, Library of Christian Classics (Philadelphia, Pa.: Westminster Press, 1953).

Augustine, *On the Spirit and the Letter* (Eng., *NPNF*, ser. 1, vol. 5, pp. 89–115); and in John Burnaby (ed.), *Augustine: Later Works*, Library of Christian Classics (Philadelphia, Pa.: Westminster Press, 1955).

*Aulén, Gustaf, *Christus Victor* (London: SPCK, 1931).

*Baillie, Donald M., *God Was in Christ: An Essay on Incarnation and Atonement* (London: Faber & Faber, 1948).

Ballard, Paul, 'Pastoral Theology', *Theology* 91 (1988).

Ballard, Paul, *Practical Theology in Action: Theology in the Service of the Church* (London: SPCK, 1996).

Balthasar, Hans Urs von, *The Glory of the Lord: A Theological Aesthetics*, 7 vols (Eng., Edinburgh: T&T Clark, 1982–9).

Balthasar, Hans Urs von, *The Theology of Karl Barth* (Eng., San Francisco, Calif.: Ignatius Press, 1992).

Balthasar, Hans Urs von, *Theo-drama: Theological Dramatic Theory*, 5 vols (Eng., Edinburgh: T&T Clark, 1988–98).

Barbour, Ian, *Religion and Science* (London: SCM Press, 1998).

Barr, James, *The Semantics of Biblical Language* (Oxford: Oxford University Press, 1961).

Barr, James, *Old and New in Interpretation: A Study of the Two Testaments* (London: SCM Press, 1966).

Barr, James, *The Concept of Biblical Theology* (Minneapolis, Minn.: Fortress Press, 1999).

*Barth, Karl, *The Word of God and the Word of Man* (Eng., London: Hodder & Stoughton, 1928).

Barth, Karl, *The Epistle to the Romans* (Eng., Oxford: Oxford University Press, 1933).

Barth, Karl, *The Resurrection of the Dead* (London: Hodder & Stoughton, 1933).

*Barth, Karl, *Church Dogmatics*, 14 vols (Eng., Edinburgh: T&T Clark, 1957).

Barth, Karl, *Protestant Theology in the Nineteenth Century* (London: SCM Press, 1972).

Bartholomew, Craig, and others (eds), *A Royal Priesthood? The Use of the Bible Ethically and Politically* (Carlisle: Paternoster, 2002).

**Bauckham, Richard, *Jesus and the Eyewitnesses: The Gospels as Eyewitness Testimony* (Grand Rapids, Mich.: Eerdmans, 2006).

Beasley-Murray, George R., *Jesus and the Last Days* (Peabody, Mass: Hendrickson, 1995).

Boman, Thorlief, *Hebrew Thought Compared with Greek* (London: SCM Press, 1960).

Bonhoeffer, Dietrich, *Ethics* (Ger., 1949; Eng., London: SCM Press, 1959).

Bonhoeffer, Dietrich, *Sanctorum Communio: A Theological Study of the Sociology of the Church* (Eng., Philadelphia, Pa.: Fortress Press, 1998).

Bornkamm, Günther, *Jesus of Nazareth* (Minneapolis, Minn.: Fortress Press, 1959).

Bornkamm, Günther, 'Faith and Reason in Paul', in *Early Christian Experience* (London: SCM Press, 1969), pp. 29–46.

Bright, John, *Early Israel in Recent History Writing* (London: SCM Press, 1956).

Brightman, Edgar, *A Philosophy of Religion* (New York, N.Y.: Skeffington and Prentice Hall, 1940).

*Brown, F., Driver, S. R. and Briggs, C. A., *The New Hebrew and English Lexicon* (Lafayette, Ind.: Associated Publishers, 1980).

Browning, Don, *Practical Theology* (San Francisco, Calif.: Harper & Row, 1983).

Brunner, Emil, *Man in Revolt* (London: Lutterworth Press, 1939).

Brunner, Emil, *Christian Doctrine of God* (Eng., London: Lutterworth Press, 1949).

Brunner, Emil, *Natural Theology*, with Karl Barth, *No!* (Eng., Eugene, Ore.: Wipf & Stock, 2002).

Buber, Martin, *I and Thou* (New York, N.Y.: Simon & Schuster, 1996).

Buber, Martin, 'Speech Is Relational', in Stahmer (ed.), *Speak That I May See Thee*, pp. 183–215.

*Bultmann, Rudolf, *Theology of the New Testament*, vol. 1 (London: SCM Press, 1952).

Bultmann, Rudolf, *Essays Philosophical and Theological* (London: SCM Press, 1955).

*Bultmann, Rudolf, 'New Testament Mythology', in H.-W. Bartsch (ed.), *Kerygma and Myth*, vol. 1 (Eng., London: SPCK, 1964).

Bultmann, Rudolf, *Faith and Understanding* (London: SCM Press, 1969).

Bultmann, Rudolf, *New Testament and Mythology and Other Basic Writings*, ed. Schubert Ogden (Philadelphia, Pa.: Fortress Press, 1984).

Caird, George B., *The Language and Imagery of the Bible* (London: Duckworth, 1980).

**Calvin, John, *Institutes of the Christian Religion*, transl. H. Beveridge, 2 vols (Grand Rapids, Mich.: Eerdmans, 1989).

Capps, David, *Pastoral Care and Hermeneutics* (Philadelphia, Pa.: Fortress Press, 1984).

Childs, Brevard S., *Myth and Reality in the Old Testament* (London: SCM Press, 1960).

Childs, Brevard S., *Biblical Theology in Crisis* (Philadelphia, Pa.: Westminster Press, 1970).

*Childs, Brevard S., *Exodus: A Commentary* (London: SCM Press, 1974).

Childs, Brevard S., *Introduction to the Old Testament as Scripture* (London: SCM Press, 1979).

Clarke, Clifton R. (ed.), *Pentecostal Theology in Africa* (Eugene: Ore.: Pickwick Publications, 2014).

Clement of Alexandria, *Stromata* (Eng., ANF, vol. 2, pp. 299–568).

Collins, John N., *Diakonia: Re-interpreting the Sources* (Oxford: Oxford University Press, 1990).

Congar, Yves, *Tradition and Traditions* (Eng., New York, N.Y.: Macmillan, 1966).

Congar, Yves, *I Believe in the Holy Spirit*, 3 vols (Eng., New York, N.Y.: Seabury Press and London: Chapman, 1983).

Conzelmann, Hans, 'On the Analysis of the Confessional Formula in 1 Cor. 15: 3–5', *Interpretation* 20 (1966), pp. 15–25.

*Cranfield, Charles E. B., *The Epistle to the Romans*, 2 vols (Edinburgh: T&T Clark, 1975–9).

Crossan, John Dominic, *The Historical Jesus: The Life of a Mediterranean Jewish Peasant* (San Francisco, Calif.: Harper-Collins, 1991).

Cullmann, Oscar, *Christ and Time* (London: SCM Press, 1951).

Cullmann, Oscar, *The Christology of the New Testament* (Eng., 2nd edn, London: SCM Press, 1963).

Cullmann, Oscar, *Salvation in History* (London: SCM Press, 1967).

*Cullmann, Oscar and Leenhardt, F. J. (eds), *Essays on the Lord's Supper* (London: Lutterworth Press, 1958).

Daly, Mary, *Beyond God the Father* (Boston, Mass.: Beacon Press, 1973).

Danby, H., *The Mishnah* (Oxford: Oxford University Press, 1933).

**Danker, Frederick W., *et al.*, *A Greek-English Lexicon of the New Testament* (3rd edn, Chicago, Ill.: University of Chicago Press, 2000).

Davies, W. D., *Paul and Rabbinic Judaism* (London: SPCK, 1955).

D'Costa, Gavin, *Theology and Religious Pluralism* (Oxford: Blackwell, 1986).

D'Costa, Gavin, 'Theology of Religions', in David Ford with Rachel Muers (ed.), *The Modern Theologians* (3rd edn, Oxford: Blackwell, 2005), pp. 626–44.

D'Costa, Gavin, *Christianity and World Religions* (Chichester: Wiley-Blackwell, 2009).

Dodd, C. H., *Gospel and Law* (Cambridge: Cambridge University Press, 1951).

Downing, F. Gerald, *Has Christianity a Revelation?* (London: SCM Press, 1964).

Dreyer, Yolanda, 'Reflections on Donald Capps' Hermeneutical Model of Pastoral Care', in *Harvard Theological Review* 70 (2005), pp. 1–37.

**Dunn, James D. G., *The Theology of Paul the Apostle* (Edinburgh: T&T Clark, 1998).

Ebeling, Gerhard, *The Word of God and Tradition* (Eng., London: Collins, 1968).

Ebeling, Gerhard, 'Time and Word', in James Robinson (ed.), *The Future of Our Religious Past* (London: SCM Press, 1971).

Ebeling, Gerhard, *The Study of Theology* (Eng., London: Collins, 1979).

Eichrodt, Walther, *Theology of the Old Testament*, vol. 1 (London: SCM Press, 1961).

Epp, Eldon Jay, *Junia: The First Woman Apostle* (Minneapolis, Minn.: Fortress Press, 2005).

*Evans, Donald D., *The Logic of Self-Involvement* (London: SCM Press, 1963).

Fairweather, E. R., (ed.), *A Scholastic Miscellany* (Philadelphia, Pa.: Westminster Press and London: SCM Press, 1956).

Farmer, H. H., *The World and God* (London: Nisbet, 1935).

Farrer, Austin, *Love Almighty and Ills Unlimited* (New York, N.Y.: Doubleday and London: Collins, 1962).

Fee, Gordon, *God's Empowering Presence* (Milton Keynes: Paternoster, 1995).

*Fiddes, Paul S., *Participating in God: A Pastoral Doctrine of the Trinity* (Louisville, Minn.: Westminster/John Knox Press, 2000).

Fiorenza, Elisabeth Schüssler, *In Memory of Her: A Feminist Theological Reconstruction of Christian Origins* (New York, N.Y.: Crossroad and London: SCM Press, 1983).

Fitzmyer, Joseph, *Romans* (New York, N.Y.: Doubleday, 1992).

Florovsky, Georgii, *Ways of Russian Theology*, <http://www.holytrinitymission. org/books/english/way_russian_theology_florovsky.htm>; also in *The Collected Works of Georges Florovsky*, 5 vols [of 14] (Belmont, Mass.: Nordland, 1972–9).

France, R. T., *The Gospel of Mark: A Commentary on the Greek Text* (Grand Rapids, Mich.: Eerdmans, 2002).

**Franks, R. S., *The Work of Christ: A Historical Study of Christian Doctrine* (London: Nelson, 1962).

Fuchs, Ernst, 'The New Testament and the Hermeneutical Problem', in James M. Robinson and John B. Cobb (eds), *New Frontiers in Theology*, vol. 2, *The New Hermeneutic* (New York, N.Y.: Harper & Row, 1964), pp. 111–45.

Gadamer, Hans-Georg, *Truth and Method* (Eng. 2nd edn, London: Sheed & Ward, 1989; 1st Ger. edn, 1960).

Gerkin, Charles, *The Living Human Document: Re-envisioning Pastoral Counseling in a Hermeneutical Mode* (Nashville, Tenn.: Abingdon, 1983).

*Gillespie, Thomas W., *The First Theologians: A Study in Early Christian Prophecy* (Grand Rapids, Mich.: Eerdmans, 1994).

*Gooch, Paul D., 'Conscience in 1 Corinthians 8 and 10', *New Testament Studies* 33 (1987), pp. 244–54.

Gregory of Nyssa, 'On "Not Three Gods"', 3 (Eng., *NPNF*, ser. 2, vol. 5, pp. 531–6).

***Gunton, Colin, *The Actuality of Atonement: A Study of Metaphor, Rationality, and the Christian Tradition* (Edinburgh: T&T Clark, 1988).

Harnack, Adolf von, *What Is Christianity?* (Eng., London: Benn, 1958).

Harrison, Glynn, 'The Ego-Trip Generation', *Commentary Magazine* (Summer 2013), p. 18; <http://www.oakhill.ac.uk/commentary/13_summer/pdfs/glynn_harrison.pdf>.

Hauerwas, Stanley, *Sanctify Them in the Truth: Holiness Exemplified* (Edinburgh: T&T Clark, 1998).

Hauerwas, Stanley, with William Willimon, *Resident Aliens: Life in the Christian Community* (Nashville, Tenn.: Abingdon, 2004).

Hawking, Stephen, *A Brief History of Time* (New York, N.Y.: Bantam, 1988).

*Haykin, Michael, *The Spirit of God: The Exegesis of 1 and 2 Corinthians in the Pneumatomachian Controversy of the Fourth Century* (Leiden: Brill, 1994).

Hegel, Georg W. F., *Lectures on the Philosophy of Religion*, 3 vols (London: Kegan Paul, Trench, 1895).

Heidegger, Martin, *Being and Time* (Eng., New York, N.Y.: Harper & Row, 1971).

Heidegger, Martin, *On the Way to Language* (Eng., New York, N.Y.: Harper & Row, 1971).

Hick, John (ed.), *Classical and Contemporary Readings in the Philosophy of Religion* (Englewood Cliffs, N.J.: Prentice Hall, 1964).

*Hick, John, *Evil and the God of Love* (2nd edn, London: Macmillan, 1977 (1966)).

Hill, David, *Greek Words and Hebrew Meanings* (Cambridge: Cambridge University Press, 1967).

**Hill, Wesley, *Paul and the Trinity: Persons, Relations, and the Pauline Letters* (Grand Rapids, Mich.: Eerdmans, 2015).

*Hodgson, Peter C., 'Georg W. F. Hegel', in Ninian Smart and others (eds), *Nineteenth Century Religious Thought in the West*, 3 vols (Cambridge: Cambridge University Press, 1985), vol. 1, pp. 81–122.

*Holleman, Joost, *Resurrection and the Parousia* (Leiden: Brill, 1996).

*Hollenweger, Walter J., *The Pentecostals* (Peabody, Mass.: Hendrickson, 1972).

Howard-Snyder, Daniel and O'Leary-Hawthorne, John, 'Transworld Sanctity and Plantinga's Free Will Defense', *International Journal for the Philosophy of Religion* 44 (1998), pp. 1–28.

Hume, David, *A Treatise of Human Nature* (3rd edn, Oxford: Oxford University Press, 1978 (1739)).

Hume, David, *Dialogue Concerning Natural Religion* (New York, N.Y.: Harper, 1948 (1779)).

Hunter, A. M., *The Teaching of Calvin* (London: James Clarke, 1950).

Ignatius, *To the Trallians*, in K. Lake (ed.), *Apostolic Fathers*, 2 vols (London: William Heinemann, 1912–17), vol. 1, pp. 213–25.

Irenaeus, *Against Heresies* (Eng., ANF, vol. 1, pp. 315–567).

Jacob, Edmond, *Theology of the Old Testament* (Eng., London: Hodder & Stoughton, 1958).

*Jeremias, Joachim, *The Parables of Jesus* (Eng., London: SCM Press, 1963).

**Jeremias, Joachim, *The Eucharistic Words of Jesus* (Eng., London: SCM Press, 1966).

**Jeremias, Joachim, *New Testament Theology* (London: SCM Press, 1971).

Jewett, Robert, *Paul's Anthropological Terms* (Leiden: Brill, 1971).

*Jones, O. R., *The Concept of Holiness* (London: Allen & Unwin, 1961).

Jung, Lee Hong, 'Minjung and Pentecostal Movements in Korea', in Anderson and Hollenweger (eds), *Pentecostals after a Century*, pp. 138–63.

Jüngel, Eberhard, *God as the Mystery of the World* (Eng., Edinburgh: T&T Clark, 1983).

Kallis, Anastasios, 'Orthodox Church', in Erwin Fahlbusch *et al.* (eds), *The Encyclopedia of Christianity*, 5 vols (Leiden: Brill and Grand Rapids, Mich.: Eerdmans, 1997), vol. 3, pp. 866–72.

Kalu, Ogbu, *African Pentecostalism: An Introduction* (New York, N.Y.: Oxford University Press, 2008).

*Käsemann, Ernst, *New Testament Questions of Today* (London: SCM Press, 1969).

Knight, George W., *The Pastoral Epistles* (Grand Rapids, Mich.: Eerdmans, 1992).

Küng, Hans, *The Living Church* (Eng., London: Sheed & Ward, 1963).

*Küng, Hans, *Justification: The Doctrine of Karl Barth and a Catholic Reflection* (Eng., New York: Nelson, 1964).

*Küng, Hans, *On Being a Christian* (London: Collins, 1976).

*Küng, Hans, *The Incarnation of God: An Introduction to Hegel's Theological Thought as Prologue to a Future Christology* (Eng., Edinburgh: T&T Clark, 1987).

*Küng, Hans, *Infallible? An Unresolved Enquiry* (London: SCM Press, 1994).

**Künneth, Walter, *The Theology of the Resurrection* (Eng., London: SCM Press, 1965).

Latimer, Hugh, *Sermons* (Cambridge: Cambridge University Press, 1844).

**Leenhardt, F. J., 'This Is My Body', in Cullmann and Leenhardt (eds), *Essays on the Lord's Supper*, pp. 39–40.

Loades, Ann, *Feminist Theology: A Reader* (London: SPCK, 1990).

Lonergan, Bernard, *Insight* (New York, N.Y.: Harper & Row, 1978 (1957)).

Lonergan, Bernard, *Method in Theology* (London: DLT, 1971).

Lossky, Vladimir, *Orthodox Theology* (New York, N.Y.: Crestwood, 1959 and New York, N.Y.: St Vladimir's Seminary Press, 1997).

*Lossky, Vladimir, *The Image and Likeness of God* (London and Oxford: Mowbray, 1974).

*Lossky, Vladimir, *The Mystical Theology of the Eastern Church* (Eng., New York, N.Y.: St Vladimir's Seminary Press, 1976; and Cambridge: James Clarke, 1991).

Lovejoy, Arthur, *The Great Chain of Being* (Cambridge, Mass.: Harvard University Press, 1936).

*Luther, Martin, 'Heidelberg Disputation', in James Atkinson (ed.), *Luther: Early Theological Works* (London: SCM Press, 1962), pp. 174–307.

Luther, Martin, *Luther's Works*, 55 vols (St Louis, Mo.: Concordia, 1950–86).

McGee, Gary B. (ed.), *Initial Evidence: Historical and Biblical Perspectives* (Eugene, Ore.: Wipf & Stock, 2007).

Mackie, J. L., *The Miracle of Theism* (Oxford: Clarendon Press, 1982).

McPherson, Aimee Semple, *The Foursquare Gospel*, ed. Raymond Cox (Los Angeles, Calif.: Foursquare Publications, 1969).

Macquarrie, John, *An Existentialist Theology: A Comparison of Heidegger and Bultmann* (London: SCM Press, 1955).

Macquarrie, John, *In Search of Humanity* (London: SCM Press, 1982).

Macquarrie, John, *Jesus Christ in Modern Thought* (London: SCM Press, 1990).

Marks, Elaine and Courtivron, Isabelle de (eds), *New French Feminisms: An Anthology* (Englewood Cliffs, N.J.: Prentice Hall, 1981).

Marxsen, W., *The Resurrection of Jesus of Nazareth* (Eng., Philadelphia, Pa.: Fortress Press, 1970).

Meister, Chad, *Introducing Philosophy of Religion* (New York, N.Y. and London: Routledge, 2009).

***Migliore, Daniel L., *Faith Seeking Understanding* (Grand Rapids, Mich.: Eerdmans, 1991).

Mill, John Stuart, *Three Essays on Religion* (London: Longmans, Green, 1875).

*Miller, Donald E. and Yamamiri, Tetsunao, *Global Pentecostalism: The New Age of Christian Social Engagement* (Berkeley, Calif.: University of California Press, 2007).

Miranda, José Porfirio, *Marx and the Bible: A Critique of the Philosophy of Oppression* (Eng., New York, N.Y.: Orbis, 1974).

*Moltmann, Jürgen, *Theology of Hope* (London: SCM Press, 1967).

*Moltmann, Jürgen, *The Crucified God* (London: SCM Press, 1974).

**Moltmann, Jürgen, *The Trinity and the Kingdom of God* (London: SCM Press, 1981).

*Moltmann, Jürgen, *God in Creation: An Ecological Doctrine of Creation* (Eng., London: SCM Press, 1985).

Moltmann, Jürgen, *The Way of Jesus: Christology in Messianic Dimensions* (London: SCM Press, 1989).

*Moltmann, Jürgen, *History of the Triune God* (London: SCM Press, 1991).

*Moltmann, Jürgen, *The Spirit of Life: A Universal Affirmation* (London: SCM Press, 1991).

*Moltmann, Jürgen, *The Coming of God: Christian Eschatology* (Eng., London: SCM Press, 1996).

Moltmann, Jürgen, *A Broad Place* (London: SCM Press, 2007).

Moore, Arthur L., *The Parousia in the New Testament* (Leiden: Brill, 1966).

Moore, Arthur L., *1 and 2 Thessalonians* (London: Nelson, 1969).

Morris, Leon, *Glory in the Cross* (London: Hodder & Stoughton, 1966).

Mounce, William D., *Pastoral Epistles* (Nashville, Tenn.: Nelson, 2000).

Niebuhr, H. Richard, *The Kingdom of God in America* (San Francisco, Calif.: Harper, 1937).

Niebuhr, H. Richard, *Christ and Culture* (New York, N.Y.: Harper-Collins, 1999).

*Niebuhr, Reinhold, *Moral Man and Immoral Society* (London: SCM Press, 1963).

O'Donovan, Oliver, *Resurrection and the Moral Order* (Leicester: IVP, 1986; 2nd edn, Grand Rapids, Mich.: Eerdmans, 1994).

*O'Donovan, Oliver, *The Desire of Nations: Rediscovering the Roots of Political Theology* (Cambridge: Cambridge University Press, 1996).

*O'Donovan, Oliver, *The Just War Revisited* (Cambridge: Cambridge University Press, 2003).

O'Donovan, Oliver, *Ways of Judgment* (Grand Rapids, Mich.: Eerdmans, 2005).

O'Donovan, Oliver, *Church in Crisis: The Gay Controversy and the Anglican Communion* (Eugene, Ore.: Cascade, 2008).

*O'Donovan, Oliver, *Self, World, and Time*, vol. 1, *Ethics as Theology: An Introduction* (Grand Rapids, Mich.: Eerdmans, 2013).

Ogungbile, David, 'African Pentecostalism and the Prosperity Gospel', in Clarke (ed.), *Pentecostal Theology in Africa*, pp. 132–49.

Olupona, J. K., 'African, West', in *NIDPCM*, pp. 11–31.

Origen, *Against Celsus* (*ANF*, vol. 4, pp. 395–669).

Origen, *De Principiis*, 4.1.16 (*ANF*, vol. 4, pp. 239–384).

Ott, Heinrich, *Reality and Faith: The Theological Legacy of Dietrich Bonhoeffer* (Philadelphia, Pa.: Fortress Press, 1972).

Paley, William, *Natural Theology, or Evidences of the Existence and Attributes of God* (Oxford: Oxford University Press, 2006 (1802)).

*Pannenberg, Wolfhart, 'The Revelation of God in Jesus of Nazareth', in James M. Robinson and John B. Cobb (eds), *New Frontiers in Theology*, vol. 3, *Theology as History* (New York, N.Y.: Harper & Row, 1967), pp. 101–33.

**Pannenberg, Wolfhart, *Jesus – God and Man* (London: SCM Press, 1968).

**Pannenberg, Wolfhart, *Basic Questions in Theology*, 3 vols (London: SCM Press, 1970–3).

Pannenberg, Wolfhart, *Theology and the Philosophy of Science* (Philadelphia, Pa.: Westminster Press and London: DLT, 1976).

***Pannenberg, Wolfhart, *Systematic Theology*, 3 vols (Edinburgh: T&T Clark, 1991–8).

Parham, Charles F., *A Voice Crying in the Wilderness* (Baxter Springs, Kans.: Apostolic Faith Bible College, 1902).

Parker, T. H. L., 'Creeds and Confessions', in F. G. Healey (ed.), *Preface to Christian Studies* (London: Lutterworth Press, 1971), pp. 137–49.

*Peirce, C. A., *Conscience in the New Testament* (London: SCM Press, 1955).

Plantinga, Alvin, 'Free Will Defence', in Max Black (ed.), *Philosophy in America* (Ithaca, N.J.: Cornell University and London: Allen & Unwin, 1965).

Plantinga, Alvin, *The Nature of Necessity* (Oxford: Clarendon Press, 1974).

*Plantinga, Alvin, *God, Freedom and Evil* (Grand Rapids, Mich.: Eerdmans, 1977).

**Plantinga, Alvin, *Warranted Christian Belief* (New York, N.Y: Oxford University Press, 2000).

*Plantinga, Alvin and Wolterstorff, Nicholas (eds), *Faith and Rationality* (Notre Dame, N.Y.: University of Notre Dame Press, 1983).

*Polkinghorne, John, *The Way the World Is* (London: SPCK, 1984 and 1992).

*Polkinghorne, John, *One World: The Interaction of Science and Theology* (Princeton, N.J.: Princeton University Press, 1987).

*Polkinghorne, John, *Quarks, Chaos, and Christianity: Questions to Science and Religion* (London: SPCK, 2005).

*Pontifical Biblical Commission, *The Interpretation of the Bible in the Church* (Collegeville, Minn.: The Liturgical Press, 1994).

Prat, F., *The Theology of St Paul*, 2 vols (London: Burns & Oates, 1945).

Pulikottil, Paulson, 'One God, One Spirit, Two Memories: A Pentecostal and Native Pentecostalism in Kerala', in Veli-Matti Kärkkäinen (ed.), *The Spirit in the World: Emerging Pentecostal Theologies in Global Contexts* (Grand Rapids, Mich.: Eerdmans, 2009), pp. 19–88.

Rahner, Karl, *The Shape of the Church to Come* (Ger., 1972; Eng., London: SPCK, 1974).

*Rahner, Karl, *Foundations of the Christian Faith* (London: DLT, 1978).

Rahner, Karl, *Theological Investigations*, 23 vols (London: DLT, 1961–92).

**Ramsey, Ian T., *Religious Language: An Empirical Placing of Theological Phrases* (London: SCM Press, 1957).

*Ramsey, Ian T., *Christian Discourse* (New York, N.Y. and London: Oxford University Press, 1965).

Reid, J. K. S., *The Authority of Scripture* (London: Methuen, 1957).

*Reid, J. K. S., *Our Life in Christ* (London: SCM Press, 1963).

*Reventlow, Henning Graf, *The Authority of the Bible and the Rise of the Modern World* (London: SCM Press, 1984).

Richards, Janet Radcliffe, *The Sceptical Feminist* (London: Penguin, 1983).

*Ricoeur, Paul, *Freud and Philosophy* (Eng., New Haven, Conn.: Yale University Press, 1970).

**Ricoeur, Paul, *Time and Narrative*, 3 vols (Eng., Chicago, Ill.: Chicago University Press, 1984, 1985, 1988).

*Ricoeur, Paul, *Oneself as Another* (Chicago, Ill.: University of Chicago Press, 1992).

Robinson, James, *A New Quest of the Historical Jesus* (London: SCM Press, 1959).

Robinson, John A. T., *The Body: A Study in Pauline Theology* (London: SCM Press, 1952).

Robinson, John A.T., 'Need Jesus Have Been Perfect?', in Stephen Sykes and J. P. Clayton (eds), *Christ, Faith and History* (Cambridge: Cambridge University Press, 1972).

Robinson, John A. T., *The Human Face of God* (London: SCM Press, 1973).

***Rogers, Eugene F., *After the Spirit* (London: SCM Press, 2006).

Rosenzweig, Franz, in Stahmer (ed.), *Speak That I May See Thee*, pp.148–82.

Roth, Cecil, *The Haggadah* (Heb. and Eng., London: Soncino Press, 1934).

Rowley, H. H., *Rediscovery of the Old Testament* (2nd edn, London: James Clarke, 1948).

Ruether, Rosemary and McLaughlin, Eleanor (eds), *Women of Spirit: Female Leadership in the Jewish and Christian Traditions* (New York, N.Y.: Simon & Schuster, 1979).

Rupp, E. Gordon, 'The Study of Church History', in F. G. Healey (ed.), *Preface to Christian Studies* (London: Lutterworth Press, 1971), pp. 105–22.

Russell, D. S., *The Method and Message of Jewish Apocalyptic 200 B.C. – A.D.100* (London: SCM Press, 1964).

Russell, Letty, *The Liberating Word* (Philadelphia, Pa.: Westminster Press, 1976).

*Ryle, Gilbert, *The Concept of Mind* (London: Hutchinson, 1949 and Penguin, 1963).

*Ryle, Gilbert, *Dilemmas* (Cambridge: Cambridge University Press, 1966).

Schleiermacher, Friedrich D. E., *A Brief Outline of the Study of Theology* (Eng., Edinburgh: T& T Clark, 1850).

Schleiermacher, Friedrich D. E., *Speeches on Religion* (Eng., New York, N.Y.: Harper, 1958).

*Schleiermacher, Friedrich D. E., *Hermeneutics: The Handwritten Manuscripts*, ed. H. Kimmerle (Eng., Missoula, Mont.: Scholars Press, 1977).

*Schleiermacher, Friedrich D. E., *The Christian Faith* (Eng., Edinburgh: T&T Clark, 1989).

Schmitt, Carl, *Political Theology* (Eng., Chicago, Ill.: University of Chicago Press, 2004 (1984)).

**Schnackenburg, Rudolf, *Baptism in the Thought of St. Paul: A Study in Pauline Theology* (Oxford: Blackwell, 1964).

Schweitzer, Albert, *The Quest of the Historical Jesus* (London: Black, 1910 and 1954).

Schweitzer, Albert, *The Mysticism of Paul the Apostle* (Eng., London: Black, 1931).

Sepúlveda, Juan, 'Indigenous Pentecostalism and the Chilean Experience', in Anderson and Hollenweger (eds), *Pentecostals after a Century*, pp. 111–34.

Smart, James, *The Strange Silence of the Bible in the Church* (London: SCM Press, 1970).

Smitherman, G., *Talking and Testifying: Language of Black America* (Detroit, Mich.: Wayne State University Press, 1977).

Stahmer, Harold (ed.), *Speak That I May See Thee: The Religious Significance of Language* (New York, N.Y.: Macmillan, 1968).

*Stanton, Graham, *Jesus of Nazareth in New Testament Preaching* (Cambridge: Cambridge University Press, 1974).

*Stendahl, Krister, 'Paul and the Introspective Conscience of the West', in *Harvard Theological Review* 56 (1963), pp. 199–215; and in Stendahl, Krister, *Paul among Jews and Gentiles*, pp. 78–96.

Stendahl, Krister, *Paul among Jews and Gentiles* (Philadelphia, Pa.: Fortress Press, 1976).

*Stowers, Stanley K., 'Paul on the Use and Abuse of Reason', in D. L. Balch and others (eds), *Greeks, Romans, Christians* (Minneapolis, Minn.: Fortress Press, 1990), pp. 253–86.

*Swinburne, Richard, *The Coherence of Theism* (Oxford: Clarendon Press, 1977).

*Swinburne, Richard, *The Existence of God* (Oxford: Clarendon Press, 1979).

**Sykes, Stephen (ed.), *Being Human: A Christian Understanding of Personhood Illustrated with Reference to Power, Money, Sex and Time: Report of the Doctrine Commission* (London: Church House Publishing, 2003).

Taylor, Vincent, *The Person of Christ in New Testament Teaching* (London: Macmillan, 1963).

Tennant, F. R., *Philosophical Theology*, 2 vols (Cambridge: Cambridge University Press, 1930).

Tertullian, *Prescriptions against Heretics* (Eng., *ANF*, vol. 3, pp. 269–427).

*Theissen, Gerd, *Psychological Aspects of Pauline Theology* (Edinburgh: T&T Clark, 1987).

Thielicke, Helmut, *Theological Ethics* (Eng., Philadelphia, Pa.: Fortress Press, 1966–9).

Thielicke, Helmut, *Modern Faith and Thought* (Eng., Grand Rapids, Mich.: Eerdmans, 1990).

Thiselton, Anthony C., *The Two Horizons: New Testament Hermeneutics and Philosophical Description* (Exeter: Paternoster and Grand Rapids, Mich.: Eerdmans, 1980).

Thiselton, Anthony C., *The First Epistle to the Corinthians: A Commentary on the Greek Text* (Grand Rapids, Mich.: Eerdmans and Carlisle: Paternoster, 2000).

Thiselton, Anthony C., *The Last Things: A New Approach* (London: SPCK, 2012).

Thiselton, Anthony C., 'The Image and the Likeness of God: A Theological Approach', in Malcolm Jeeves (ed.), *The Emergence of Personhood: A Quantum Leap?* (Grand Rapids, Mich.: Eerdmans, 2015), pp. 184–201.

***Thiselton, Anthony C., *Systematic Theology* (Grand Rapids, Mich.: Eerdmans and London: SPCK, 2015).

Thornton, Lionel S., *The Common Life in the Body of Christ* (3rd edn, London: Dacre Press, 1950).

*Thrall, Margaret, 'The Pauline Use of Syneidēsis', *New Testament Studies* 14 (1967), pp. 118–25.

*Tillich, Paul, *Systematic Theology*, 3 vols (Chicago, Ill.: University of Chicago Press and London: Nisbet, 1953, 1957, 1963).

Tillich, Paul, *The Shaking of the Foundations* (Eng., New York, N.Y.: Scribner, 1955).

Tillich, Paul, 'The Religious Symbol', in S. Hook (ed.), *Religious Experience and Truth* (Edinburgh: Oliver & Boyd, 1962).

Tillich, Paul, *Theology of Culture* (Eng., Oxford: Oxford University Press, 1964).

Trible, Phyllis, 'Depatriarchalizing in Biblical Tradition', *Journal of the American Academy of Religion* 41 (1973), pp. 35–42.

Trible, Phyllis, *God and the Rhetoric of Sexuality* (Philadelphia, Pa.: Fortress Press, 1978).

Trible, Phyllis, *Texts of Terror* (Philadelphia, Pa.: Fortress Press, 1984).

Tyndale, William, *A Pathway into the Holy Scripture*, in *Doctrinal Treatises* (Cambridge: Cambridge University Press, 1846 (*c.* 1530)), pp. 7–29.

Vanstone, W. H., *Love's Endeavour, Love's Expense* (1st edn, 1977; London: DLT, 2007).

Warner, E. E., 'Elim Fellowship', in *NIDPCM*, p. 598.

Watson, Francis, 'The Triune Identity', *Journal for the Study of the New Testament* 80 (2000), pp. 99–124.

*Webster, John, *The Domain of the Word: Scripture and Theological Reason* (London and New York, N.Y.: Bloomsbury, 2012).

Weil, Simone, *Waiting for God* (London: Routledge, 1974 (1939)).

Weiss, Johannes, *Earliest Christianity* (Eng., New York, N.Y.: Harper, 1959).

Whiteley, D. E. H., *The Theology of St Paul* (2nd edn, Oxford: Blackwell, 1971).

Wiesel, Elie, *Night* (New York, N.Y.: Hill & Wang, 1960 and 1969).

Williams, N. P., *The Ideas of the Fall and Original Sin* (London: Longmans, Green, 1929).

*Williams, Rowan, 'Eastern Orthodox Theology', in David Ford (ed.), *The Modern Theologians* (3rd edn, Oxford: Blackwell, 2005), pp. 572–88.

Wilson, E. A., 'Latin America', in *NIDPCM*, pp. 157–67.

Witherington III, Ben, *1 and 2 Thessalonians: A Socio-rhetorical Commentary* (Grand Rapids, Mich.: Eerdmans, 2006).

*Wittgenstein, Ludwig, *Philosophical Investigations* (Oxford: Blackwell, 1967).

Wolff, Hans Walter, *Anthropology of the Old Testament* (London: SCM Press, 1974).

*Wolterstorff, Nicholas, *Divine Discourse* (Cambridge: Cambridge University Press, 1995).

*Wolterstorff, Nicholas, *John Locke and the Ethics of Belief* (Cambridge: Cambridge University Press, 1996).

Wood, Nicholas J., *Faiths and Faithfulness: Pluralism, Dialogue and Mission* (Milton Keynes: Paternoster, 2009).

Wood, Skevington, *Captive to the Word* (Exeter: Paternoster, 1969).

Wright, G. Ernest, *The Challenge of Israel's Faith* (Chicago, Ill.: University of Chicago Press, 1944).

Wright, G. Ernest, *The Old Testament against Its Environment* (London: SCM Press, 1950).

Wright, G. Ernest, *God Who Acts: Biblical Theology as Recital* (London: SCM Press, 1952).

*Wright, N. T., *Jesus and the Victory of God* (London: SPCK, 1996).

*Wright, N. T., *Scripture and the Authority of God* (London: SPCK, 2005).

**Wright, N. T., *Surprised by Hope* (London: SPCK, 2007).

Wycliffe, John, *De Veritate Sacrae Scripturae* (Eng., London: Wycliffe Society and Trubner, 1907).

Yoder, John H., *The Politics of Jesus* (Grand Rapids, Mich.: Eerdmans, 1972).

Ziesler, John, *The Meaning of Righteousness in Paul: A Linguistic and Theological Enquiry* (Cambridge: Cambridge University Press, 1972).

**Zizioulas, John D., *Being as Communion: Studies in Personhood and the Church* (New York, N.Y.: St Vladimir's Seminary Press, 1985 and 1997).

Zizioulas, John D., *Eucharist, Bishop and Church: The Unity of the Church in the Divine Eucharist and the Bishop during the First Three Centuries* (Brookline, Mass.: Holy Cross, 2001).

*Zizioulas, John D., *Communion and Otherness: Further Studies in Personhood and the Church* (London: T&T Clark, 2007).

Index of Scripture and patristic references

225

Index of authors

Index of subjects

Note: entries in **bold print** indicate the main treatment of a topic.